The English Tenses Exercise Book

Phil Williams

MMXIX

Copyright

Cover design by Phil Williams

Cover images © Bob Wright, © schiva (Depositphotos)

ISBN: 978-1-913468-06-4

Published by English Lessons Brighton, an imprint of Rumian Publishing

Contents

Contents i

Introduction 3

How to Use This Book 4

Tense Forms 5

Forming the Past 6

    1. Past Simple 6

    2. Past Continuous 13

    3. Past Perfect 19

    4. Past Perfect Continuous 25

Forming the Present 30

    5. Present Simple 30

    6. Present Continuous 37

    7. Present Perfect 43

    8. Present Perfect Continuous 49

Forming the Future 55

    9. Future Simple 55

    10. Future Continuous 62

    11. Future Perfect 69

    12. Future Perfect Continuous 76

Forming Mixed Tenses 82

    13. Mixed Simple Tenses 82

    14. Mixed Continuous Tenses 91

15. Mixed Perfect Tenses 99

16. Mixed Perfect Continuous Tenses.. 109

Tenses in Use... 117

17. The Past in Use.. 118

18. The Present in Use... 142

19. The Future in Use 167

20. Mixed Tenses in Use 189

Infinitives and Participles 218

21. Identifying Bare Infinitives 219

22. Participles 221

23. Mixed Verb Types... 223

A Note from the Author... 226

Answers 227

Introduction

Welcome to *The English Tenses Exercise Book* – a collection of 161 exercises designed to drill the 12 key tenses of English: the **past**, **present** and **future** in their **simple**, **continuous**, **perfect** and **perfect continuous** forms. This book can be used for general, independent practice, though the exercises roughly match the guidelines laid out in *The English Tenses Practical Grammar Guide*.

This book is designed to make you fully comfortable with forming and using the tenses, both on their own and in conjunction with other tenses. Many other excellent grammar guides and exercise books exist, but it is rare that they offer more than one or two exercises on a particular topic. This book does the opposite: the topic is narrow, but the quantity of exercises and number of examples is vast. Some examples repeat similar ideas or themes – this is to reinforce lessons, demonstrate different usage and (in some cases) provide extra continuity or engagement.

As a writer and teacher for over fifteen years, I have devised these exercises and examples with the aim of presenting English in natural use, considering various styles and subjects. You will find everyday sentences and more unusual examples; short stories and non-fiction passages; academic English and business English; and more. Regardless of your level, my hope is that the examples will help familiarise you with the tenses across a broad range of usage. The vocabulary I have chosen is generally at an intermediate level, occasionally using more basic or advanced language, and the majority of verbs come from lists of those most commonly used. The prose exercises particularly aim to present more varied and fluent use of English, and for wider exposure, some examples have been included to demonstrate how a particular tense *could* be used. Please do complete the book with an accompanying dictionary if necessary and feel free to get in touch if anything is unclear.

And if you find some examples lean towards life in an English seaside town, that reflects my own setting, and the setting for my website, *English Lessons Brighton*.

How to Use This Book

The exercises in this book primarily concern verb forms, asking you to choose and correctly form the appropriate tense for each sentence. Sentences are either presented in isolated lists or in prose format. Instructions are given for each exercise as to the tense or tenses being tested, usually indicated in **bold**.

These exercises usually provide a space for you to fill in the correct tense. The information in brackets lets you know which verb to use and whether any additional words are necessary, such as a subject or adverbs. The spaces are standard sizes depending on the exercise and do not specifically indicate how long the answer should be.

The book is organised into two main sections, **Tense Forms** and **Tenses in Use**. These are divided into groups covering the **past, present** and **future** tenses, and each also contains mixed tense exercises. Within each grouping, you will find more basic list exercises and more complex prose exercises for comparative use. You may complete the exercises in any order you choose, but be aware that the book becomes more complex as it builds to more comparative use at the end of each section, particularly with the mixed tenses exercises. To present more natural use, there are occasional passive or modal examples to demonstrate wider contexts of the tenses. An additional section, **Infinitives and Participles**, is included at the back to specifically drill understanding of the verb forms that help complete the more complicated tenses.

You can complete the exercises writing directly in the spaces provided, and generous space around the exercises is given to aid note-taking, but you may wish to use a separate piece of paper or notebook so you can practise the exercises more than once. You can photocopy these exercises for personal or class use, but please be conscious of wasting paper and always credit the book.

Tense Forms

The following section drills forming the tenses, to get you used to quickly identifying and using different verb forms in the **past**, **present** and **future**. Each section includes exercises for the **simple**, **continuous**, **perfect** and **perfect continuous**, covering affirmative and negative statements, questions with and without question words, negative questions and mixed tenses.

The focus here is always on the required tense form. This means that the example sentences in this section are not necessarily the only way to express these points, but are used for illustrative purposes. This is particularly true of the **perfect** and **perfect continuous** forms, which can be relatively rare in practice, and usually require specific contexts to make complete sense. The mixed tenses passages are designed to include as many instances of these forms as possible, though in everyday use such passages may be expressed in simpler ways.

grew   *build*   *built*

Forming the Past

1. Past Simple

1.1 Past Simple Statements

Form complete sentences in the **past simple** (affirmative or negative), without contractions, using the information provided.

For example:

Q: I / to know / not / where he lived

A: I did not know where he lived.

1. the postman / to be / late again

   _____

2. Felicity / to grow / tomatoes in her garden

   _____

3. he / to understand / not / the project

   _____

4. we / to fail / to finish in time

   _____

5. they / to give / not / us the bag of flour

   _____

6. Liam / to ask / not / the question politely

   _____

7. the hummingbirds / to build / a nest in our attic

   _____

said   were

8. the piano / to look / too old to use

_____

9. she / to say / we / to be / wrong

_____

10. I / to pick / not / the right flowers

_____

11. our cake / to taste / not / right

_____

12. we / to drive / all the way to Scotland

_____

13. you / to bring / not / the green umbrella

_____

14. they / to arrest / the wrong man

_____

15. the lady of the manor / to write / not / a convincing memoir

_____

drove

1.2 Past Simple Questions 1

Convert the following past simple statements into **past simple** *yes* **or** *no* **questions** (they do not require question words). First person statements should become second person questions. Remember that past simple questions require the auxiliary **to do** or **to be**.

For example:

Q: We went to Bali on our honeymoon.

A: Did you go to Bali on your honeymoon?

1. Our dogs were very messy.

    _____

2. The chef cooked something spectacular.

    _____

3. I read all three of my textbooks this weekend.

    _____

4. She asked him to go on a date.

    _____

5. You knew about the rotten fruit!

    _____

6. The priests demanded that the film be banned.

    _____

7. I bought a new bicycle.

    _____

8. He hoovered the house because of the dust.

    _____

9. The children played on the swings.

    _____

10. She was very disappointed with the presentation.

    _____

11. We misjudged the time it would take to get to the party.

_____

12. I lost my keys again.

_____

13. The story got a lot more interesting after the main character died.

_____

14. They sent a replacement cabinet after ours broke.

_____

15. The council banned parking on my road.

_____

16. She ran a marathon last spring.

_____

17. It (was) the hottest day of the year.

Was it _____ ?

18. Ulric visited the doctor for the first time.

_____

19. My computer stopped working.

_____

20. They prepared for the storm months in advance.

_____

1.3 Past Simple Questions 2

Convert the following past simple statements into **past simple questions,** using the question words provided. First person statements should become second person questions. Remember that past simple questions require the auxiliary **to do** or **to be.**

For example:

Q: He purchased two bottles of wine. (what)
A: What did he purchase?

1.   I helped the old man in the market. (where)

_____

2.   Julian sang a beautiful ballad. (what)

_____

3.   We searched for the doctor in the jungle. (where)

_____

4.   She was very angry because of the train delays. (why)

_____

5.   After the competition, everyone went for ice cream. (when)

_____

6.   They stole the gold necklaces, but not the silver ones. (which)

_____

7.   I gave the homeless man £20. (how much)

_____

8.   The critic hated the director's latest film. (what)

_____

9.   He had a disagreement with the man who sold him his car. (who)
        HAVE

_____

10. The great oak tree was cut down yesterday. (what)

_____

Cut Cut

11. Tyler wanted to free the guinea pigs. (what)

_____

12. The family took the bottles to the new recycling centre. (where)

_____

13. The girl believed in magic, but not dwarves. (what)

_____

14. We <u>tied</u> the knots by following the instructions on the internet.
    (how / to tie)

_____

15. Someone ate her last cupcake! (who)

_____

1.4 Past Simple Negative Questions

Complete the following sentences in the **past simple negative question
form**, without contractions, using the subjects and verbs in brackets.
Remember that past simple questions require the auxiliary **to do** or **to be**.
    For example:
    Q: Why _____ his trumpet? (Timmy / to play)
    A: Why <u>did</u> **Timmy not play** his trumpet?

1. What _____ us? (he / to tell)
2. _____ like an easy task? (it / to seem)
3. Where _____ the students? (Mindy / to take)
4. Why _____ locked? (the door / to be)
5. How _____ there in time? (we / to get)
6. _____ any water on the hike? (they / to bring)
7. _____ supposed to be in Italy this week? (she / to be)
8. _____ for very long? (the spiders / to live)
9. _____ sad about the game being cancelled? (you / to be)
10. When _____ a manager? (the football team / to have)

11

eat (ate) eaten

1.5 Mixed Past Simple ✓

Complete the following sentences in the appropriate **past simple affirmative, negative or question form**, without contractions, using the information provided in brackets.

For example:

Q: _____ happy with the result? (she / to be / not)

A: Was she not happy with the result?

1. We were not very good at sports. (to be / not)
2. The Morrisons owned too many chickens. (to own)
3. Herman did not get on with his neighbours. (to get on / not)
4. Where did I parked my car? (I / to park) time
5. Did you see that new ballet? (you / to see)
6. The builders ete a large breakfast. (to eat)
7. Was she not a good swimmer? (she / to be / not)
8. The lady did not decide to buy the dress. (to decide / not)
9. Did they not listen to the radio? (they / to listen / not)
   'e'stening
10. She run all the way around the park. (to run)

are
are
were
were

2. Past Continuous

2.1 Past Continuous Statements

like *lying*

Form complete sentences in the **past continuous** (affirmative or negative), without contractions, using the information provided.

For example:

Q: the man / to run / for his train

A: The man was running for his train.

1. the giraffe / to lie down

   _____

2. they / to draw / not / pictures of fruit

   _____

3. it / to get / dark outside

   _____

4. you / to tell / me about your new phone

   _____

5. they / to fly / not / over Mongolia

   flying
   _____

6. I / to clean / the pans when the police arrived

   _____

7. the animals / to dig / a hole

   _____

8. Kyle / to read / not / novels this summer

   _____

9. we / to paint / the house all day

   _____

10. no one / to help / with the display

_____

11. the computer / to load / not / properly

_____

12. you / to sleep / not / in the right room

_____

13. she / to brush / her teeth

_____

14. I / to test / the light switch

_____

15. the rodents / to plan / something

planning _____

2.2 Past Continuous Questions 1

Form complete **past continuous** *yes* or *no* **questions**, without question words, using the information provided. First person statements should become second person questions.

For example:

Q: he / hang / washing / outside

A: Was he hanging his washing outside?

1. they / to build / a new school

_____

2. Lily / to hide / something

_____

3. the days / to get / longer

getting _____

4. you / to ask / about my van

_____

5. the light / to work / when you got home

    _____

6. his father / to try / to play the piano

    trying
    _____

7. the students / to travel / through Bolivia

    _____

8. everyone / to wait / for me

    _____

9. I / to say / the right word

    saying
    _____

10. the sailors / to load / the correct boat

    _____

11. the bus / to stop / everywhere

    stopping
    _____

12. we / to sing / in tune

    _____

13. Rupert and Jim / to fight / again

    fighting
    _____

14. the sun / to shine / on your wedding day

    shining
    _____

15. the trains / to arrive / on time last weekend

    arriving
    _____

2.3 Past Continuous Questions 2

Convert the following past continuous statements into **past continuous questions**, using the question words provided. First person statements should become second person questions.

For example:

Q: They were cycling in Sweden. (where)

A: Where were they cycling?

1. The students were doing very well. (how)

    _____

2. Tim was studying French. (what)

    _____

3. You were flying to Ireland. (where)

    _____

4. The cat was running away. (why)

    _____

5. They were singing the national anthem. (what)

    _____

6. I was living in America for three years. (how long)

    _____

7. Someone was leaving dirty dishes out. (who)

    _____

8. Her husband was watching a detective show on TV. (what)

    _____

9. The tour guide was taking them to the cathedral. (where)

    _____

10. Hailey was smiling because she had flowers. (why)

    _____

11. The Japanese investors were meeting with someone. (who)

_____

12. The restaurant was getting crowded because it was so busy. (why)

_____

13. The new shoes were arriving at noon. (when)

_____

14. Alison was preparing a banner for the carnival. (what)

_____

15. We were picking up bad habits from our friends. (what)

_____

2.4 Past Continuous Negative Questions

Complete the following sentences in **past continuous negative question form**, without contractions, using the subjects and verbs in brackets.
For example:
Q: Why _____ to the radio? (you / to listen)
A: Why **were you not listening** to the radio?

1. enjoying _____ the party? (you / to enjoy)
2. What _____ them? (the man / to show)
3. _____ the right pen? (I / to hold)
4. Why _____ warmer? (the weather / to get)
5. Where _____ during the cruise? (the boat / to stop)
6. Using _____ the correct ingredients? (you / to use)
7. When _____? (the bell / to ring)
8. _____ more sandwiches? (they / to bring)
9. sitting _____ at the back of the class? (he / to sit)
10. Why _____ the teacher? (the children / to follow)

17

2.5 Mixed Past Continuous

Complete the following dialogue with the appropriate **past continuous** **affirmative**, **negative** or **question form**, using the information in brackets.

The Ice Cream Van

Simon: Do you know what I just saw? An ice cream van (1) _____ (to drive) down our road.

Carl: Really? (2) _____ (they / to sell) ice cream? It's November!

Simon: Well, (3) _____ (it / to play) music, so I think they wanted customers.

Carl: (4) _____ (the van / to go) to the beach?

Simon: It couldn't have been; (5) _____ (the driver / to head / not) in the right direction.

Carl: Then where (6) _____ (he / to plan) to park?

Simon: Hmm. (7) _____ (something / happen / not) in the town centre earlier today?

Carl: Of course! (8) _____ (they / open) a new sports shop this morning!

Simon: Oh! I (9) _____ (to think) about going to that, but I decided not to.

Carl: But (10) _____ (you / to expect / not) ice cream! Let's go!

3. Past Perfect

3.1 Past Perfect Statements

Form complete sentences in the **past perfect** (affirmative or negative), without contractions, using the information provided.

For example:

Q: it / to be / twenty long years since he was there

A: It had been twenty long years since he was there.

1. they / to start / the party early

    _____

2. it / to snow / overnight

    _____

3. the delivery truck / to park / outside

    _____

4. I / to hear / not / about the Incas before

    _____

5. you / to warn / me not to go there, but I did

    _____

6. she / to arrive / too late for the exam

    _____

7. Simone realised / she / to listen / not / to this tune yet

    _____

8. before finding the lecture hall, we / to go / to Room 2b

    _____

9. we / to agree / not / on a price for the painting by noon

    _____

10. he / to read / the book thirteen times

_____

11. the picnic was ruined; the rats / to eat / everything

_____

12. the shop / to close down / for good

_____

13. I / to ask / not / for a map, because I knew the way

_____

14. she / to forgot / where the cups were kept

_____

15. Ryan went to see a film, but they / to sell / all the tickets

_____

3.2 Past Perfect Questions 1

Convert the following past perfect statements into **past perfect *yes* or *no* questions** (they do not require question words). Use the information in brackets when necessary. First person statements should become second person questions.

For example:

Q: Maria had studied all night to pass the test.

A: Had Maria studied all night to pass the test?

1. They had been to California before.

_____

2. I had already asked you about your toe.

_____

3. He hadn't worn his coat to the park.

_____

4.   The horse had eaten already.

_____

5.   Someone had broken the window.

_____

6.   The mice had infested the house.

_____

7.   I had never been able to juggle.

_____

8.   Roger had repaired the bicycle.

_____

9.   Jonas had taken the wrong bag.

_____

10. The cleaners hadn't emptied the bins.

_____

3.3 Past Perfect Questions 2

Convert the following past perfect statements into **past perfect questions,** using the question words provided. First person statements should become second person questions.

For example:

Q: They had driven to the coast for the weekend. (where)
A: Where had they driven to for the weekend?

1.   Lisa had added something to the soup. (what)

_____

2.   The cows had escaped from the field. (how)

_____

3.   We had discussed many topics in the previous two lessons. (what)

_____

4.   I had put my glasses on the table. (where)

_____

5.   The clock had stopped at 1 p.m. (when)

_____

6.   She had changed her clothes during the break. (when)

_____

7.   The President had appointed a new secretary. (who)

_____

8.   Harry had heard something behind the shed. (what)

_____

9.   All the eggs had gone. (where)

_____

10. We had stayed in an excellent hotel last time. (where)

_____

3.4 Past Perfect Negative Questions

Complete the following sentences in **past perfect negative question form**, without contractions, using the subjects and verbs in brackets.

For example:

Q: Why _____ your homework? (you / to finish)

A: Why **had you not finished** your homework?

1.   _____ her about the invitation? (he / to tell)

2.   _____ in Boston? (where / Charlene / to be)

3.   _____ together? (the team / to work)

4.   _____ the cooker before going out? (I / to turn off)

5.   _____ the radiator to the right temperature? (the plumber / to set)

6.   _____ in his report? (what / the night manager / to include)

7. _____ at 7 a.m.? (why / the alarm / to go off)

8. _____ to the soup? (what / the chef / to add)

9. _____ the situation clearly? (I / to explain)

10. _____ the car's engine before travelling? (why / they / to check)

3.5 Mixed Past Perfect

Complete the following text with the appropriate **past perfect affirmative, negative** or **question form**, using the information in brackets.

A Fresh Cake

Stephen was looking forward to a freshly baked cake. (1) _____ (he / to leave) it baking for 45 minutes now. This was the final step in a process (2) _____ (Stephen / start) four hours earlier, after (3) _____ (his wife / to suggest) that he try a new recipe (4) _____ (she / to find). (5) _____ (he / not / to plan) to spend the day baking, but (6) _____ (they / to buy) all the ingredients already, and (7) _____ (they / not / to make) homemade cake for a long time, so he agreed to give it a go.

Once he started, he realised it was actually good fun. (8) _____ (he / to measure) everything carefully before combining the ingredients, and then made a terrible mess mixing the batter. It was too sticky. His wife asked: (9) _____ (why / he / not / to use) more flour? (10) _____ (he / read) the recipe correctly?

Eventually, (11) _____ (Stephen / to wrestle) the mixture under control, and he cleaned the whole kitchen while they waited for it to rise. (12) _____ (it / to turn out) to be quite simple

23

really. When he put the mix in the oven, he asked himself, (13) _____ (why / he / not / to try) this sooner?

After half an hour, (14) _____ (the kitchen / to start) to smell amazing.

Finally, 45 minutes were almost over, and Stephen's mouth was watering. He opened the oven to find (15) _____ (the cake / to rise) beautifully, and (16) _____ (it / to develop) a firm, golden top. They would definitely enjoy this, and Stephen admitted, (17) _____ (his wife / to be) right. It was a good idea.

4. Past Perfect Continuous

4.1 Past Perfect Continuous Statements

Form complete sentences in the **past perfect continuous** (affirmative or negative), without contractions, using the information provided.

For example:

Q: the circus / to come / to town for twenty years

A: The circus had been coming to town for twenty years.

1. they / to travel / all night

   _____

2. I / to listen / not / during the lecture

   _____

3. she / dance / with Raul

   _____

4. the bird / to sing / for hours

   _____

5. it / to snow / not / before they left the hotel

   _____

6. the traffic lights / to work / not / that morning

   _____

7. Sidney / to learn / to play the bassoon

   _____

8. strange symbols / to appear / all over town

   _____

9. the price of cauliflower / to rise / throughout January

   _____

10. Tina / to wait / for the right man

    _____

11. we / to go / to the same holiday villa for years

    _____

12. wild dogs / to steal / from the pantry

    _____

13. the children / to practise / not / their handwriting

14. they / to camp / not / in Wales before

15. I / to hope / for a good result

4.2 Past Perfect Continuous Questions 1

Convert the following past statements into **past perfect continuous *yes* or *no* questions** (they do not require question words). Use the information in brackets when necessary. First person statements should become second person questions.

For example:

Q: It had been raining during the night.

A: Had it been raining during the night?

1. We had been watching Channel 4.

2. The garden seemed dry. (Jim / to water)

3. There was cat hair in the bedroom. (the cat / to sleep)

4. They had been training together for a long time.

5. The carpenter had new chairs in the window. (to make)

6. I had been snoring in my sleep.

7. She knew what they said in their phone call. (to listen)

8.   The door had been closing on its own.

    _____

9.   She had received help with her studies. (Winston / to help)

    _____

10. The bracelet had been sitting on the table all along.

    _____

4.3 Past Perfect Continuous Questions 2

Convert the following past statements into **past perfect continuous questions**, using the question words provided. First person statements should become second person questions.

For example:

Q: They had been searching for cheap train tickets for hours. (how long)
A: How long had they been searching for cheap train tickets (for)?

1.   She had been hiding the cake. (where)

    _____

2.   We had been listening to classical music in the car. (what)

    _____

3.   The dog had been barking at squirrels. (what)

    _____

4.   Clive had been planning to go on holiday that April. (when)

    _____

5.   The man had been playing the trumpet all morning. (how long)

    _____

6.   Mum had been preparing burritos for dinner. (what)

    _____

7.   I had been sitting on a wet patch of grass. (where)

    _____

8. You had been working at the weekend because you wouldn't say "no". (why)

   _____

9. They had been thinking about banning whistles. (what)

   _____

10. Fiona had been cooking bagels in the oven before she bought the toaster. (how)

    _____

4.4 Past Perfect Continuous Negative Questions

Complete the following sentences in **past perfect continuous negative question form**, without contractions, using the subjects and verbs in brackets.

For example:

Q: What _____ at school? (they / to learn)

A: What **had they not been learning** at school?

1. _____ in the right space? (we / to park)
2. Where _____ a mess? (the boys / to make)
3. _____ to the teacher? (she / to listen)
4. Why _____? (the water / to boil)
5. _____ fast enough? (I / to walk)
6. _____ all day? (it / to rain)
7. Why _____ the books I gave her? (Lily / to read)
8. When _____ the truth? (the politician / to tell)
9. _____ in the morning? (they / to run)
10. Why _____ the roses? (the gardener / to trim)

4.5 Mixed Past Perfect Continuous

Complete the following text with the appropriate **past perfect continuous affirmative**, **negative** or **question form**, without contractions, using the information in brackets.

A Ruined Allotment

(1) _____ (it / to rain) all night, we could tell. The allotment was flooded. (2) _____ (I / to warn / not) everyone about this for months? If they had listened, we could have built a shelter. But (3) _____ (they / to do) other things, like swimming in the lake. Besides, Barry kept arguing, (4) _____ (the potatoes / to grow / not) anyway. Why bother?

(5) _____ (the weather / to get) more unpredictable, that was the main problem. Some months we had no rain at all. As much as two months ago, (6) _____ (people / to say) we might have a completely dry season. But I remembered the storms, three years ago, when I lost everything. (7) _____ (I / not / to listen) when the forecasts offered warnings that time. (8) _____ (why / I / not / to pay) more attention during that period? Back when it would have helped ... The same reason no one listened to me this time. (9) _____ (things / to go) so well!

Forming the Present

5. Present Simple

5.1 Present Simple Statements

Form complete sentences in the **present simple** (affirmative or negative), without contractions, using the information provided.

For example:

Q: I / to eat / not / eggs every day

A: I do not eat eggs every day.

1. Billy / to like / cats

   _____

2. trains in Japan / always / to run / on time

   _____

3. Tina / to drink / not / banana milkshakes

   _____

4. the shopping centre / to open / every day at 6 a.m.

   _____

5. all cookies / to taste / amazing

   _____

6. I / to find / biology / interesting

   _____

7. Fred and Shirley / to eat / not / after midnight

   _____

8. unhappy employees / to be / not / good for business

   _____

9. the last house on my street / to look / haunted

    _____

10. my car / to have / climate control / but / it / to work / not

    _____

11. flocks of birds / to fly / in interesting formations

    _____

12. peanut butter and cheese / to go / not / well together

    _____

13. reading books definitely / to make / you smarter

    _____

14. we / to travel / not / to the lakes more than twice a year

    _____

15. Grandma's stuffed animal collection / to scare / everyone who / to come / to visit

    _____

5.2 Present Simple Questions 1

Convert the following present simple statements into **present simple *yes* or *no* questions** (they do not require question words). First person statements should become second person questions. Remember that present simple questions require the auxiliary **to do** or **to be**.

For example:

Q: I own a red bicycle.

A: Do you own a red bicycle?

1. I am hungry.

    _____

2. Lily listens to heavy metal music.

    _____

3. All parrots have colourful feathers.

    _____

4. The carnival is safe for children.

_____

5. Uncle Jeff knows the way to the beach.

_____

6. You speak a foreign language.

_____

7. I want another cup of tea.

_____

8. You are sure this milk is non-dairy.

_____

9. Howard always talks during class.

_____

10. Your parents live near your house.

_____

11. Exercise is important to you.

_____

12. The campers sleep in tents.

_____

13. My cat seems fat because he is so fluffy.

_____

14. Good grades matter if I want to be an artist.

_____

15. The path under the bridge is safe at night.

_____

16. Abigail works in the library.

_____

17. I need to keep taking these pills.

_____

18. This cauliflower smells strange.

_____

19. Glass bottles are good for storing hot liquids.

_____

20. That man is a friend of yours.

_____

(5.3) Present Simple Questions 2

Convert the following present simple statements into **present simple questions**, using the question words provided. First person statements should become second person questions. Remember that present simple questions require the auxiliary **to do** or **to be**.

For example:

Q: She lives in Spain now. (where)
A: Where does she live now?

1. There is something in your backpack. (what)

_____

2. The sun rises at 6 a.m. (when)

_____

3. You boil perfect eggs. (how)

_____

4. Brianne buys her hats in the market. (where)

_____

5. The boys play in the park every Tuesday. (where)

_____

6. We always visit the same café. (why)

_____

7. Michael always knows the answers to these questions. (how)

_____

8. You want to go to the cinema. (when)

_____

9.   Your father works near here. (where)

_____

10. The running club meets on Saturday mornings. (when)

_____

11. Those teachers wear such smart clothes. (why)

_____

12. I have to do something to open this tin of beans. (what)

_____

13. The gardeners cut the grass twice a week. (how often)

_____

14. The cutlery goes in the middle drawer. (which)

_____

15. The children get home from school at 4 p.m. (when)

_____

5.4 Present Simple Negative Questions

Complete the following sentences in **present simple negative question form**, without contractions, using the subjects and verbs in brackets. Remember that present simple questions require the auxiliary **to do** or **to be**.
   For example:
   Q: What food _____? (you / to eat)
   A: What food **do you not eat**?

1. Des _____ milk? (that chocolate / to contain)

2. _____ the owner of this car? (he)

3. Which _____ a swimming pool? (hotel / to have)

4. _____ expected before 7 p.m.? (the guests)

5. _____ a good time to visit? (when)

6. Why _____ more tennis? (Ben / to play)

7. _____ the colour of their bedroom? (they / to like)

8. Why _____ the boss already? (she)

9. _____ right in this picture? (what / to look)

10. _____ if we go to the beach this weekend? (it / to matter)

5.5 Mixed Present Simple

Complete the following text with the appropriate **present simple affirmative**, **negative** or **question form**, using the information in brackets.

Bonfire Night in Lewes

Every year on November 5th, (1) _____ (Lewes / to host) one of the largest bonfire nights in the UK. (2) _____ (some people / to call) Lewes the "Bonfire Capital of the World". (3) _____ (what / to be) so special about these evenings?

(4) _____ (the festivities / to mark) Guy Fawkes Night by bringing together bonfire societies from across Sussex. (5) _____ (seven local societies / run) six separate parades and firework displays, but (6) _____ (they / to be / not) alone. (7) _____ (the town / to draw in) as many as 30 other societies from across Sussex. (8) _____ (the evening / to be / not) a small event: up to 5,000 people take part in the celebrations, and (9) _____ (the town / to welcome) tens of thousands of spectators; as many as 80,000 one year!

On these evenings, (10) _____ (the trains / take) a long time to queue for, and the locals might complain: (11) _____ (why / these people / to go / not) somewhere else?! With a population of only 17,500, (12) _____ (the market town / to have / not) the facilities for such a big crowd.

(13) _____ (why / so many people / to travel) so far for these parades?

(14) _____ (the history / to go) back a long way. In the past, the celebrations were more like riots, which gradually became the processions (15) _____ (we / to see) today. Even now, (16) _____ (the evenings / to stir) controversy: many people ask that (17) _____ (the societies / to burn / not) effigies that cause offence. Between the many memorable evenings, the rich history and the media attention, (18) is it _____ (it / to be / not / inevitable) that so many people should visit?

36

6. Present Continuous

6.1 Present Continuous Statements

Form complete sentences in the **present continuous** (affirmative or negative), without contractions, using the information provided.

For example:

Q: Freddie / to play / in the garden

A: Freddie is playing in the garden.

1. my mother / to watch / the television

    _____

2. the cat / to sleep / on the sofa

    _____

3. it / to rain / not / anymore

    _____

4. the phone / to ring

    _____

5. you / to learn / very fast

    _____

6. we / to work / not / together today

    _____

7. the tap / to drip / again

    _____

8. I / to write / not / about the Egyptians

    _____

9. the nuns / to dance / to disco music

    _____

10. she / to sing / far too loudly

    _____

11. the plants / to grow / very fast

    _____

12. Oliver / to sleep / not / in his own bed

_____

13. raccoons / to steal / from our bins

_____

14. that man / to stare / at you

_____

15. you / to sit / not / in the right seat

_____

6.2 Present Continuous Questions 1

Convert the following statements into **present continuous** *yes* or *no* **questions** (they do not require question words). First person statements should become second person questions.

For example:

Q: Tim plays the flute.

A: Is Tim playing the flute?

1. You are writing an essay.

_____

2. The council are building a new swimming pool.

_____

3. He is avoiding his boss.

_____

4. We are heading north.

_____

5. That girl is carrying too many books.

_____

6. Your son behaves well at school.

_____

7. I feel like I am catching a cold.

_____

8. Chelsea are winning the match.

    _____

9. Melissa eats healthy food.

    _____

10. There could be buns baking in the oven.

    _____

11. Her pregnancy shows.

    _____

12. The walls in our building are getting dirty.

    _____

13. Our creative team generates a lot of ideas.

    _____

14. Henry is sharing his cake with everyone.

    _____

15. I could be looking at this picture the wrong way around.

    _____

6.3 Present Continuous Questions 2

Convert the following present continuous statements into **present continuous questions**, using the question words provided. First person statements should become second person questions.

For example:

Q: Julie is applying to a college. (which)

A: Which college is Julie applying to?

1. I am trying to do something. (what)

    _____

2. He is drilling into that wall. (why)

    _____

3. Nancy is thinking about something. (what)

    _____

4.   We are walking to the casino. (where)

_____

5.   They are investing their savings. (how)

_____

6.   The business is expanding slowly. (why)

_____

7.   Hank is storing his old photos in a strange box. (where)

_____

8.   Something is drawing lots of birds to the garden. (what)

_____

9.   The wind is blowing from the north. (which direction)

_____

10.   The councillors are insisting on raising taxes. (why)

_____

11.   The kitchen staff are preparing food for many guests. (how many)

_____

12.   Lula is parking the car in the street. (where)

_____

13.   The nurse is giving you medicine. (what)

_____

14.   Something is making that awful sound. (what)

_____

15.   Thirteen visitors are waiting in the hall. (how many)

_____

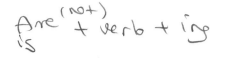
Are (not) + verb + ing
is

6.4 Present Continuous Negative Questions

Complete the following sentences in **present continuous negative question form**, without contractions, using the subjects and verbs in brackets.

For example:

Q: Which dish _____ for dinner? (we / to prepare)

A: Which dish **are we not preparing** for dinner?

+ ing

1. Is _____ his dog? (Charles / to bring)

2. _____ enough homework? (the teachers / to set)

3. Which ingredient _____? (I / to taste)

4. Where _____ the children? (she / to take)

5. Why _____ their juice? (my children / to drink)

6. _____ wet in the rain? (the bikes / to get)

7. Which places _____ on your honeymoon? (you / to visit)

8. Why _____ in this room? (the towels / to dry)

9. _____ her boyfriend? (she / to miss)

10. _____ the poetry competition? (Joe and Kyle / to enter)

6.5 Mixed Present Continuous

Complete the following text with the appropriate **present continuous affirmative, negative** or **question form**, using the information in brackets.

Proud Mr Duff

(1) _____ (Mr Duff / to build) a new shed in his garden.
(2) _____ (he / to borrow) tools from his neighbour, Mr Benton, but (3) _____ (they / to work / not) well because Mr Duff has not fully charged them. (4) _____ (the shed / to fall) behind

41

schedule. Mr Duff's wife has asked, "(5) _____ (things / to go / not) to plan?"

Mr Duff is a proud man. Though the problem persists, (6) _____ (he / to admit / not) it, so over time (7) _____ (his wife / to ask) more questions about the delayed shed. (8) _____ (winter / to come), and while Mr Duff works on the shed (9) _____ (the family / to store) their outdoor things under the porch.

"(10) _____ (you / to do) something wrong," Mrs Duff insists.

"(11) _____ (what / you / to talk) about?" Mr Duff replies, stubbornly.

(12) _____ (the situation / to worry) Mrs Duff. (13) _____ (her husband / to get) upset and (14) _____ (he / to spend) too much time out there. (15) _____ (how / she / to go) to help? She decides to ask Mr Benton.

Mr Benton suggests that (16) _____ (Mr Duff / to take / not) proper care of the tools. Benton listens, and realises (17) _____ (the tools / to make) the wrong noises. (18) _____ (why / the man / to charge / not) them properly?! Knowing Mr Duff is proud, Mr Benton suggests Mrs Duff charge the tools at night, when (19) _____ (her husband / to watch / not). She does, and soon the construction speeds up. (20) _____ (everything / to come) together – just in time.

7. Present Perfect

7.1 Present Perfect Statements

Form complete sentences in the **present perfect** (affirmative or negative), without contractions, using the information provided.

For example:

Q: the engineer / to repair / the van

A: The engineer has repaired the van.

1. Remi / to choose / her dress carefully

   _____

2. the sailors / to paint / the boat bright green

   _____

3. the dentists / to order / a new chair

   _____

4. my father / to retire / not / yet

   _____

5. you / to create / a wonderful display

   _____

6. the Robinsons / to prepare / not / the table for dinner

   _____

7. we / to pay / the delivery man for the pizza

   _____

8. I / to refuse / to take part in the parade

   _____

9. the police / to identify / not / the thief

   _____

10. she / to mention / her family's wealth many times

   _____

11. Edward / to believe / not / in Santa since he was young

_____

12. the bus service / to improve / not

_____

13. I / recommend / this movie many times

_____

14. the storm / to destroy / our fence

_____

15. my parents / to decide / not / which house to buy

_____

7.2 Present Perfect Questions 1

Convert the following statements into **present perfect _yes_ or _no_ questions** (they do not require question words). First person statements should become second person questions.

  For example:

  Q: She has visited over 50 countries.

  A: Has she visited over 50 countries?

1. You have seen the newspaper this morning.

_____

2. The weather is getting better. (to improve)

_____

3. All the boxes are gone. (they / to take)

_____

4. We have got some bread.

_____

5. Drew has told you about her exam results.

_____

6. The postman has delivered your package.

_____

7. Your wife has agreed to a colour for the walls.

8. I'm unsure if we've brought enough cheese.

9. The teacher set some homework.

10. The grass looks like it has been cut. (the gardener / to cut)

11. Carl and Harry spent all their holiday money.

12. You must listen to this new song. (to hear)

13. My mother is going to the market.

14. I understand this correctly.

15. All the teams are submitting their final answers.

7.3 Present Perfect Questions 2

Convert the following statements into **present perfect questions**, using the question words provided. First person statements should become second person questions.

For example:

Q: They have offered us a free box of muffins. (what)

A: What have they offered you?

1. I received this package. (why)

2. You have not been in the office this month. (where)

3.   Rebecca did something with her hair. (what)

_____

4.   Something fell out of the basket. (what)

_____

5.   The farmer has raised many pigs. (how many)

_____

6.   The club has closed. (why)

_____

7.   My sweets are gone. (where)

_____

8.   You have chosen some socks to wear. (which)

_____

9.   The scientist has never been wrong. (when)

_____

10. The company supplied us with recycled paper. (which paper)

_____

11. She has failed to convince them. (why)

_____

12. This musician remains unknown. (how)

_____

13. You put my violin somewhere. (where)

_____

14. You have fed something to those ducks. (what)

_____

15. Sally flew to Portugal. (why)

_____

7.4 Present Perfect Negative Questions

Complete the following sentences in the **present perfect negative question form**, without contractions, using the subjects and verbs in brackets.
For example:
Q: _____ to Belgium? (who / to be)
A: Who has not been to Belgium?

1.   _____ the news? (you / to hear)
2.   _____ him? (why / his sister / to forgive)
3.   _____ ? (what / the mice / to eat)
4.   _____ yet? (the meeting / to finish)
5.   Which rooms _____? (they / to clean)
6.   _____ enough? (these people / to suffer)
7.   _____ more umbrellas? (why / the store / to sell)
8.   _____ in this report? (what problems / the team / to analyse)
9.   _____ about the cinema? (Terry / to reply)
10. _____ of? (what / we / to think)

7.5 Mixed Present Perfect

Complete the following text with the appropriate **present perfect affirmative**, **negative** or **question form**, using the information in brackets.

Molly's Travels

(1) _____ (Molly / to return) after a year of travelling. (2) _____ (she / to bring) her family many gifts, but they are more interested in her stories. (3) _____ (where / she / to be)? What fascinating sights (4) _____ (she / to see)?

   "(5) _____ (I / to experience) many things," Molly says.

"(6) _____ (I / to wasted / not) the time I had. (7) _____ (you / to read / not) my blog about it?"

Most of her family read the blog, but (8) _____ (her Dad / to find / not) the time yet. He asks, "What exotic foods (9) _____ (you / to try)?"

"(10) _____ (I / to write) so many things about the dishes in China already!" Molly says. "(11) _____ (one blog post / to reach) 5,000 visitors so far."

Everyone congratulates her. Dad wonders, (12) _____ (why / so many people / to visit) Molly's blog? He did not know she was a talented writer.

"Which country did you like most?" Mum asks.

"America is nice," Molly says, "but (13) _____ (Australia / to steal) my heart for good. (14) _____ (I / to enjoy / not) better weather anywhere else in my life! (15) _____ (my new friends / to invite) me back to Melbourne already."

(16) _____ (she / to make) new friends across the world, to go with this successful blog? (17) _____ (travelling / to change) his daughter, Dad can see. (18) _____ (where / his shy little girl / to go)? Perhaps now the better question is, (19) _____ (where / she / to be / not)? He is happy for her, though, and (20) _____ (he / to learn) his lesson. Next time she goes away, he will pay more attention!

8. Present Perfect Continuous

8.1 Present Perfect Continuous Statements

Form complete sentences in the **present perfect continuous** (affirmative or negative), without contractions, using the information provided.

For example:

Q: Billy / to feed / the ducks all week

A: Billy has been feeding the ducks all week.

1. we / to live / here for eight years

   _____

2. I / to listen / to pop music

   _____

3. it / to get / harder to park on my road

   _____

4. those boys / to sit / there for hours

   _____

5. Ferdinand / to take / not / French lessons

   _____

6. our car / to make / strange noises

   _____

7. he / to talk / for 30 minutes

   _____

8. pigeons / to nest / on our roof

   _____

9. the pie shop / to turn / people away

   _____

10. she / to sell / her paintings cheaply

   _____

11. you / to watch / not / TV all morning

   _____

12. Eric / to draw / not / funny cartoons

_____

13. the phone / to ring / non-stop

_____

14. I / to read / a book about trees

_____

15. more raccoons / to steal / from our bins

_____

8.2 Present Perfect Continuous Questions 1

Convert the following statements into **present perfect continuous** *yes* or *no* **questions** (they do not require question words). First person statements should become second person questions.

For example:

Q: I have been running today.

A: Have you been running today?

1. I haven't been practising hard enough.

_____

2. We have been making too much noise.

_____

3. She has been swimming in the lake.

_____

4. I'm not sure if you heard. (to listen)

_____

5. The days seem to be getting dark earlier.

_____

6. No one has watered the plants.

_____

7. They have been waiting for a long time.

_____

8.   Tim might be working for your father.

_____

9.   I might have been paying too much for soap.

_____

10. The fox has been sleeping in the garden.

_____

8.3 Present Perfect Continuous Questions 2

Convert the following statements into **present perfect continuous questions**, using the question words provided. First person statements should become second person questions.

For example:

Q: William has been feeding his rabbit grass. (what)

A: What has William been feeding his rabbit?

1.   This story has been going somewhere. (where)

_____

2.   My computer has been heating up. (why)

_____

3.   Oliver has been riding horses for many years. (how long)

_____

4.   She has been sending out invitations. (why)

_____

5.   Something has been happening in town this weekend. (what)

_____

6.   They have been delivering our mail to the wrong address. (where)

_____

7.   I don't know what the trucks have been carrying this week. (what)

_____

8.   The geography club has been exploring in a jungle. (which)

_____

9. Mr Jones has been teaching us anatomy. (what)

_____

10. The batteries have been charging for two hours. (how long)

_____

8.4 Present Perfect Continuous Negative Questions

Complete the following sentences in the **present perfect continuous negative question form**, without contractions, using the subjects and verbs in brackets.

For example:

Q: Where _____ cookies? (the girl / to deliver)

A: Where **has the girl not been delivering** cookies?

1. What _____ us? (Len / to tell)

2. _____? (anyone / to study)

3. _____ this weekend? (who / to read)

4. What _____ right? (she / to do)

5. _____ to dance class regularly? (you / to go)

6. _____ Wanda enough attention? (I / to give)

7. Why _____ this spring? (the wind / to blow)

8. What questions _____? (the reporters / to ask)

9. _____ you? (that sound / to worry)

10. Why _____ harder? (the team / to work)

8.5 Mixed Present Perfect Continuous

Complete the following text with the appropriate **present perfect continuous affirmative**, **negative** or **question form**, using the information in brackets.

Cleaning the Beach

(1) _____ (the council / to make) efforts to improve Worthing's beach. For a long time, (2) _____ (the beach / to suffer) from soiled water. (3) _____ (the daily tests / to meet / not) expected hygiene levels. (4) _____ (what / to cause) this?

The council claims there are two main problems with the water. One is waste from people, where (5) _____ (holiday-makers / to pick up / not) after themselves. Another is waste from animals – where (6) _____ (people / to clean up / not) after their dogs.

(7) _____ (what / the council / to do) to change this?

Litter pick stations have been set up. (8) _____ (visitors / to collect) rubbish whilst walking on the beach. (9) _____ (the council / to provide) bags and "grab sticks" to encourage this. (10) _____ (children / to treat) this as a game: how much litter can they pick up in an hour?

Meanwhile, dogs are no longer allowed on the beach during summer. (11) _____ (dog walkers / to ignore) the signs, so there are now big fines in place. (12) _____ (beach patrols / to warn) dog walkers not to use certain areas to avoid being fined. Not everyone is happy about this. Hillary Menrose complained, "(13) _____ (why / they / to focus) so hard on dogs, when seagulls make just as much mess. We always pick up after Fluff Doogle on our walks, but (14) _____ (I / to watch) those birds, and they drop litter, too!"

There were big protests when the council wished to further limit dog walkers, and (15) _____ (the truth / to come out). Actually, there is a third reason that the sea is dirty: (16) _____ (the water company / to dump) waste into the sea. (17) _____ (why / the council / to focus / not) on them? One thing's for sure: (18) _____ (the beach / to get / finally) the attention it deserves!

Forming the Future

9. Future Simple

9.1 Future Simple Statements

Form complete sentences in the **future simple** (affirmative or negative), without contractions, using the information provided. The questions indicate whether to use the **will** or **going to** form.

For example:

Q: we / to be going to / not / to travel / for three months
A: We are not going to travel for three months.

1. the final exam / will / to be / difficult

   _____

2. our friends / will / to come / for dinner

   _____

3. they / to be going to / not / to watch / the show together

   _____

4. Sasha / will / not / to buy / the next round of drinks

   _____

5. Amy / to be going to / to regret / her decision

   _____

6. my shoes / to be going to / not / to last / another winter

   _____

7. you / will / not / to agree / with me

   _____

8. the church bells / to be going to / to ring / today

   _____

9.   those geese / will / to steal / your bread

_____

10.   the client / will / to approve / these new designs

_____

11.   I / to be going to / not / to lend / Charles any more money

_____

12.   Mrs Freda / will / not / to teach / noisy children

_____

13.   the festival / to be going to / to include / a lot of musicians

_____

14.   your new table / will / to arrive / tomorrow

_____

15.   this course / to be going to / not / to take / very long

_____

9.2 Future Simple Questions 1

Convert the following statements into **future simple** *yes* **or** *no* **questions** (they do not require question words). The questions indicate whether to use the **will** or **going to** form when necessary. First person statements should become second person questions.

For example:

Q: I'm not sure if the waiter will clear away my dirty dishes.

A: Will the waiter clear away your dirty dishes?

1.   You are going to the party on Saturday.

_____

2.   I wonder if he is going to give back my book.

_____

3.   The actor must remember his lines. (will)

_____

4. I'm not sure if this bus stops in Portsmouth. (to be going to)

    _____

5. The performance had better start on time. (will)

    _____

6. Vera hopes to meet the man of her dreams. (will)

    _____

7. The Olympics might be held in Italy. (to be going to)

    _____

8. Tom will admit that he ate the cake.

    _____

9. Our house should sell by September. (to be going to)

    _____

10. You have not finished your coffee. (to be going to)

    _____

11. The old bicycle might need to be repaired. (will)

    _____

12. James should bring his wife to the concert. (will)

    _____

13. The doors need to be replaced. (to be going to)

    _____

14. That truck might not fit in the parking space. (to be going to)

    _____

15. I think the T-shirt is going to shrink in the washing machine.

    _____

16. We want to split the bill evenly. (will)

    _____

17. She must learn these words by Tuesday. (will)

    _____

18. I am hoping to see my cousins at the weekend. (to be going to)

    _____

19. Our town might change over the next five years. (will)

_____

20. It looks like that young man is about to propose to his girlfriend. (to be going to)

_____

9.3 Future Simple Questions 2

Convert the following statements into **future simple questions**, using the question words provided. First person statements should become second person questions.

For example:

Q: Dom is going to ask for a raise tomorrow. (when)

A: When is Dom going to ask for a raise?

1. Someone must pay for this damage. (who / to be going to)

_____

2. The builders will finish the roof soon. (when)

_____

3. Something is going to happen to the vacant beach huts. (what)

_____

4. Harry intends to climb that tree. (how / to be going to)

_____

5. The papers are writing about the new President. (what / will)

_____

6. You are going to lose your job. (why)

_____

7. My father will return from his holiday this Monday. (when)

_____

8. The barbecue is going to be held in the park. (why)

_____

9. We need to find a good carpet. (where / to be going to)

_____

10. The mice will cause havoc. (how)

_____

11. I must do something while my computer is updating. (what / will)

_____

12. She is going to cook something for her lunch. (what)

_____

13. The new product is going to be ready by autumn. (when)

_____

14. I need someone to volunteer to take my Saturday shift. (who / will)

_____

15. You will go somewhere for your summer holiday. (where)

_____

9.4 Future Simple Negative Questions

Complete the following sentences in **future simple negative question form**, without contractions, using the subjects and verbs in brackets.
    For example:
    Q: What _____ her parents? (Olivia / to be going to / to tell)
    A: What **is Olivia not going to tell** her parents?

1. _____ next year? (you / will / to return)
2. When _____ at home? (they / to be going to / to be)
3. _____ on his trip? (what / Drew / to be going to / to take)
4. _____ TV for a week? (how / I / will / to watch)
5. _____ pasta for dinner? (we / to be going to / prepare)
6. Why _____ them more toys? (their mother / to be going to / to buy)
7. What terms _____ to? (they / will / to agree)

8. _____ with us to Kent? (who / will / to come)

9. _____? (that tall cake / to be going to / to fall over)

10. _____ to her wedding? (who / she / will / to invite)

9.5 Mixed Future Simple

Complete the following text with the appropriate **future simple affirmative**, **negative** or **question form**, using the information in brackets.

The Spaceship

(1) _____ (we / to be going to / to build) a spaceship in our back garden. (2) _____ (it / will / not / to be) easy, but we have the plans and the right tools. (3) _____ (my Uncle Jimmy / will / to help) put it together, as (4) _____ (he / to be going to / to need) to earn his keep while he stays with us this summer. We haven't asked him yet, but (5) _____ (he / will / to say) yes, I am sure. But (6) _____ (we / to be going to / to share) all our plans with him? I hope (7) _____ (he / will / to agree) without knowing how valuable the project is.

(8) _____ (the rocket / will / to fly) faster and higher than any before. (9) _____ (it / to be going to / not / to cost) much to make, because (10) _____ (my dad / will / to find) good materials in the dump. I do have some unanswered questions, though: (11) _____ (how many / people / will / to fit) inside? (12) _____ (the government / to be going to / to notice) what we are doing? If they hear about our amazing rocket, (13) _____ (they / will / not / to allow) us to succeed. The government does not want competition – (14) _____ (our rocket / to be going to / to reach)

Venus. (15) _____ (we / will / to discover) valuable diamonds before they do.

Mum thinks I can't do it. She says, "(16) _____ (what / you / will / to use) to fuel the rocket?"

"Hope," I tell her. "(17) _____ (it / to be going to / to work) because we have hope."

And anyway, (18) _____ (we / will / to persuade) Jimmy to deal with the other problems. We are the brains and the planners, after all: (19) _____ (the adults / will / to build) it. As long as (20) _____ (Uncle Jimmy / to be going to / not / to steal) our ideas.

10. Future Continuous

10.1 Future Continuous Statements

Form complete sentences in the **future continuous** (affirmative or negative), without contractions, using the information provided. The questions indicate whether to use the **will** or **going to** form.

For example:

Q: Jamie / will / to attend / the conference with Howard.

A: Jamie **will be attending** the conference with Howard.

1. I / will / to ask / everyone two questions

   _____

2. the days / to be going to / to get / longer

   _____

3. my friend / will / to drive / us to Oxford

   _____

4. we / will / to play / football all morning

   _____

5. you / to be going to / to wait / for hours

   _____

6. Richard / to be going to / not / to research / traffic control this week

   _____

7. she / will / to sweep / the floor

   _____

8. the company / to be going to / to organise / a trip soon

   _____

9. I / to be going to / not / to work / this afternoon

   _____

10. Penny / will / to aim / for the best results

   _____

555

11. he / to be going to / to add / songs to his playlist all night

12. the bank / will / not / to open / a new branch in Rye

13. we / to be going to / to dance / on stage this Friday

14. you / to be going to / not / to sit / there when I get back

15. the baby / will / to wake up / soon

10.2 Future Continuous Questions 1

Convert the following statements into **future continuous** *yes* or *no* **questions** (they do not require question words). The questions indicate whether to use the **will** or **going to** form and particular verbs. First person statements should become second person questions.

For example:

Q: I would like a break soon. (to be going to / to get)

A: Are you going to be getting a break soon?

1. You are going to be washing these dishes.

2. Jools should go to Detroit by train. (will / to take)

3. They might supply us with milk. (will / to supply)

4. Eric is going to be expanding his gallery.

5. I hope she is going to be speaking on the panel.

6. The badgers might be sleeping during the day. (will)

    _____

7. No one is sure if the producers will be continuing the radio show. (will)

    _____

8. They might be closing more stores. (to be going to)

    _____

9. The planes could be landing at this airport. (will)

    _____

10. Mrs Antwerp may spend time here during her visit. (to be going to)

    _____

11. The Duke might discuss his retirement this week. (to be going to / to announce)

    _____

12. We will be meeting the neighbours together.

    _____

13. They said they might collect the sofa today. (will / to collect)

    _____

14. That field is where the farmer should grow wheat. (to be going to / to plant)

    _____

15. I heard you might perform at the Royal Albert Hall. (to be going to)

    _____

10.3 Future Continuous Questions 2

Convert the following statements into **future continuous questions**, using the question words and other information provided. The questions indicate whether to use the **will** or **going to** form. First person statements should become second person questions.

For example:

Q: The boat is leaving at 3 p.m. (when / to be going to)

A: When is the boat going to be leaving?

1. Everyone will be sitting in the living room this evening. (where)

    _____

2. You are going to be doing lots in Bali. (what)

    _____

3. Tristan plans to exercise more this month. (how often / to be going to / to exercise)

    _____

4. Greta is giving a speech on Wednesday. (what / will / to talk about)

    _____

5. I must share a room. (who / to be going to / with)

    _____

6. She should be jogging tomorrow. (when / to be going to)

    _____

7. They need to clear away this mess. (will)

    _____

8. I will read a crime thriller next week. (what)

    _____

9. The barman is hanging his new fairy lights all over the bar. (where / will)

    _____

10. Clive has been fixing that van for a long time. (how long / to be going to / to fix)

    _____

11. We are going to be skating outside tomorrow. (where)

    _____

12. There will be a prize for the best costume. (who / will / to wear)

    _____

13. The school is starting to teach Pilates this spring. (what / to be going to / to teach)

    _____

14. The bakers sell their doughnuts at unusual times. (when / to be going to / to sell)

    _____

15. Someone must accept the award. (who / to be going to / to accept)

    _____

10.4 Future Continuous Negative Questions

Complete the following sentences in **future continuous negative question form**, without contractions, using the subjects and verbs in brackets. The questions indicate whether to use the **will** or **going to** form.

For example:

Q: Why _____ his calls? (will / Grant / to answer)

A: Why **will Grant not be answering** his calls?

1. When _____ this week? (you / will / to study)
2. _____ tomorrow? (the girls / to be going to / to swim)
3. Where _____ the horse? (he / to be going to / to ride)
4. Why _____ the party? (they / will / to attend)
5. _____ a new dish? (the chef / will / to prepare)
6. _____ for the President's arrival? (the flag / to be going to / to fly)

7. Why _____ for the escaped mongoose with us? (they / will / to look)

8. What _____ on this trip? (Liz / will / to bring)

9. Why _____ the badminton club? (you / to be going to / to join)

10. _____ the boiler over lunch? (the plumber / to be going to / to repair)

10.5 Mixed Future Continuous

Complete the following text with the appropriate **future continuous affirmative**, **negative** or **question form**, using the information in brackets. The questions indicate whether to use the **will** or **going to** form.

The Scout Trip

The Wood Row (1) _____ (scouts / will / to go) to the New Forest for four days next week. (2) _____ (they / to be going to / to camp) in a field where they will study the local wildlife. Their leader, Mr Ryan, said, "(3) _____ (the children / to be going to / not / to laze) about. (4) _____ (they / will / to challenge) themselves all weekend, so they can learn more."

(5) _____ (what / will / the scouts / to do) on their adventure? A full itinerary has been prepared:

(6) _____ (the children / will / to make) notes about the animals they see. (7) _____ (they / will / to hike) for three hours each day, and (8) _____ (they / will / not / to rest) much at camp, as (9) _____ (everyone / to be going to / to cook) two meals each day. Phones are banned, so

(10) _____ (the children / will / not / to call) home.

(11) _____ (what else / to be going to / to happen) over the weekend? Well, (12) _____ (the weather / will / to change) on Saturday morning – from sunny to rainy – but (13) _____ (Mr Ryan / will / not / to let) that stop them. He asked himself, "When (14) _____ (it / will / not / to rain)?" and made sure that (15) _____ (their activities / to be going to / to occur) at those times.

"(16) _____ (I / will / to prepare) alternative indoor activities, too", he said. "(17) _____ (what / we / will / to do) while it's raining? Well, there's a nice old car museum to explore, for starters."

One thing is for sure: the young scouts are going to be tired.

11. Future Perfect

11.1 Future Perfect Statements

Form complete sentences in the **future perfect** (affirmative or negative), without contractions, using the information provided. The questions indicate whether to use the **will** or **going to** form.

For example:

Q: the burritos / will / to eat / by dawn

A: The burritos will have been eaten by dawn.

1. we / will / to decide / by 1 p.m.

   _____

2. she / will / to sell / the dress before noon

   _____

3. I / to be going to / not / to finish / this book by nightfall

   _____

4. the workers / will / to paint / our bedroom

   _____

5. you / will / to accept / my proposal by Friday

   _____

6. Regina / to be going to / to design / a new logo before the meeting

   _____

7. the champion / to be going to / to play / his last game by December

   _____

8. the scientists / will / to add / the new planets to the map

   _____

9. the council / will / to clear / the roads for the festival

   _____

10. our neighbours / to be going to / to replace / their windows by Monday

    _____

11. the keys / will / not / to be / find / by then

_____

12. the university / will / to award / my niece a prize

_____

13. Victor / to be going to / to escape / before we get back

_____

14. the groundsmen / will / to plant / new grass over the old field

_____

15. the eggs / will / not / to go / bad

_____

11.2 Future Perfect Questions 1

Convert the following statements into **future perfect** *yes* or *no* **questions** (they do not require question words). The questions indicate whether to use the **will** or **going to** form. First person statements should become second person questions.

For example:

Q: I am not sure if I will finish my essay in time.
A: Will you have finished your essay in time?

1. They have to replace the batteries by tomorrow. (will)

_____

2. You are going to measure the temperature.

_____

3. You must wash the dishes in time for dinner. (will)

_____

4. I wonder if the dentist has raised her prices. (will)

_____

5. They are going to have fixed the leaking sink by 10 a.m.

_____

6. I am not sure if I am going to have managed this project well.

   _____

7. The new batteries are going to arrive in time.

   _____

8. Perhaps the hats will have sold.

   _____

9. Billie will have brought her best socks.

   _____

10. Mrs Carter should have visited her daughter. (to be going to)

    _____

11. Petrol prices might have risen again. (will)

    _____

12. The priest must learn to dance before the ball. (to be going to)

    _____

13. The geese are going to have left the park.

    _____

14. We must make enough scones for everyone. (will)

    _____

15. The panel will have discussed the important issues.

    _____

11.3 Future Perfect Questions 2

Convert the following statements into **future perfect questions**, using the question words provided. The questions indicate whether to use the **will** or **going to** form. First person statements should become second person questions.

For example:

Q: They will have built three new condos by spring. (what)

A: What will they have built by spring?

1.   Some people are going to have eaten before the party. (who)

_____

2.   The wall will have been damaged. (what / to happen)

_____

3.   You are going to have stayed in many places this summer. (where)

_____

4.   Manny must not have returned that book yet. (when / to be going to)

_____

5.   The pirates will have hidden the treasure. (where)

_____

6.   The manager will have handled his own accounts. (how)

_____

7.   Our clients are going to have paid us by Wednesday. (when)

_____

8.   I will have learned many things on the course. (what)

_____

9.   The sandwiches will have been prepared before lunch. (when)

_____

10. The traders are going to have docked the ship in Portsmouth. (where)

_____

11.4 Future Perfect Negative Questions

Complete the following sentences in **future perfect negative question form**, without contractions, using the subjects and verbs in brackets. The questions indicate whether to use the **will** or **going to** form.

For example:

Q: _____ the assignment on time? (who / will / to complete)

A: Who will have not completed the assignment on time?

1. Where _____? (Darren / to be going to / to be)

2. What _____ through? (the gerbils / will / to bite)

3. Why _____ from their mistakes? (they / will / to learn)

4. How many _____ by Saturday? (cakes / you / to be going to / to make)

5. _____ her article on time? (the reporter / will / to write)

6. _____ this puzzle before the bell? (who / to be going to / to solve)

7. Why _____ her dress before tomorrow? (Mrs Harris / to be going to / to fix)

8. _____ a delay? (the traffic / will / to cause)

9. Where _____ by the end of my reading tour? (I / to be going to / to speak)

10. Why _____ the bad news before he arrives? (they / will / to deliver)

11.5 Mixed Future Perfect

Complete the following text with the appropriate **future perfect affirmative**, **negative** or **question form**, using the information in brackets. The questions indicate whether to use the **will** or **going to** form.

The Big Presentation

Bob and Charlotte are giving a big presentation tomorrow at 2 p.m. Their (1) _____ (German clients / will / to arrive) by then, and it is important to impress them. There is lots to do. (2) _____ (they / will / to finish) the overall report by this evening, but the graphs will be incomplete as (3) _____ (they / to be going to / not / to process) all the data in time. Charlotte is worried because she has to take her children to school before work in the morning, but (4) _____ (Bob / will / to start) on the graphs before she arrives.

(5) _____ (what / he / will / to do)? She hopes (6) _____ (he / to be going to / to call) the research department and compiled their data. (7) _____ (what / he / will / not / to complete)? The graphs themselves. Unfortunately, Bob is not very good with graph software. But Charlotte imagines (8) _____ (she / will / to create) all the necessary graphs before noon. That will give them time to prepare to greet the clients.

Charlotte will be so busy, she will not have time for lunch. (9) _____ (she / will / to prepare) smoothies in the morning, though. Hopefully the clients won't notice (10) _____ (she / to be going to / to eat / not) lunch. (11) _____ (the pair / will / to polish) their presentation to such a high standard, the clients should be too impressed to care about anything else. By tomorrow afternoon, Charlotte imagines (12) _____ (they / will / to seal) the deal.

12. Future Perfect Continuous

12.1 Future Perfect Continuous Statements

Form complete sentences in the **future perfect continuous** (affirmative or negative), without contractions, using the information provided. The questions indicate whether to use the **will** or **going to** form.

For example:

Q: Herman / will / to live / in Dresden for two years by this summer

A: Herman will have been living in Dresden for two years by this summer.

1. I / will / to learn / Mandarin for a month by this Friday

    _____

2. soon, the couple / will / to argue / for 20 minutes

    _____

3. we / to be going to / to dance / all night long

    _____

4. you / will / to choose / the flowers carefully

    _____

5. the storm clouds / to be going to / to gather / for a while

    _____

6. Georgie / will / to listen / to pop music again

    _____

7. our dog / will / to sleep / while we were out

    _____

8. I / to be going to / to cycle / all morning, so I'll need a shower

    _____

9. Carl / will / to practise / for the Olympics

    _____

10. the boats / will / to bump / into each other overnight

    _____

11. the spies / will / to listen

   _____

12. my uncle / to be going to / to research / our family history ahead of
    the reunion

   _____

13. it / will / to get / hotter before we go on holiday

   _____

14. the tree / will / to shed / its leaves for weeks

   _____

15. she / to be going to / to laugh / at her own radio show

   _____

12.2 Future Perfect Continuous Questions 1

Convert the following statements into **future perfect continuous** *yes* or *no*
questions (they do not require question words). Where necessary, the
questions indicate whether to use the **will** or **going to** form. First person
statements should become second person questions.

For example:

Q: He will have studied in Wales for a long time.

A: Will he have been studying in Wales for a long time?

1. We might be waiting all morning. (to be going to)

   _____

2. Nancy will have been singing throughout the first act.

   _____

3. They will bake a cake. (will)

   _____

4. I am going to have been wasting my time.

   _____

5. The shoppers are going to queue for hours.

   _____

6. I hope Charlie shaves regularly during the holiday. (will)

_____

7. We will have been writing to each other a for long time.

_____

8. Sally is going to have been working in insurance for two years.

_____

9. The tide should have been going out. (to be going to)

_____

10. The grapes might have been getting mouldy. (will)

_____

12.3 Future Perfect Continuous Questions 2

Convert the following statements into **future perfect continuous questions**, using the question words provided. The questions indicate whether to use the **will** or **going to** form. First person statements should become second person questions.

For example:

Q: They will have been travelling by boat. (why)
A: Why will they have been travelling by boat?

1. She will have been practising for a long time. (how long)

_____

2. Jim will have been swimming in the creek. (where)

_____

3. You are going to have been travelling a great distance. (how far)

_____

4. The trucks are going to have been carrying crackers. (what)

_____

5. The children will have been walking home. (why)

_____

6. We are going to have been working on this project for months. (how long)

_____

7. They are going to have been waiting for a decision. (what)

_____

8. The foxes will have been gathering in the garden. (why)

_____

9. He is going to have been asking for help. (who)

_____

10. The intern is going to have been saying good things about his job. (what)

_____

12.4 Future Perfect Continuous Negative Questions

Complete the following sentences in **future perfect continuous negative question form**, without contractions, using the subjects and verbs in brackets. The questions indicate whether to use the **will** or **going to** form.

For example:

Q: Why _____? (the surgeon / will / to operate)

A: Why **will the surgeon not have been operating**?

1. Where _____? (the tractor / will / to go)

2. _____ enough? (I / to be going to / to participate)

3. How long _____ for? (your aunt / to be going to / to work)

4. What _____? (we / to be going to / to see)

5. _____ hope? (they / will / to lose)

6. Why _____ for the test? (he / to be going to / to prepare)

7. Which buildings _____? (the company / will / to develop)

8. _____ in the right places? (the coats / to be going to / to hang)

9. _____ upright? (the guard / will / to stand)

10. What _____ us? (our friends / will / to show)

12.5 Mixed Future Perfect Continuous

Complete the following text with the appropriate **future perfect continuous affirmative**, **negative** or **question form**, using the information in brackets. The questions indicate whether to use the **will** or **going to** form.

The Fish of Mugrub

Things have been changing in the fishing village of Mugrub. By November, (1) _____ (things / will / to change) for five years. Lots of new buildings have been built there; some residents feel that when the next few projects begin (2) _____ (they / will / to build) apartments forever. Resident Liam McDonald said, "And because of the noise, when they finish, (3) _____ (we / will / not / to sleep) for years!"

Tourists and researchers have been coming to Mugrub to see a new glowing fish, discovered almost five years ago. If projections are met this December, (4) _____ (the population / will / to grow) by 25% each year. Should the latest tackle shop get permission, (5) _____ (new shops / will / to open) at a rate of four a year. But has happiness been increasing in the same way?

"(6) _____ (I / will / to live) here for three decades this August," McDonald said. "And (7) _____ (I / will / not to work) for almost half of that. I liked the peace and quiet before. The mayor says it will calm down, but (8) _____ (these outsiders / to be going to / not / to hovering) around for five years, soon?"

Not everyone is as unhappy with the changing village. Shop owner Jenny McCluck looks forward to the future: "I imagine (9) _____ (we / will / to get) visitors from all over the world during the summer. They cannot resist the village, and though (10) _____ (they / to be going to / not / to expect) to stay long, they will do. It's good for business."

It's also good for the glowing fish. This summer, (11) _____ (local researchers / will / to apply) for grants each year for the past five years – and they are confident Mugrub's popularity will finally secure funding this time. Dr Bailey said, "Next year, we expect to uncover the mysteries of the glowing fish, as (12) _____ (we / to be going to / not / to waste) time searching for funding!"

Forming Mixed Tenses

13. Mixed Simple Tenses

13.1 Simple Tenses Scramble

The following sentences have been scrambled. Form complete **past simple**, **present simple** or **future simple statements and questions** using the words provided.

For example:

Q: washed / Mary / in the river / her clothes

A: Mary washed her clothes in the river.

1. isn't / ? / this / easy

   _____

2. too many people / were / on the boat / there

   _____

3. not / seem / Paul / does / ? / quiet today

   _____

4. loud / swans / very / are

   _____

5. to go swimming / not / is / it / a good day

   _____

6. will / to the gala / wear / ? / what / you

   _____

7. waited / we / for hours

   _____

8. be / before noon / they / at the dock / will

    _____

9. this photo / ? / real / to you / does / look

    _____

10. did / her house / ? / Nina / when / buy

    _____

11. she / for more mushrooms / to the shop / went

    _____

12. always / I / my wallet behind / leave

    _____

13. later / your room / won't / ? / tidy / you

    _____

14. too tired / you / to swim / look

    _____

15. a new boat / the fisherman / did / ? / how / buy

    _____

16. to me most / this tie / appeals

    _____

17. their medicine / who / ? / did / take / not / this morning

    _____

18. give up / not / on this reform / will / the President

    _____

19. over a period of many years / fell apart / our house

    _____

20. perfect / practice / makes

    _____

13.2 Simple Questions

Form **past simple**, **present simple** or **future simple questions** using the information provided. Use the **will** form for future questions. First person statements should become second person questions.

For example:

Q: I could not find my book. (where / to be)

A: Where was your book?

1. I'm not sure what rabbits eat. (to eat / grass)

    _____

2. Jimmy was muddy. (to fall / the mud)

    _____

3. The circus always makes you happy. (you / to enjoy)

    _____

4. Wendy should be in the market tomorrow, but she hasn't confirmed.

    _____

5. The river runs through the north part of town. (where / to run)

    _____

6. Dozens of men waited in the street. (how many)

    _____

7. The man was still on the bench, two hours later. (he / to sit / for two hours)

    _____

8. There should be twenty people at dinner.

    _____

9. We cannot wait past noon for the delivery. (what time / the delivery / to arrive)

    _____

10. They study very hard just before exams. (when)

    _____

11. Cape Town was the busiest city that year. (which)

_____

12. Someone must watch my child tomorrow. (who)

_____

13. He claims men are less healthy than women. (men)

_____

14. The squirrels will steal those nuts.

_____

15. The radio stopped working. (the radio's battery / to run out)

_____

16. She likes many flowers, but especially marigolds. (the marigold / to be / her favourite)

_____

17. I saw Polly with a bicycle but I'm not sure if it is hers. (Polly / to own)

_____

18. The lifeguards saved all the children. (who)

_____

19. When I am older, I intend to get twenty cats.

_____

20. Before the war, this shop had fresh bread. (to sell)

_____

13.3 Simple Negative Questions

Form **past simple**, **present simple** or **future simple negative questions** using the information provided, with or without contractions. Use the **will** form for future questions. First person statements should become second person questions.

For example:

Q: Children are playing outside today when they should be in school. (the school / to open)

A: Is the school not open today? *or* Isn't the school open today?

1. Robert only has vegetables on his plate. (to eat / meat)

   _____

2. The investigator wrote a confusing summary of the report. (to understand / the report)

   _____

3. Our charity isn't getting donations. (why / people / will / to give)

   _____

4. She refuses to see her mother again. (she / to visit)

   _____

5. You don't look happy about the bagpipes playing. (you / to like)

   _____

6. Harry is unwell, perhaps he will not go to school tomorrow.

   _____

7. Our friends did not meet until college.

   _____

8. These questions are very strange.

   _____

9. Running every day might make me fit, but I'm not sure.

   _____

10. The ducks look hungry again. (you / to feed)

    _____

11. Julian does not practise guitar very often. (who)

_____

12. The council did not remove our rubbish this week. (why)

_____

13. There is nowhere to park, but our friends are coming. (they / to be able to / their car)

_____

14. Simon took his driving test but is not driving. (Simon / to pass)

_____

15. Something is not right. (what / to look)

_____

13.4 Mixed Simple Corrections

Identify grammatical mistakes in the following **simple** tense sentences, marking the sentences as either **correct** or **incorrect**.

For example:

Q: She watch TV every day.

A: Incorrect – *She **watches** TV every day.*

1. The employee will wait until he is called.

_____

2. I do live there anymore.

_____

3. The kitchen smell like sweet apple pie.

_____

4. I did not pass my exams last week.

_____

5. Herman and Claire enjoys playing chess on Saturdays.

_____

6.   That woman is exactly who she says she is.

_____

7.   You will not improve if you do not study.

_____

8.   This aeroplane will flies if it is repaired.

_____

9.   He did not arrived in time for the show last night.

_____

10. The greyhounds returns after they escaped.

_____

11. The little children seem tired at the moment.

_____

12. The car looked dirty now.

_____

13. The toaster works when we tried it earlier.

_____

14. Dani will not come to the seminar this evening.

_____

15. They want all the different flavoured pizzas available now.

_____

13.5 Mixed Simple Tenses

Complete the following text with the appropriate **past simple**, **present simple** or **future simple** forms, using the information in brackets.

A House by the Sea

(1) _____ (Bill / to live) in a bungalow by the sea, now.
(2) _____ (his house / to sit) opposite the beach.
(3) _____ (he / always / to dream) of owning a house with a sea view, and (4) _____ (he / finally / to have) it.
(5) _____ (it / to take) him fifteen years to find the right home.
At times, (6) _____ (he / not / to believe) it would be possible.
(7) _____ (his friends / often / to ask), "(8) _____
(why / you / to want) a home by the sea? (9) _____ (did / anyone / not / to tell) you that the sea is dangerous? (10) _____ (you / will / not / to drown)?"

Indeed, before he moved, (11) _____ (many people / to say) that storms and floods could damage a seaside home. (12) _____ (beach property / to tend) to be expensive, too. And in England, (13) _____ (it / to be / not / easy) to find space along the sea, certainly not near big towns. (14) _____ (these details / to bother / not) Bill. Whatever the price, (15) _____ (he / to determine), his dream would come true.

Finally, (16) _____ (he / to save) enough money and found exactly the right place. (17) _____ (he / to buy) his bungalow outright. Now, (18) _____ (he / to enjoy) sitting on the porch watching the waves. (19) _____ (the water / to come / not) high· enough to damage the house. (20) _____ (Bill / to be going to /

invite) all his friends down during the summer, and (21) _____

(they / will / to see) for themselves how wonderful it is here.

But now Bill has achieved his dream, (22) _____ (what / will /

he / to do) next? (23) _____ (he / to have) other plans? Yes.

(24) _____ (Bill / to imagine) what life would be like *on* the sea.

(25) _____ (he / to be going to / to study) to become a boat

captain. Then, (26) _____ (he / to buy) a boat.

(27) _____ (nothing / to be going to / to stop) him.

14. Mixed Continuous Tenses

14.1 Continuous Tenses Scramble

The following sentences have been scrambled. Form complete **past continuous**, **present continuous** or **future continuous** **tense statements** using the words provided.

For example:

Q: in the parade / to carry / will / Carlos / the flag

A: Carlos will be carrying the flag in the parade.

1. here after he buys some wine / to come back / will / he

     _____

2. to enjoy / everyone / themselves before we got there

     _____

3. Rita / to sew / a new dress two days ago

     _____

4. exceptionally well today / Joe / to dance

     _____

5. to perform / you / will / first tonight

     _____

6. will / people / this for a long time to come / to discuss

     _____

7. I / to party / all night, so I needed to rest

     _____

8. to sit / she / in the wrong seat, someone tell her

     _____

9. in the street / we / to arguing / but got told to stop

     _____

10. the giraffe / while it rained / to stand / under the tree

     _____

11. their wounds later / the defeated team / to lick / will

     _____

12. to try / to sleep but / it is too noisy outside / I

_____

13. will / to learn / exciting new techniques / we / next week

_____

14. the cleaners / to empty / the bins right now

_____

15. to annoy / you / me, please go away

_____

14.2 Continuous Questions

Form **past continuous**, **present continuous** or **future continuous questions** using the information provided. Use the **will** form for future questions. First person statements should become second person questions.

For example:

Q: Kim has the TV on. (what / she / to watch)

A: What is she watching?

1. It seemed like we were working all night. (how long)

_____

2. They will be climbing the mountain in the morning. (when)

_____

3. Our boy is not improving with his studies. (to study / enough)

_____

4. Jenny has booked another language test. (to take / again)

_____

5. He was fighting with a gorilla in the jungle. (where)

_____

6. She has prepared an entry for the contest. (to enter)

_____

7. Rupert is getting very fit. (to do / lots of exercise)

_____

8. Everyone seemed angry at the volume of my voice. (to talk / too loudly)

___

9. The gang was hanging out near the club. (where)

___

10. Everyone is getting sweets from Charlotte! (Charlotte / to give out)

___

11. The police suspect a pink car was used in the crime. (why / the police / to search)

___

12. She's not sure how long this mess will take to clean up.

___

13. I've arranged to meet Bob in the foyer at 9 p.m. (Bob / to wait)

___

14. The unhappy workers were gathering below the balcony. (who)

___

15. Wait for Charles, I think his shoelaces are undone! (Charles / to tie)

___

14.3 Continuous Negative Questions

Form **past continuous**, **present continuous** or **future continuous negative questions** using the information provided, without contractions. Use the **will** form for future questions. First person statements should become second person questions.

For example:

Q: We are not travelling to Scotland.

A: Are you not travelling to Scotland?

1. You are not eating well.

___

2. They arrived unexpectedly. (they / to plan / to come)

___

3. I hope you will be joining us.

    _____

4. I feel like it is getting warmer.

    _____

5. You must recycle more plastic. (why)

    _____

6. The coastguard is patrolling the east beach. (where)

    _____

7. Henry has decided not to give any presents this Christmas. (why)

    _____

8. The foxes were not standing on the roof.

    _____

9. The bookshop is opening late today. (why / early)

    _____

10. I don't think our team is playing in the match this weekend.

    _____

11. Sheila would not reveal the truth about her birdcage. (what / to reveal)

    _____

12. The girl was not standing there when you took the photo.

    _____

13. We have no fresh water for the campers. (the campers / will / to expect)

    _____

14. Should that lion be this close to the shelter? (that lion / to get)

    _____

15. You weren't waiting in the parlour last night. (why)

    _____

14.4 Continuous Contractions

Form **past continuous**, **present continuous** or **future continuous negative questions** using the information provided, with contractions. Use the **will** form for future questions. First person statements should become second person questions.

For example:

Q: They were not listening to the professor during the lecture.

A: Weren't they listening to the professor during the lecture?

1. You are not reading that magazine.

    _____

2. They stopped work during yesterday's storm. (they / to work)

    _____

3. We have hardly any tissues left. (your tissues / to run out)

    _____

4. I'm not sure if Danny will be waiting at home.

    _____

5. It seemed like you took a long break from studying. (how long / to study / for)

    _____

6. We are not sitting close to the stage. (why)

    _____

7. Hailey will not be skiing with us.

    _____

8. They were fighting over the last piece of cheese.

    _____

9. The weather is changing rapidly.

    _____

10. Something was definitely missing from the recipe. (what / they / to include)

    _____

11. The field seems very empty. (the farmers / to work)

    _____

12. Howard may have been pretending to gather mushrooms last week. (to gather)

_____

13. The fireman is not listening. (why)

_____

14. The tulips are turning a curious shade of purple.

_____

15. Your notepad was empty! (to take / notes)

_____

14.5 Mixed Continuous Corrections

Identify grammatical mistakes in the following **continuous** tense sentences, marking the sentences as either **correct** or **incorrect**.

For example:

Q: He was not listen to the teacher.

A: Incorrect – *He was not **listening** to the teacher.*

1. You was singing the right tune.

_____

2. The band will not be coming unless we pay them more.

_____

3. He is moving to Seattle today.

_____

4. I are baking a wonderful cake.

_____

5. His parents will visiting tomorrow.

_____

6. The birds were not sit there yesterday.

_____

7. It is raining too heavily for us to go out.

_____

8.   We are shopping in the mall when the alarm went off.

   _____

9.   The guards are not watching the diamonds right now.

   _____

10.   She was practising piano last summer.

   _____

11.   We will not be waited very long if you call ahead.

   _____

12.   The men will be drinking all night, now the bar has a new license.

   _____

13.   Brenda was washing the windows last week.

   _____

14.   The cat are staring out of the window again.

   _____

15.   They will not performing this evening, after all.

   _____

14.6 Mixed Continuous Tenses

Complete the following dialogue with the appropriate **continuous** forms, using the information in brackets. Use contractions where possible.

Going to the Cinema

Billy: (1) _____ (to book) tickets for the cinema. Do you want to come?

Angela: Hmm. (2) _____ (what / to play)?

Billy: It's a superhero movie. (3) _____ (it / will not / show) for much longer, so we need to go now.

Angela: Another superhero movie! (4) _____ (why / they / to make / still) them?

Billy: This is the best one yet – (5) _____ (it / to get) amazing reviews.

Angela: I don't care – (6) _____ (I / not / to go) to another superhero film.

Billy: Well, (7) _____ (I / to watch) it whether you come or not. (8) _____ (what / you / to do), anyway?

Angela: (9) _____ (I / to be / study) for my exam on Friday before you interrupted, actually.

Billy: (10) _____ (you / to revise / not) all day yesterday?

Angela: Yes, and (11) _____ (I / will / to read) all day tomorrow, too. So what?

Billy: (12) _____ (you / to work) too hard! Come to the cinema and have a break.

Angela: Fine. I'll come, but (13) _____ (we / to see / not) that superhero film.

Billy: (14) _____ (what / you / to think) of watching instead?

Angela: There's a new thriller. With a twist. (15) _____ (Bridget / tell) me about it last week.

Billy: Hmm. Fine. But (16) _____ (I / drive)!

15. Mixed Perfect Tenses

15.1 Perfect Tenses Scramble

The following sentences have been scrambled. Form complete **perfect tense statements** and **questions**, without contractions, using the words provided.

For example:

Q: to fifteen countries / Felicity / to be / so far

A: Felicity has been to fifteen countries so far.

1. my essay but / I / to finish / was not happy with it

    _____

2. Ryan / a new camera / and cannot stop talking about it / to buy

    _____

3. before you get there / to close / the shop / will

    _____

4. you / to prepare / have you / ? / the salad, / not

    _____

5. to record / many artists / the tune / before John produced a cover

    _____

6. the door / ? / forced open / to be

    _____

7. to arrive / yet, by this time tomorrow / will / our friends / not

    _____

8. will / the weather / to change / by the weekend / ?

    _____

9. she / a new book / to start / even though she was still reading one

    _____

10. Sam / will / to walk / home, if he is not at the school

    _____

11. this film before; / to see / I / it looks good / not

    _____

12. they / so many scones / to eat / ? / that they could not have cake

_____

13. to build / the children / a den, so the living room is a mess

_____

14. the priest / to go / ? / before she arrived

_____

15. will / dinner / the restaurant / to serve / not / by 7 p.m., as the chef is missing

_____

15.2 Perfect Questions 1

Form **past perfect, present perfect** or **future perfect questions** using the information provided. Use the **will** form for future questions. First person statements should become second person questions.

For example:

Q: Frederick has passed his written exam.

A: Has Frederick passed his written exam?

1. You have been to Hungary before.

_____

2. They weren't sure if they'd locked the door before going out. (to lock)

_____

3. I hope we have soup today. (the chef / to cook)

_____

4. We need time to rest before the train comes. (will / to rest)

_____

5. Someone had punctured the wheel deliberately.

_____

6. I feel like I have told her this before.

_____

7. The water might have boiled. (to boil / yet)

    _____

8. The minister discovered his backpack was full of oranges. (to take / the wrong backpack)

    _____

9. Hopefully the snow will have cleared by morning.

    _____

10. You seem to like Japanese cinema. (you / to see / many Japanese films)

    _____

11. I have not heard from the university about my application yet. (the university / to receive)

    _____

12. They should have released the lobsters later. (to release / too early)

    _____

13. She was unsure if she entered the right answer. (to write)

    _____

14. I think Maria will have done the pies by 2 p.m. (Maria / will / to cook)

    _____

15. They say it has become harder to buy property.

    _____

15.3 Perfect Questions 2

Form **past perfect, present perfect** or **future perfect questions** using the information provided. Use the **will** form for future questions. First person statements should become second person questions.

For example:

Q: The postman has left something by the door. (what)

A: What has the postman left by the door?

1. Shirley has done something bad. (what)

   _____

2. He was inside, but no one knew how. (how / to get)

   _____

3. The courier will have left the package under the porch. (where)

   _____

4. Luke has put all the empty milk cartons in the garage. (where)

   _____

5. I did not hear what the man at the front desk had said. (what / the man)

   _____

6. It is stuffy in here and the windows are closed. (why / no one / to open)

   _____

7. My papers have been drawn all over. (who / to draw)

   _____

8. We could not find the badgers. (where / the badgers / to hide)

   _____

9. The boats will have docked by sunset. (when)

   _____

10. Tim's phone was broken. (how / to break)

    _____

11. She has lost the remote control. (where / to put)

    _____

12. The caretaker had cleaned the floor with a new product. (what)

_____

13. The package was waiting when we got home. (when / the package / to arrive)

_____

14. The award will go to whoever has showed the most potential this year. (who / to show)

_____

15. We have stored some decorations in the garage. (what / to store)

_____

15.4 Negative Perfect Questions

Form **past perfect, present perfect** or **future perfect negative questions** using the information provided, without contractions. Use the **will** form for future questions. First person statements should become second person questions.

For example:

Q: I have not received any emails today. (why)
A: Why have you not received any emails today?

1. You have not seen Alfred this month.

_____

2. The mail is not here yet. (to arrive)

_____

3. It seemed the explorers had taken the wrong turn. (to take / the correct turn)

_____

4. The hosts will not have prepared for 100 guests.

_____

5. I think we put the bread in the oven 45 minutes ago. (to be / 45 minutes / since)

_____

6. I needed a new question to ask. (what question / to ask / before)

_____

7. Their seats at the theatre will not be reserved. (to reserve)

_____

8. The cupboard had not squeaked as loudly that morning.

_____

9. She is waiting for her boyfriend to return. (her boyfriend / to return)

_____

10. I thought we paid for this meal already. (to pay)

_____

11. I fear the shops will have closed by 7 p.m.

_____

12. Harriette had not packed the correct shoes. (why)

_____

13. He seemed tired when he started work. (to rest / before)

_____

14. I don't see your name on the list for lessons. (to sign up)

_____

15. The taxi might not arrive by midnight.

_____

15.5 Perfect Contractions

Form **past perfect, present perfect** or **future perfect negative questions** using the information provided, with contractions. Use the **will** form for future questions. First person statements should become second person questions.

For example:

Q: They will never complete the project before sundown.

A: Won't they have completed the project before sundown?

1. The President has not achieved all his goals. (which goals)

_____

2. I can't believe you have not heard this tune before. (why)

    _____

3. The thieves had not hidden the jewels.

    _____

4. The men will not have distributed the presents in time.

    _____

5. She had not wanted everything that she received. (what)

    _____

6. The tour group has not visited the Alps. (where)

    _____

7. They hadn't known the door would be locked. (how)

    _____

8. Our opponents cannot plan for everything. (what / to plan)

    _____

9. I thought I helped with the dishes.

    _____

10. The kitten has not damaged all the chairs. (which / chair)

    _____

11. The creature was following him, unnoticed. (he / to notice)

    _____

12. Let's consider what we will not have completed by New Year.

    _____

15.6 Mixed Perfect Corrections

Identify grammatical mistakes in the following **perfect** tense sentences, marking the sentences as either **correct** or **incorrect**.

For example:

Q: Clive has eat all the pudding.

A: Incorrect – *Clive has **eaten** all the pudding.*

1. I have not see that play, but I hear it is good.

   _____

2. Gill has not eaten her carrots because they looked green.

   _____

3. The team will have repaired the boat in time for the race this Saturday.

   _____

4. Victor has learned to play the piano yet.

   _____

5. Why have you not given me my watch back?

   _____

6. It had not was easy, but the girls replaced the punctured tyre.

   _____

7. We hadn't bring a map and got hopelessly lost.

   _____

8. Had Sue feed animals before or not?

   _____

9. He will has heard the good news before the meeting.

   _____

10. Hadn't I seen Martin's new guitar somewhere before?

    _____

11. They will have collect all the flowers before the wedding day.

    _____

12. The magicians have not agreed on a trick, so we have cancelled the performance.

_____

13. She have not lived here for long, have she?

_____

14. I will recovered by the time they arrive tomorrow.

_____

15. The project won't exceed its budget if we stay on track.

_____

15.7 Mixed Perfect Tenses

Complete the following text with the appropriate **perfect** forms, using the information in brackets. Use contractions where possible.

The House that Would Not Sell

The building on Grand Avenue (1) _____ (to be) up for sale for a long time now. The owners (2) _____ (to renovate) it recently: (3) _____ (they / decorate) all the rooms, and are currently building a new garage. They claim (4) _____ (they / will / to spend) more than £10,000 on these improvements once they are done. But (5) _____ (the house / will / to be) on the market six months by next week.

(6) _____ (why / it / to fail) to sell?

The property probably (7) _____ (to sell) because of the damp problems. One couple who went to view it complained that (8) _____ (the owners / to paint) over mould on one wall before they visited. The real estate agent expressed frustration: "I wish (9) _____ (we / to ask) more questions before taking on the house.

(10) _____ (why / the owners / to hire) two different estate agents already? Because the others quit after they discovered the damp!"

The owners, Jeff and Winn Murray, insist (11) _____ (they / to do / not) anything wrong. Jeff said, "(12) _____ (we / to live) here for ten years and (13) _____ (the damp / never / to bother) us. When we first moved in, (14) _____ (mushrooms / to grow) on the carpet. Did we complain? No, because (15) _____ (we / to expect) a few problems beforehand. (16) _____ (anyone / to move / ever) house without problems?"

(17) _____ (Mr Murray / to find / not) his potential customers forgiving, however. Buyers can easily spot damp now, as moisture scanners (18) _____ (to become) so effective. Winn Murray said, "One young couple's clothes beeped while we showed them around. (19) _____ (what / they / to bring) in their pockets? A damp-measuring device! Perhaps we need a new estate agent, who will bring less devious buyers. But (20) _____ (how many agents / we / will / to try) then? Perhaps we should just keep the house!"

16. Mixed Perfect Continuous Tenses

16.1 Perfect Continuous Scramble

The following sentences have been scrambled. Form complete **perfect continuous tense statements** and **questions**, without contractions, using the words provided.

For example:

Q: the sea / to get / warmer since April

A: The sea has been getting warmer since April.

1. Ben / TV for an hour / to watch / while the soup simmered
    _____

2. your phone / why / to ring / your shower / ? / since you started
    _____

3. our friends / to visit / us once a week until they left town
    _____

4. the gate / to open / properly for a week now / not
    _____

5. to study / medicine for / you / two years last time I saw you
    _____

6. they / you get to the party / will / to wait / all evening by the time
    _____

7. Jason / to call / the council every day / not / this week
    _____

8. to travel / I / for / how / will / when I finally get home / ?
    _____

9. to see / each other / we / for a year before we got married
    _____

10. the men / they reach the summit / to climb / for days before / will
    _____

11. she / to learn Spanish before / to try / ? / her holiday next month
    _____

12. whether or not to / I / to consider / go out this evening
    _____

16.2 Perfect Continuous Questions 1

Form **past perfect continuous, present perfect continuous** or **future perfect continuous questions** using the information provided. Use the **will** form for future questions. First person statements should become second person questions.

For example:

Q: I estimate that the bus has been stopping every two minutes.

A: Has the bus been stopping every two minutes?

1. He had been studying for a long time before the exam.

   _____

2. They will have been building that wall all summer.

   _____

3. I'm not sure if we were sitting or standing when the bell rang.

   _____

4. I have been reading about giraffes this week.

   _____

5. They say Ben will have been living on a boat for two years this August.

   _____

6. I'm worried she has been staring at me all morning.

   _____

7. I think you had been looking for a new bag last time I saw you.

   _____

8. Someone, possibly my wife, has been cooking something that smells delicious.

   _____

9. We were afraid that mushrooms had been growing under the floorboards.

   _____

10. Our nephew will have been walking for months before we see him.

11. The neighbours seem angry with Hillary. (Hillary / to argue)

12. The squirrels will have been sleeping all winter.

16.3 Perfect Continuous Questions 2

Form **past perfect continuous**, **present perfect continuous** or **future perfect continuous questions** using the information provided. Use the **will** form for future questions. First person statements should become second person questions.

For example:

Q: Bob has been making a model aeroplane. (what)

A: What has Bob been making?

1. There was lots of banging on the door that night. (who / to bang)

2. She must be hiding her silverware in the cellar. (where / to hide)

3. Greg has sent the TV station angry letters. (why)

4. The plumber has been in the basement for a long time. (what / to do)

5. Jane will have been learning to ride camels for a year come March. (how long)

6. Simon had an important phone call before dinner. (who / to talk to)

7. The cake will cool on the windowsill for three hours before tea. (where)

8. The birds arrived at the lake after two hours of flying. (how long / to fly)

    _____

9. You keep writing things in your journal. (what)

    _____

10. We will need two weeks to practise this dance before the show.

    _____

16.4 Negative Perfect Continuous Questions

Form **past perfect continuous**, **present perfect continuous** or **future perfect continuous negative questions** using the information provided, without contractions. Use the **will** form for future questions. First person statements should become second person questions.

For example:

Q: Clive has not been swimming this week.

A: Has Clive not been swimming this week?

1. I don't think the tomatoes have been growing in this soil. (the tomatoes / to grow)

    _____

2. Veronica had refused to send the letters. (to send)

    _____

3. They claimed they had collected no names during the survey. (to collect)

    _____

4. You will not have been working here long enough for a raise this month.

    _____

5. She might not have been paying attention when the homework was set.

    _____

6. The old man still has a full cupboard of beans. (to eat / his beans)

    _____

7. The couple will not have been renting for long before they buy.

    _____

8. Roger and Kelly's towels seem very dirty. (to wash / their towels)

    _____

9. My aunt had not been buying anything online.

    _____

10. Sandy will not have been working today. (why)

    _____

16.5 Perfect Continuous Contractions

Form **past perfect continuous**, **present perfect continuous** or **future perfect continuous negative questions** using the information provided, with contractions. Use the **will** form for future questions. First person statements should become second person questions.

For example:

Q: I have not been making pies. (what)
A: What haven't you been making?

1. The Queen had not been wearing her crown at night. (who)

    _____

2. He might not have been travelling through Europe next month.

    _____

3. Sally had not been sharing her chocolate with anyone. (what)

    _____

4. I think you should have been using the blue pen.

    _____

5. Dennis thought he had been searching for this wallet all morning.

    _____

6. I have been trying to watch all the new cookery shows, but might have missed some. (which / cookery shows / to watch)

    _____

7. She has been ignoring my messages for weeks. (how long / she / to reply)

    _____

8. It's uncertain if the club will have been expanding quickly enough to earn a bonus.

9. The charity has not been accepting donations since January. (why)

10. He claimed the cupboard had not been squeaking last time we were there.

16.6 Mixed Perfect Continuous Corrections

Identify grammatical mistakes in the following **perfect continuous** tense sentences, marking the sentences as either **correct** or **incorrect**.
    For example:
    Q: The children have been gathered flowers for hours.
    A: Incorrect – *The children have been **gathering** flowers for hours.*

1. The pot plants will have been getting enough water this week.

2. The Smiths have not been closing their windows at night, even when it rained.

3. The children have playing outside this week.

4. Will they have been preparing for long enough by next week?

5. We have not to be meeting as often now as we used to.

6. The goats had not been cooperating with the farmer yesterday.

7. Mandy had been let her sister use the computer that summer.

8. You have not been listening to me, please do!

    _____

9. Won't Felicity have been cycling at all this winter?

    _____

10. She will has been reading the correct book.

    _____

11. Jim had been working for eight days by tomorrow morning.

    _____

12. Had Ralph been putting the clean cups in the wrong cupboard all along?

    _____

13. People had not been returning books to the library last month.

    _____

14. Has our guests been waiting long? They look bored.

    _____

15. My car will have not been starting since the accident last Thursday.

    _____

16.7 Mixed Perfect Continuous

Complete the following text with the appropriate **perfect continuous** forms, using the information in brackets. Use contractions where possible.

Extreme Endurance

Janet (1) _____ (to train) to complete the Extreme Endurance Race in July. The race (2) _____ (to take place) in Devon for eight years now, and involves swimming, running, cycling and climbing. Janet (3) _____ (to run) and cycling since she was young, but before last January she (4) _____ (to swim / not) for a long time and she (5) _____ (to climb / never). By the time of the race, she

(6) _____ (to learn) to climb for only six months!

(7) _____ (why / she / to work) so hard for this? Before Christmas, (8) _____ (Janet / to get) ill frequently. (9) _____ (she / to see) doctors two or three times a week, and all of them said she needed more exercise. Her friend (10) _____ (Claude / to compete) in tough races for decades, and he suggested she try one. So she chose the toughest. (11) _____ (what / she / to think)?

By February, (12) _____ (she / to rise) every morning at 5 a.m. for two months. (13) _____ (her diet / not / to help), so she cut out sugar and dairy. The improvements were rapid. Janet has not only lost weight and raised her stamina, (14) _____ (she / to feel) more awake and alive. What's more – (15) _____ (she / not / to get) ill anymore. (16) _____ (her life / to improve / also) in other ways she did not expect – (17) _____ (she / even / to sleep) better.

But the Extreme Endurance Race is quickly approaching, and (18) _____ (she / to grow) more nervous by the day. (19) _____ (she / to practise) for long enough to face it? She isn't sure, but one thing is certain: by the time it's over, (20) _____ (Janet / to work) hard enough to form a habit. Now she's started getting fit, she doesn't expect to stop.

Tenses in Use

The following section is designed to drill usages of the different tenses, so you can get a feel for the appropriate application of each tense in context. These are divided into the **past**, **present** and **future**, with each section including exercises that cover the uses of the **simple**, **continuous**, **perfect** and **perfect continuous** forms. There are also comparative exercises that relate the tenses to each other, as referenced in the book *The English Tenses Practical Grammar Guide*. Following the specific uses, there is a group of mixed tenses exercises, drawing all the tenses together for drills of more free and flexible use.

17. The Past in Use

17.1 Complete or Process 1

Complete the following sentences by putting the verb in brackets in either the **past simple** or **past continuous** form. Remember, we use the past simple for actions completed in the past, while we use the past continuous for ongoing or interrupted processes.

For example:

Q: I _____ my dog when it started to rain. (to walk)

A: I **was walking** my dog when it started to rain.

1.   Billy _____ his homework before tea. (to complete)

2.   We _____ to meet at 4 p.m. (to agree)

3.   Lynn called while I _____ for a bus. (to wait)

4.   He is only here because you _____ him. (to invite)

5.   We could see that the ship _____. (to sink)

6.   John _____ into the room to deliver the news. (to burst)

7.   She _____ her glasses under the sofa. (to find)

8.   Only three students _____ their essays early. (to submit)

9.   They left early because they _____ the film. (to enjoy / not)

10. The boy cried when a bee _____ him. (to sting)

11. I lost my phone while I _____ in Spain. (to relax)

12. Vera _____ to lock the door again. (to forget)

13. Ruth _____ for her mother, so could not go to the party. (to care)

14. The dog snarled because it _____ its toy. (to protect)

15. Fred _____ the car when he remembered his goggles. (to load)

16. We discovered our parents _____ too much for gas. (to pay)

17. What _____ at the time that the fire started? (you / to do)

18. When _____ how to turn on the fridge? (she / explain)

19. Where _____ the diamonds? (the thieves / to hide)

20. Why _____ during the meeting? (Julia / to laugh)

17.2 Complete or Process 2

Complete the following sentences by putting the verb in brackets in either the **past simple** or **past continuous** form. Remember, we use the past simple for actions completed in the past, while we use the past continuous for ongoing or interrupted processes. Use contractions where possible.

For example:

Q: "Is the new cinema open yet?"
"I think so – when I looked, they _____ tickets online."
(to sell)

A: "Is the new cinema open yet?"
"I think so – when I looked, they **were selling** tickets online."

1. "Are you going on holiday this year?"

    "No, I _____ on one already." (to go)

2. "I heard you gave up science classes."

    "Yes, I thought I _____ enough." (to learn / not)

3. Penny collected model buses for many years. She _____

    to get enough to start a museum. (to try)

4. "Why did we stop using disposable cups?"

    "Because management _____ to reduce plastic." (to decide)

5. Sparrows _____ in our loft. We could hear them above us. (to nest)

6. "What did that sign say?"

    "I couldn't see, it _____ in the wind." (to sway)

7. The new restaurant was a massive success. Hundreds of customers
    _____ in the first two days. (to come)

8. "You're home early tonight."
    "Yes, I _____ back to watch the game." (to hurry)

9. Didn't that man look terribly cold? _____ all over? (he /
    to shake / not)

10. "Look at how many burgers I have!"
    "Wow, _____ them all?" (to buy)

11. "Your father called to ask where you were. _____ him
    we were going to the beach?" (you / to tell / not)

12. "I heard they gave Michelle a first-class ticket to Bali."
    "Yes, I think so – _____ on the site of a new hotel?"
    (she / to consult / not)

17.3 Complete or Process 3

Complete the following sentences by putting the verb in brackets in either the
past perfect or **past perfect continuous** form, without contractions.
Remember, we use the past perfect for actions completed at a particular point
in the past, while we use the past perfect continuous for processes ongoing or
interrupted at a particular point in the past.

For example:
Q: We _____ the sink before John came home. (to fix)
A: We **had fixed** the sink before John came home.

1. There were no biscuits left because she _____ them all.
    (to eat)

2. The guests surprised her, as their flight _____ early. (to
    arrive)

3. Our neighbours _____ for hours when we asked them to
    stop. (to shout)

4. All our lights went out. I _____ to pay the meter. (to forget)

5. Raccoons _____ our bins every night, so we added locks. (to raid)

6. She _____ a presentation but went out before it was finished. (to prepare)

7. He left the café because his friends _____ at him. (to laugh)

8. Anna _____ all the author's books except one. (to read)

9. Which book _____ before she found this one? (she / to read)

10. When _____ the new bar? It looked very vibrant. (they / to open)

17.4 Past States 1

Complete the following sentences by putting the verb in brackets in either the **past simple** or **past continuous** form, without contractions. Remember, the past simple is used for states, for existence, possession and senses, even in temporary conditions.

For example:

Q: The postman arrived when I _____ in the shower. (to be)

A: The postman arrived when I **was** in the shower.

1. Sheila _____ her dress during a storm. (to iron)

2. When we arrived at the hotel, it _____ closed. (to look)

3. Though they _____ dim, the lights were on. (to seem)

4. By 3 p.m. all his shares had risen; he _____ a good day. (to have)

5. No one moved: the man _____ a gun. (to have)

6. Her husband always bought books when he _____ bored. (to feel)

7. You _____ a bad dream, so I woke you. (to have)

121

8. At the time, they _____ the problem. (to understand / not)
9. Throughout July, we _____ to paint our shed. (to try / often)
10. Geoff _____ to the radio at 11 a.m. (to listen)
11. She had not fully decided, but she _____ the yellow curtains. (to prefer)
12. I _____*War and Peace* but took a break to read a comic. (to read)
13. The man _____ a tie for so long that they closed the shop. (to choose)
14. As she entered the garage, Enid _____ a curious sound. (to hear)
15. Luke studied hard because he _____ to get top marks. (to aim)
16. Would work send me to Italy? It was exactly what I _____. (to want)
17. He waited for a decision. _____ his story? (they / to believe)
18. When we met Lana, _____ of smoke? (she / to smell)
19. The parrots surprised everyone – why _____ so angry? (they / to appear)
20. While I made tea, _____ in my diary? (you / to look)

17.5 Past States 2

Complete the following sentences by putting the verb in brackets in either the **past perfect** or **past perfect continuous** form, without contractions. Remember, the past perfect is used for states, for existence, possession and senses, even in temporary conditions.

For example:

Q: The guard investigated after he _____ that something was wrong. (to sense)

A: The guard investigated after he **had sensed** that something was wrong.

1. I was tired because I _____ in the library. (to study)

2. Jolene _____ her backpack, but it was time to give it away. (to love)

3. We _____ success while working at the bank. (to taste)

4. Two wolves _____ near the camp at night. (to lurk)

5. Though he _____ kind when he visited, he stole my ring. (to seem)

6. The shop _____ from a lack of donations, so they ran an advert to help. (to suffer)

7. Marius _____ in Lewes for thirteen years before he moved to Germany. (to live)

8. Claude _____ in Lewes for thirteen years when he was asked to move. (to live)

9. The cheese _____ fine in the morning, but was bad by lunch. (to smell)

10. Tammy _____ it was impossible until she discovered the answer. (to believe)

17.6 Past Sequences 1

Complete the following sentences by putting the verb in brackets in either the **past simple** or **past perfect** form, without contractions. Remember, the past perfect indicates an action was completed at a particular point in the past.

For example:

Q: We _____ (to prepare) dinner before we _____ (to go) out.

A: We **had prepared** dinner before we **went** out.

1. The hotel _____ (to cost) a lot because it _____ (to be) the height of summer.

2. They _____ (to exchange) letters only after they _____ (to separate).

3. My father _____ (to buy) a new car two days before he _____ (to visit) us.

4. I _____ (to pass) my driving test once I _____ (to take) 40 lessons.

5. She _____ (to want) to ride her bike but the chain _____ (to break) the day before.

6. Miles _____ (to play) the guitar for three years before he _____ (to lose) interest in it.

7. Where _____ (to be) the water he _____ (to ask) for?

8. Shelly _____ (to leave) early because she _____ (to complete) her assignment.

9. The doctor _____ (to prescribe) some medicine but Jim _____ (to stop) taking it after a day.

10. By the time the firemen _____ (to arrive), the building _____ (to be) evacuated.

11. I _____ (to want) boiled eggs but they _____ (to give) me beans on toast.

12. The bridge _____ (to need) repairing because the river _____ (to flood) that morning.

13. The children who _____ (to achieve) the best results _____ (to study) hardest.

14. By the time the procession _____ (to start), thousands of people _____ (to gather) to see the Queen.

15. Our aunt _____ (to retire) early because she _____ (to start) saving at an early age.

17.7 Past Sequences 2

Complete the following sentences by putting the verb in brackets in either the **past continuous** or **past perfect** form, without contractions. Remember, the past continuous indicates an action was in progress at a particular point in the past, while the past perfect indicates the action was completed.

For example:

Q: When I _____ every day, I felt very healthy. (to swim)

A: When I **was swimming** every day, I felt very healthy.

1. They needed to hurry because the ice _____. (to melt)

2. Roland could not find the toy because his friend _____ it. (to hide)

3. The pie _____, so I switched the oven off. (to burn)

4. Grandma _____, so we sent out a search party. (to escape)

5. Hillary knew a lot because she _____ all the books in the library. (to read)

6. I could not hear the news because my son _____. (to talk)

7. Though Tom _____ his computer, the screen still did not work. (to repair)

8. She called her mum while she _____ home. (to walk)

9. The family _____ a garden party until they forecast rain. (to plan)

10. Claus could not go to the shops because Herman _____ his car that morning. (to borrow)

11. Though the game _____, the crowd did not go home. (to end)

12. We sat on the bench as the bus _____ a long time to arrive. (to take)

13. Neil stopped studying the letter; he _____ the answer. (to find)

14. When she _____ across Europe, Gina visited Switzerland. (to travel)

15. Because the tree _____, the road was blocked. (to fall)

17.8 Processes in the Past

Complete the following sentences by putting the verb in brackets in either the **past continuous** or **past perfect continuous** form. Remember, the past perfect continuous is used to demonstrate duration before a particular time in the past.

For example:

Q: Her dress won the contest because she _____ it for three days. (to improve)

A: Her dress won the contest because she **had been improving** it for three days.

1. By the time I left Romania, I _____ there for three years. (to teach)

2. While Jen _____ the dishes, Roy cleaned the table. (to wash)

3. We sheltered in the barn because it _____. (to rain)

4. The track was impassable as it _____ heavily. (to snow)

5. Alan _____ to his bank manager all morning. (to speak)

6. You would have heard my answer if you _____. (to listen)

7. I didn't use the sink as the tap _____ lately. (to leak)

8. The bus _____ funny noises, so we pulled over. (to make)

9. He could not drive home because he _____ wine. (to drink)

10. The cleaners _____, and decided it was time to take action. (to talk)

17.9 Mixed Past Simple in Use

Complete the text below by putting the information in brackets into the most appropriate **past simple** form, without contractions.

Felix and the Umbrella

Felix (1) _____ (to decide) to go the park last Saturday. He (2) _____ (to want) to see the pond and feed the ducks. It (3) _____ (to be / not) a sunny day, so he needed an umbrella. The umbrella (4) _____ (to be / not) in its usual place. He (5) _____ (to ask) his sister: (6) _____ (to have / she) his umbrella? She (7) _____ (to say) no.

"(8) _____ (to leave / you) it at school?" she replied.

He (9) _____ (to know / not). He (10) _____ (to have) the umbrella when he (11) _____ (to walk) home on Thursday. He (12) _____ (to remember) leaving it to dry in the bathroom.

Felix (13) _____ (to find) the bathroom door locked. His father (14) _____ (to tell) him the bath (15) _____ (to need) replacing.

"(16)_____ (to see / you) my umbrella in there?" Felix (17) _____ (to ask).

"Why (18) _____ (to put / not / you) it back by the door?" his dad (19) _____ (to answer).

Felix (20) _____ (to explain) that it had been wet. But the umbrella (21) _____ (to be / not) in the bathroom when he (22) _____ (to lock) the door, his dad (23) _____ (to be) sure. (24) Where _____ (to be) it?

Felix (25) _____ (to sit) on the stairs, sad. It (26) _____ (to be / not) possible to visit the park without the umbrella. What else (27) _____ (he / can / to do)?

Just as he (28) _____ (to be) about to give up hope, his mother (29) _____ (return) from shopping. She (30) _____ (to have) the umbrella!

Felix (31) _____ (to grab) the umbrella from her startled hands, and (32) _____ (to charge) outside, finally ready to visit the park. He (33) _____ (to run) down the road, and (34) _____ (to stop / not) for anything on the way. He (35) _____ (to arrive) at the pond, at long last. The ducks (36) _____ (to be / not) there. (37) _____ (where / they / to go)?

Of course, Felix (38) _____ (to understand), standing in the rain. The ducks (39) _____ (to like / not) the rain either. They (40) _____ (to be) safe, inside, out of sight.

He would have to come back another day.

17.10 Mixed Past Continuous in Use

Complete the text below by putting the information in brackets into the most appropriate **past continuous** form, without contractions.

An Unsatisfactory Restaurant

When I (1) _____ (to search) for a new restaurant, I discovered Calbini's had opened in the town centre. They (2) _____ (to run) a promotion that week: three courses for £12.95. Very cheap, as others nearby (3) _____ (to provide) a main course for £18! (4) _____ (the place / to sell) itself short? Or (5) _____ (it / to offer) a worse service?

I visited on a Wednesday night with my colleague Gunther. He (6) _____ (to try) to decide what to eat on the way, from the online menu, but he (7) _____ (to discuss / not) it with me. Gunther is a quiet man.

On our arrival to the restaurant, the building (8) _____ (to bustle) with people. Very busy for a Wednesday night! And the staff (9) _____ (to handle / not) it well: waiters (10) _____ (to run) around, hot-faced, and the man who welcomed us was tired and (11) _____ (to smile / not). Moreover, what (12) _____ (he / to wear)? Not a smart uniform, but brightly patterned rags covered in stains. Why (13) _____ (the managers / dressing) their staff like clowns?

Our table was at the back of the room, next to the kitchen. The door (14) _____ (to open / and / to close) constantly. Even worse, we (15) _____ (to wait) for fifteen minutes before a waiter gave us a menu. The writing was badly printed: (16) _____ (how / they /

to expect) anyone to read this?

We used Gunther's online menu instead. By then, my stomach (17) _____ (to rumble). We had to give our orders twice because the waiter (18) _____ (to listen / not). He (19) _____ (to watch) the other tables; with so many people there, (20) _____ (to plan / he) a route of attack?

Eventually, our order was placed: for the main course, I (21) _____ (to have) the calzone and Gunther chose tortellini.

Our starters arrived – prawns for both of us. The prawns (22) _____ (to swim) in brine. Undercooked. I stood and demanded to know if they (23) _____ (to serve) us garbage.

The waiters, of course, were too busy to notice. The other customers (24) _____ (to become) noisier as the restaurant only got busier. And now, as I (25) _____ (to stand), I saw the food on other tables. All as bad as ours.

I told Gunther we (26) _____ (to leave) at once, only to discover he (27) _____ (to eat) the vile prawns!

"It's not bad," he told me. Clearly he (28) _____ (to come / not) with me.

He wasn't the only one happy. Other people (29) _____ (to laugh). They (30) _____ (to enjoy) this cheap, busy restaurant! (31) _____ (the chefs / to put) something special in the food? Or (32) _____ (everyone / to question / not) the quality because it was so cheap?

Either way, it (33) _____ (to fool / not) me. I gathered my things and left. The last time I saw him, Gunther (34) _____ (to devour) my meal, too.

17.11 Mixed Past Perfect in Use

Complete the text below by putting the information in brackets into the most appropriate **past perfect** or **past perfect continuous** form, without contractions.

The Mystery of the Missing Sandwich

Lunch was approaching. Xavier (1) _____ (to look) forward to his sandwich all morning. He (2) _____ (to prepare) a special sandwich today: halloumi, salad with hummus that his wife (3) _____ (to make). She (4) _____ (to make) her own hummus for years, and it (5) _____ (to reach) perfection.

But when Xavier opened the fridge, the sandwich (6) _____ (to disappear). He stared in disbelief: he (7) _____ (to put) it there last night. His wife (8) _____ (to comment) on it at 9 a.m., when she took milk for her tea, "That looks nice!" Where (9) _____ (it / to go)?

Xavier was alone that morning. His wife (10) _____ (to take) the train to York for the day. (11) _____ (someone / to sneak) in while he (12) _____ (to watch) TV? He (13) _____ (to hear / not) anything, but he (14) _____ (to listen / not) carefully.

Xavier searched the house for signs of an intruder – or clues to what (15) _____ (to become) of the missing sandwich. His daughter's room was locked, because she (16) _____ (to leave) for university a week ago. The other bedroom and the living room (17) _____ (to disturb / not).

The garden door was open, because Xavier (18) _____ (to want)

131

some fresh air. He stood checking the trees. (19) _____ (a squirrel / to come) inside and opened the fridge? (20) _____ (he / to notice / not) a genius thief?

After searching the garden for crumbs, Xavier returned to the kitchen. He (21) _____ (to find / not) any evidence of an intruder or the sandwich's fate. Why (22) _____ (he / to play) the TV so loud? His distraction (23) _____ (to let) some terrible person steal his amazing sandwich.

Finally, Xavier decided to call his wife and tell her about this tragedy. But first, he saw he (24) _____ (to receive) a message from her already.

"Thank you for preparing that lovely sandwich – it was everything I (25) _____ (to dream) of all morning!"

Xavier stared in horror. His wife (26) _____ (to think) the sandwich was for her. She (27) _____ (to take) it with her when she left! But he could only blame himself. Why (28) _____ (he / to prepare / not) one for her, too?

17.12 Mixed Past Matching

Form logical past sentences using the fragments below. Each collection of eight fragments forms four complete sentences. Note that some clauses may fit flexibly, but only one combination should satisfy all four sentences of each question.

For example:

a. The detective followed the clues	when the thief struck again.
b. The detective was following the clues	before he found the suspect.
c. The detective had followed many clues	for three days while the thief was still out there.
d. The detective had been following clues	to the creepy house.

a. The detective followed the clues to the creepy house.
b. The detective was following clues when the thief struck again.
c. The detective had followed many clues before he found the suspect.
d. The detective had been following clues for three days while the thief was still out there.

1.

a. Neil was cycling	since 9 a.m., so he stopped for lunch.
b. Neil had cycled home	in the rain yesterday.
c. Neil cycled home	when it started raining.
d. Neil had been cycling	in the rain, so he arrived wet.

2.

a. Carla passed	the same man all year when she walked to work.
b. Carla had been passing	the salt to Jeremy after he asked for it.
c. Carla was passing	this shop before, was she going the right way?
d. Carla had passed	the shop when a bracelet caught her eye.

3.

a. Our teacher had given us	too much homework ever since term started.
b. Our teacher gave us	an exam when the bell rang.
c. Our teacher had been giving us	a difficult assignment, so I could not go out.
d. Our teacher was giving us	too much homework this afternoon.

4.

a. The band played	all the songs they knew and had to stop.
b. The band had been playing	until 3 a.m. last night.
c. The band were playing	when the lights went out.
d. The band had played	for five hours before they had to stop.

17.13 Past Time Sequences

The following sentences include multiple **past** tense clauses. Put the subjects and verbs into the order of which started first, or indicate if the first action is unknown.

For example:

Q: When his patient arrived, the doctor was having a coffee.

A: A) the doctor was having B) his patient arrived

was having = past continuous, action was in process

arrived = past simple, action completed

1.   Carl washed the dishes after he ate dinner.

      A) _____ B) _____

2.   She was preparing her speech when the ambassador arrived.

      A) _____ B) _____

3.   I had been studying for weeks by the time I took the exam.

      A) _____ B) _____

4. The cat slept in the living room because Boris closed the door to the garden.

        A) _____ B) _____

5. Helga was listening to music while she travelled on the bus.

        A) _____ B) _____

6. We could not enter the house because someone had taken the spare key.

        A) _____ B) _____

7. While he was fixing the sink, the post arrived.

        A) _____ B) _____

8. Kim went to the gym after she finished work.

        A) _____ B) _____

9. Our neighbours were talking loudly before they left this morning.

        A) _____ B) _____

10. Roland returned the bike that he had borrowed.

        A) _____ B) _____

11. What were you eating when you stayed in Japan?

        A) _____ B) _____

12. Did he wipe his feet when he came in from the rain?

        13. A) _____ B) _____

14. Had Jim been asking for volunteers when you sent the email?

        A) _____ B) _____

15. Who was playing the piano while we were painting in the attic?

        A) _____ B) _____

16. The cake tasted incredible – what did they put in it?

        A) _____ B) _____

17.14 Past Tenses in Use: Identifying Times

The following passage describes the everyday routine of Jen the Magician. Indicate which states are true at the listed times.

Jen the Magician wakes each day at 07:00. She has a shower before breakfast and she finishes eating by 07:30. She does not own a car, so Jen catches the 07:45 bus for a twenty-minute journey into town. She listens to music and checks her emails on the way. Jen starts her workday at the Friends Centre at 08:30, after buying a coffee. She entertains children for an hour, then walks for fifteen minutes to perform at a care home.

Jen usually has lunch at 12:00, at *Buster's Burritos*. She stays there for an hour, reading magazines about magic. Her friend Mary comes in around 12:30. They have tea, but do not eat together as Jen usually finishes her burrito before Mary arrives.

In the afternoon, Jen visits schools in the suburbs. She demonstrates magic to classes of children, and teaches them tricks. This occupies her until 16:00, at which time she travels back to the Friends Centre. Jen runs magic classes for adults from 17:00 until 19:30, then takes the bus home. Usually, she cooks dinner and eats before practising new tricks from 21:00 to 22:00. Then she settles down with a good book before falling asleep at 23:00.

For example:
At 07:45 yesterday ...
  a. ... Jen had a shower.
  b. **... Jen was getting the bus. – TRUE**
  c. ... Jen drove to work.
  d. **... Jen had eaten breakfast. – TRUE**

1. At 07:55 yesterday ...
  a. ... Jen was on the bus.
  b. ... Jen was listening to music.
  c. ... Jen was checking her make-up.
  d. ... Jen arrived at the Friends Centre.

2. At 09:35 yesterday ...

    a.   ... Jen was entertaining children.

    b.   ... Jen had drunk a coffee.

    c.   ... Jen was walking through town.

    d.   ... Jen had started her second job.

3. At 12:45 yesterday ...

    a.   ... Jen had eaten a burrito.

    b.   ... Jen was reading a magazine.

    c.   ... Jen had been reading a magazine.

    d.   ... Mary bought a burrito.

4. At 15:30 yesterday ...

    a.   ... Jen was travelling to the Friends Centre.

    b.   ... Jen had been visiting schools for over two hours.

    c.   ... Jen was teaching adults.

    d.   ... Jen finished visiting schools.

5. At 19:30 yesterday ...

    a.   ... Jen finished work for the day.

    b.   ... Jen had taught magic to adults.

    c.   ... Jen was cooking dinner.

    d.   ... Jen went to get the bus.

6. At 10:30 yesterday ...

    a.   ... Jen practised new tricks.

    b.   ... Jen fell asleep.

    c.   ... Jen had eaten dinner.

    d.   ... Jen was reading a book.

17.15 Past Tenses in Use: Identifying Uses

To practise understanding of the different uses of the **past** tenses, the following passage contains many highlighted verb phrases. Choose which use is being demonstrated for each phrase from the list below:

- Past Action
- Past State / Possession / Sense
- Ongoing Past Process
- Past Action Completed Earlier
- Earlier Past State / Possession / Sense
- Earlier Ongoing Past Process

The Forgotten Book

Richard **(1) was standing** at the Petersons' door, trying to decide if he should knock. It **(2) was cold and dark**, and very late. The lights **(3) were off**. He **(4) had noticed** that from the road; everyone inside **(5) had gone** to bed. They **(6) had probably been sleeping** for hours. But he **(7) needed** to get his book back. He **(8) had an exam** the next day, and he needed to study. **(9) Why had he left the book there** this afternoon? Was it because **(10) he had been flirting** with Paula?

He **(11) wished** he **(12) had not been so foolish**. Last time this happened, her parents **(13) had been** angry at him for weeks. They **(14) had been sleeping** when he knocked then, too, and they **(15) had shouted** at him. He **(16) did not want** that to happen again.

He **(17) chose** not to knock.

He **(18) began to walk** quietly away. As he **(19) was leaving**, someone shouted from the window. It was Paula! She **(20) was waving** at him.

"Richard!" she **(21) called** out. "You left your book behind!"

He **(22) smiled**, this **(23) was going** well, after all.

Paula **(24) threw** the book, and it hit him on the nose. As he stumbled in pain, she **(25) was laughing** hysterically. He suspected that she **(26) had done** that on purpose.

17.16 Past Tenses in Use: Narrative 1

Complete the following text with the appropriate **past** forms, without contractions, using the information in brackets and the context of the text.

A New Pier

In April, the seaside town of Trilby-on-Sea (1) _____ (to announce) plans to build a new pier. Before this decision, Trilby's council (2) _____ (to meet) with local charities and tourist organisations for six months. A Scottish architect (3) _____ (to submit) designs including shops and rides. Most of the town (4) _____ (to love) the designs, but the council were unsure. They (5) _____ (to experience) budget cuts for the past few years.

Local residents (6) _____ (to form) a group called Pier Alliance in January to convince the council. They (7) _____ (to argue) that the new pier would bring wealth to Trilby. Visitor numbers (8) _____ (to decrease) since two summers before, and everyone (9) _____ (to try) to find a solution. They remembered: Trilby's old pier (10) _____ (to draw) massive crowds, many decades ago.

Newspaper clippings (11) _____ (to show) that hundreds of people (12) _____ (to gather) on the pier daily. It (13) _____ (to become) unstable in the 1980s, when the supports (14) _____ (to get) damaged in a terrible storm. The council (15) _____ (to remove) the pier, saying they (16) _____ (can / not) afford to maintain it.

Technology (17) _____ (to improve) a lot since then, so Pier Alliance (18) _____ (to insist) the new pier would be cheaper and safer. By time of the final decision, they (19) _____ (to ask) ten different experts to speak to the council about it. In March, a gentleman from America (20) _____ (to visit) the town. He (21) _____ (to research) piers for thirteen years and said he (22) _____ (to see / not) a better design than Trilby's new proposal. Slowly, Pier Alliance (23) _____ (to persuade) the council. The men in charge (24) _____ (to delay) the decision, so the town finally (25) _____ (to hold) a rally to demonstrate how support (26) _____ (to grow) for the new pier.

Finally, the council (27) _____ (to give) in, and the April announcement (28) _____ (to lead) to great celebrations. The new pier (29) _____ (to come) at last!

17.17 Past Tenses in Use: Narrative 2

Complete the following text with the appropriate **past** forms, without contractions, using the information in brackets and the context of the text.

The Pen Thief

Vicky was certain Clive (1) _____ (to take) her pen. It (2) _____ (to disappear) while she (3) _____ (to repair) the printer.

"What (4) _____ (to do) ten minutes ago?" Vicky asked. "You (5) _____ (to sit / not) at your desk, I am sure."

"(6) _____ (you / to watch) me?" Clive replied.

She (7) _____ (to look / not) his way, no. But he (8) _____ (to work / not) when she fixed the printer, not if he stole her pen. She (9) _____ (to ask) him to answer her question.

"I (10) _____ (to make) tea," he told her.

Vicky (11) _____ (to see / not) a mug of tea on his desk. (12) _____ (he / to drink) it already? She (13) _____ (to suspect) not. "You (14) _____ (to wander) around my desk, weren't you?"

"Absolutely not!" Clive protested. He (15) _____ (to be / not) near her desk since Vicky (16) _____ (to catch) him stealing her paper a month ago. She (17) _____ (to tell) him to stay away, and she (18) _____ (to enjoy) the results ever since.

(19) _____ (she / to let) her guard down too soon?

"(20) _____ (you / to take) my pen?" she asked, plainly.

Clive shook his head, but (21) _____ (to look) scared. "I did not, I would not, I never!"

He (22) _____ (to admire) her pen ever since she bought it; it (23) _____ (to have) a platinum grip. Vicky decided he (24) _____ (to be / not) honest. But she (25) _____ (to get) nowhere with words. She (26) _____ (to grab) him quickly, and he (27) _____ (to cry) out when she found the pen in a pocket. He (28) _____ (to lie) all along!

Vicky (29) _____ (to run) to her manager, but when she got there Clive (30) _____ (to leave / already). The manager (31) _____ (to stand) nearby. (32) _____ (he / to watch) all along?

"What (33) _____ (he / to steal) this time?" the manager asked.

Vicky (34) _____ (to show) him the pen, and the manager sighed sadly. Clive (35) _____ (to get) away with these thefts for too long. But they (36) _____ (to expose) him, at last.

18. The Present in Use

18.1 Timeless or Temporary 1

Complete the following sentences by putting the verb in brackets in either the **present simple** or **present continuous** form, without contractions. Remember, the present simple is mostly used for timeless actions while we use the present continuous for ongoing or interrupted temporary processes.

For example:

Q: Brianne _____ green beans every week. (to buy)

A: Brianne **buys** green beans every week.

1.   My family usually _____ dinner at 7 p.m. (to eat)

2.   He _____ for this meal. (to pay)

3.   Jonas _____ at St Mary's High School. (to teach)

4.   Our children _____ any instruments. (to play / not)

5.   This bed always _____ noisily. (to creak)

6.   We _____ a new house. (to buy)

7.   Albert _____ hard enough – he can do better. (to try / not)

8.   You _____ in my chair, please move. (to sit)

9.   Every time I _____ Gran, she _____ me sweets. (to visit / to give)

10. Her friends _____ her this time. (to help / not)

11. This professor's course _____ very quickly each year. (to fill)

12. Sam _____ food at the soup kitchen on Tuesdays. (to serve)

13. I _____ to become a lawyer anymore. (to study / not)

14. Why _____ south each winter? (the geese / to fly)

15. How _____ through the mountains on her trip? (Jenna / to travel)

16. _____ a new tie for the wedding ceremony? (you / to choose)

17. Which shops _____ non-dairy chocolates? (to offer / not)

18. What _____ on the beach right now? (to happen)

19. Who _____ that bright pink car? (to own)

20. Where _____ this weekend? (your parents / to stay)

18.2 Timeless or Temporary 2

Complete the following sentences in the **present simple** or the **present continuous** form, without contractions, using the information in brackets.
    For example:
    Q: Alexa gets up at 6 a.m. every day. Today, _____. (later)
    A: Today, **Alexa is getting up later**.

1. Dominic is usually so nice. Why _____? (naughty)

2. The sun is setting very late this month. Usually, _____. (earlier)

3. She refuses to say sorry. She _____. (to apologise / not)

4. Harry just climbed a tree. He _____. (to swing / a branch)

5. You will love the way Deidre cooks potatoes. She always _____. (to fry / them)

6. Mia has not given an answer yet – she _____. (to think / it)

7. I never usually buy nectarines for myself, but today I _____. (to buy / some / for my mother)

8. The boy is watching TV. He _____. (to bounce / not / his ball)

143

9. "Where is my magazine?"

 "I think it _____." (to lie / by the sofa)

10. "We are decorating our living room."

 "Oh, what colour _____?" (to paint)

11. "Mr Harris is not coming to dinner."

 "Strange. He _____." (to cancel / not / often)

12. "The volleyball team surprised everyone by reaching the final."

 "_____?" (to win / not / normally)

13. "_____ a bottle of wine?" (to hold / you)

 "No, it's a bottle of olive oil."

14. The building supervisor does not allow smoking. We _____! (to break / the rules)

15. "I drew this picture."

 "Ah, you _____!" (to improve / quickly)

18.3 Present States

Complete the following sentences by putting the verb in brackets in either the **present simple** or **present continuous** form, without contractions. Remember, the present simple is used for states, for existence, possession and senses, even in temporary conditions.

 For example:

 Q: I _____ you have a new puppy. (to hear)

 A: I **hear** you have a new puppy.

1. This fish _____ strange, is it old? (to taste)

2. Caroline _____ very elegant in her new dress. (to look)

3. My uncle _____ a biography of Julius Caesar. (to read)

4. I _____ your banana, thank you. (to want / not)

5. The cows _____ on all the flowers. (to stomp)

6. Leo _____ to understand algebra. (to struggle)

7. Our neighbours _____ very quiet today. (to seem)

8. Laila and Howard _____ their peanuts. (to share / not)

9. Finley _____ all the best Xbox games currently available. (to have)

10. The customers _____ that they are being given a good deal. (to doubt)

11. Eli _____ everyone a round of beers. (to get)

12. I might not go to Calcutta – I _____ second thoughts about it. (to have)

13. Though she needs a new chair now, Anna _____ all the options first. (to compare)

14. We _____ to deliver the table by Friday. (to promise)

15. Why _____ to be so dirty? (my hands / appear)

16. _____ new batteries too, now? (that clock / to need)

17. Who _____ to my radio show this week? (to listen)

18. What _____ to school today? (you / to wear)

19. _____ that singing bird? (Maria / to hear / not)

20. Why _____ building dams? (beavers / to love)

18.4 Mixed Simple or Continuous

Complete the following sentences with either the **present simple** or the **present continuous** form, without contractions, using the information provided.

For example:

Q: I _____ (to wash) my car every Tuesday.

A: I **wash** my car every Tuesday. (repeated event)

1. She's frustrated because she _____. (to clean up / always)

2. The beach _____ crowded today. (to be)

3. It _____ dark, I don't think we should walk home. (to get)

4. They usually _____ in the dining room. (to eat)

5. When you flick a switch, the light _____ on. (to come)

6. This cheese _____ awful. (to smell)

7. "Now, I _____ this store open!" (to declare)

8. I _____ for new books to read. (to look / always)

9. Our grandparents _____ twice a month. (to visit)

10. They say actions _____ louder than words. (to speak)

11. The swimmers _____ for the gold medal. (to compete)

12. Gary is not home, he _____ the dog. (to walk)

13. I _____ we take a different route home. (to propose)

14. Seagull numbers _____ because tourists _____ food around. (to increase, to leave)

15. Look, that tree _____ in the wind! (to sway)

18.5 Past and Present Complete Actions

Complete the following sentences by putting the verb in brackets in either the **past simple** or **present perfect** form, without contractions. Remember, the past simple only tells us something was completed in the past, while the present perfect shows it is relevant to the present.

For example:

Q: You _____ the door open – please close it. (to leave)

A: You **have left** the door open – please close it.

1. This bread _____ mouldy. (to go)

2. Alison _____ a website this morning. (to create)

3. He _____ the floor before dinner. (to sweep / not)

4. The boiler _____ again, so there is no hot water. (to break)

5. I cannot come to class. Last time, Mr Rogers _____ me not to come back. (to tell)

6. Nathan has passed his driving test because he _____. (to quit / not)

7. My cousin hates spiders, so he _____ all of his windows. (to seal)

8. The garden _____ with the recent hot weather. (to bloom)

9. The sailors _____ quickly because the winds were favourable. (to move)

10. Chloe is visiting, but she _____ how long she will stay. (to say / not)

11. My phone battery _____, can I use your charger? (to die)

12. She could not find her purse, so _____ with her credit card. (to pay)

13. The school want to speak to me because my essay _____ the competition. (to win)

14. Did you receive the coffee machine you _____? (to order)

15. We put our poster up in the hall, _____ it? (you / to see)

16. _____ the candles when you went shopping yesterday? (you / to buy)

17. _____ in your assignment yet? (you / to give / not)

18. Why _____ all the baguettes? There are none left! (that woman / to take)

19. Lola is telling everyone about her new job, _____ to you about it? (you / to speak)

20. _____ (the farmer / to deliver) that milk, or have you been to the shop?

18.6 Past and Present Continuous Actions

Complete the following sentences by putting the verb in brackets in either the **past continuous** or **present perfect continuous** form. Remember, the past continuous tells us an action was ongoing in the past, while the present perfect continuous shows an action started in the past is ongoing in the present.

For example:

Q: Our relatives _____ us every Christmas since 1987.
A: Our relatives **have been visiting** us every Christmas since 1987.

1. I _____ to pottery classes earlier this year. (to go)

2. Tristan _____ fake money and now he is in jail. (to print)

3. You _____ too hard this month, take a break. (to work)

4. She _____ her dad build the shed until Friday. (to help / not)

5. The teenagers _____ the streets last week. Are they back? (to clean)

6. Hundreds of thousands of people _____ the petition. It could reach a million by tomorrow. (to sign)

7. We _____ lessons since January, to improve our pronunciation. (to take)

8. The king _____ his responsibilities, so a committee was formed. (to avoid)

9. The ivy _____ over our wall. We must cut it back before it gets worse. (to spread)

10. They _____ the window – it stinks in here! (to open / not)

11. _____ here before me? (you / to wait)

12. _____ this exhibit for long? (the museum / to show)

13. _____ you today? (the children / to bother)

14. _____ when you used the bike? (the wheel / to squeak)

18.7 Past Present Emphasis

Complete the following sentences by putting the verb in brackets in the **past simple** or **present perfect** form, without contractions. The past simple may be used instead of the present perfect when we wish to emphasise completion or to emphasise the subject that completed an action.

For example:

Q: Yes, the dishes are clean. I _____ them, not Harry. (to wash)

A: Yes, the dishes are clean. I **washed** them, not Harry.

1. Who left this bag here? It _____ a stain. (to leave)

2. You _____ me to come to the game. (to convince / not)

3. I know Germany well, because I _____ there for six months last year. (to live)

4. The car just made an awful noise – I think we _____ a log. (to hit)

5. She was sure about it: Simon _____ the vase. (to break)

6. I could not bring the book home. The librarian _____ to lend it to me. (to refuse)

7. This kitchen is unsanitary. Rats _____ the cellar. (to infest)

8. My phone _____ working. Can I borrow yours? (to stop)

9. What is in the oven? _____ potatoes? (you / to cook)

10. Who designed these wonderful curtains? _____ them? (you / to do)

11. Someone is stealing my socks. _____ them? (Billie / to take)

12. How is your degree? _____ any easier? (it / to get)

18.8 Duration in the Present 1

Complete the following sentences by putting the verb in brackets in either the **present continuous** or **present perfect continuous** form, without contractions. Remember, the present continuous tells us an action is ongoing now, while the present perfect continuous shows an ongoing action started in the past.

For example:

Q: I _____ to download this movie for hours. (to try)

A: I **have been trying** to download this movie for hours.

1. We _____ this washing machine for fifteen years. (to use)

2. I _____ to work for the whole week, starting today. (to walk)

3. She _____ which scarf to buy. (to consider)

4. The couple _____ for a while. (to shop)

5. William _____ computer games for very long. (to play / not)

6. You _____ me since I came in – stop it! (to watch)

7. Alice _____ doughnuts every day this week, we have decided. (to buy)

8. That man _____ hats at a discount for the next two hours. (to sell)

9. You've been quiet. _____ all morning? (you / to read)

10. I need the car later. _____ it all day? (you / to use)

11. She has been unwell for weeks. _____ her medicine? (she / to take / not)

12. Why _____ me so many questions right now? (he / to ask)

151

18.9 Duration in the Present 2

Complete the following sentences by putting the verb in brackets in either the **present perfect** or **present perfect continuous** form, without contractions. Remember, the present perfect is used for states and to discuss occasional events, while the present perfect continuous shows an ongoing process.

For example:

Q: I _____ to Vilnius many times. (to go)

A: I **have gone** to Vilnius many times.

1.   Martha _____ six shops in Brighton. (to open)

2.   We _____ in hotels many times this year. (to stay)

3.   The sea _____ warmer all summer. (to get)

4.   He _____ to class a single time this week. (to go / not)

5.   You _____ the dishes twice today. (to wash)

6.   I _____ as many letters as I used to, and hope that will change. (to receive / not)

7.   Claudia _____ on her brother for fifteen minutes. (to spy)

8.   Eliot _____ any television since yesterday. (to watch / not)

9.   Margaret _____ her geography textbook since last Wednesday. (to study)

10. You _____ your shoes in the wrong cupboard for months. (to put)

11. The boy _____ his teacher an apple once a week this year. (to give)

12. The girl _____ the bus to school almost every day this year, but sometimes walks. (to take)

13. How many times _____ they would repair the road? (they / to say)

14. _____ in Oxford recently? (you / to bowl)

15. _____ her hair short for a long time? (she / to cut)

16. How long _____ for? Get them some water! (the clients / to wait)

18.10 Duration in the Present 3

Complete the following sentences by putting the verb in brackets in the **present perfect** or **present perfect continuous** form, without contractions. Remember that the present perfect is used for states, possession and senses.

For example:

Q: I _____ in Hamburg for sixteen months. (to live)

A: I **have lived** in Hamburg for sixteen months.

1. We _____ each other for twenty years. (to love)

2. They _____ in magic ever since they saw the Great Roberto perform. (to believe)

3. I _____ to rap music for the past three weeks. (to listen)

4. Axel _____ tired since he woke up. (to be)

5. She _____ Victorian ghost stories all night. (to read)

6. You _____ during this holiday. (to relax / not)

7. Doris _____ all the children's speeches today. (to hear)

8. What _____ in his shed all morning? (Carter / to do)

9. How long _____ about the secret passage for? (they / to know)

10. Why _____ everything he has been saying? (we / to understand / not)

11. How long _____ on our fence for? (that fox / to sit)

12. _____ restless for long? (the villagers / to seem)

18.11 Present Continuous Emphasis

The following sentences are in the **present continuous** or **present perfect continuous** forms, which can be used to emphasise tasks or continuous temporary states. Indicate if the sentences are correct or incorrect. Try to explain why.

For example:

Q: Clarice has been knowing her friends for years.

A: Incorrect – *to know* is not typically temporary

1.   Fred is constantly practising the violin at night.

2.   Violet is always asking the wrong questions.

3.   You are not understanding the question, let me explain.

4.   The women are never being unkind to animals.

5.   She is looking rather elegant today.

6.   The garage has been smelling strange lately.

7.   This parade is taking place each winter.

8.   Our streets flood because leaves are blocking the drains.

9.   Are you seeing what's happening outside?

10. Is he believing in aliens?

11. Is Mario liking the shirt we gave him?

12. Are you loving this weather or what?

18.12 Mixed Present Matching

Form logical present tense sentences using the fragments below. Each collection of eight fragments forms four complete sentences. Note that some clauses may fit flexibly, but only one combination should satisfy all four sentences of each question.

For example:

a. I drink tea	because I am cold.
b. I am drinking tea	that you gave me.
c. I have drunk the tea	since I was seven.
d. I have been drinking tea	because it tastes great.

    a.   I drink tea because it tastes great.
    b.   I am drinking tea because I am cold.
    c.   I have drunk the tea that you gave me.
    d.   I have been drinking tea since I was seven.

1.

a. The pie is cooling	we can eat it.
b. The pie has cooled	for an hour already.
c. The pie has been cooling	enough to eat.
d. When the pie cools,	on the shelf.

2.

a. Tania has had	strange dreams constantly this week.
b. Tania has been having	her dinner, and is going to bed.
c. Tania has	a party, so no one can sleep.
d. Tania is having	lots of friends, because she is nice.

3.

a. The professor is studying	languages as a hobby.
b. The professor has studied	ten languages already.
c. The professor studies	languages for 50 years.
d. The professor has been studying	a new language right now.

4.

a. What have you done with my pen?	You've had it all morning.
b. What are you doing with my pen?	It always comes back wet!
c. What do you do with my pen when you borrow it?	Use your own!
d. What have you been doing with my pen?	I can't find it.

18.13 Present Time Sequences

The following sentences include multiple **present** tense clauses. Put the subjects and verbs into the order of which started first, or indicate if the first action is unknown.

For example:

Q: I am attending college because I have finished school.

A: A) I have finished B) I am attending

have finished = present perfect, action completed with present result

am attending = present continuous, action in progress now

1.   I live in Surrey, but I commute to London every day.

        A) _____ B) _____

2.   My sister is asking if the teacher has marked her paper.

        A) _____ B) _____

3.   He is reading because the TV is not working.

        A) _____ B) _____

4.   We have been visiting this campsite for years, but it is getting more crowded.

        A) _____ B) _____

5. My mother cooks an excellent soup which has been in the family for generations.

        A) _____ B) _____

6. The hotel seems empty – perhaps the guests are sleeping.

        A) _____ B) _____

7. They are repairing the door I have been complaining about since Tuesday.

        A) _____ B) _____

8. Lottie has learned to walk and she is wandering about everywhere.

        A) _____ B) _____

9. What are you watching? Have you seen it before?

        A) _____ B) _____

10. I want to get to Kings Cross – is this bus going the right way?

        A) _____ B) _____

18.14 Present Tenses in Use: Present Narration

Choose the best **present** form (**simple**, **continuous**, **perfect** or **perfect continuous**), without contractions, using the information provided in brackets and the context of the text.

A Difficult Interview

Emma (1) _____ (to write) for the Daily Sentinel newspaper. She (2) _____ (to work) on a feature article about pop icon, Natalie Reid. It is a very important piece for the newspaper, because Reid (3) _____ (to become) one of the most famous musicians in the world, and she (4) _____ (to grant) Emma an exclusive interview. Emma (5) _____ (to research) the singer for a month, to make sure she (6) _____ (to have) an informed set of questions to ask.

　　Today, Emma (7) _____ (to edit) her interview questions. Some of her examples (8) _____ (to include):

　　What (9) _____ (you / to like) to do in your free time?

　　How (10) _____ (fame / to change) your life?

　　Where (11) _____ (you / to get) your ideas from?

　　How long (12) _____ (you / to write) music for?

　　What (13) _____ (you / to like / not) about being famous?

　　Emma (14) _____ (to be) worried, because these questions (15) _____ (to seem) too ordinary. (16) _____ (Reid / to hear / not) them a hundred times before? Reid (17) _____ (to tour) the world for the past six months. She (18) _____ (to meet) thousands of people who probably asked the same things.

　　Emma (19) _____ (to want) to ask something different. Reid

(20) _____ (to come) from an unusual background; she (21) _____ (to live) in a poor neighbourhood all her life, and (22) _____ (to give) generously to charities. The singer (23) _____ (to fund / now) the construction of new housing. But Emma (24) _____ (to fear) asking questions about these topics, because she (25) _____ (to visit / not) Reid's neighbourhood herself. The area (26) _____ (to frighten) her. And (27) _____ (her readers / to care) about these things? On social media, Reid's fans (28) _____ (to raise / only) questions about her relationships for the past few months.

(29) _____ (Emma / to make) things too complicated?

No, Emma (30) _____ (to think), now; it's time to get on with it. She (31) _____ (to be) foolish to avoid these topics. And she (32) _____ (to waste) time worrying about it. Most likely, Reid (33) _____ (to wait) for someone to ask the important questions!

18.15 Present Tenses in Use: Routines

Barry works as a part-time school caretaker. The following passage describes what he did yesterday. Mostly, he followed a typical routine. Convert this passage to the **present** tense to describe his everyday routine or variations from it. The first two sentences have been done for you.

Q: Barry got to work at 6 p.m. He talked with Year 2 teacher, Mrs Jones, as she was still in the school.

A: Barry **gets** to work at 6 p.m. He **talks** with the teachers, **if they are** still in the school.

Barry started work by vacuuming all the carpets. He lifted the chairs onto tables to clear the floors, and emptied the bins in each room. Barry wiped the boards clean, which is sometimes necessary.

Then, Barry swept the tiled floors in the corridors and halls. Because it was Friday, he mopped these floors. He used two buckets, one for soapy water and one for rinsing.

Once all the floors were finished, Barry cleaned the washrooms. He sprayed them with disinfectant and scrubbed the toilets. He replaced the soap and toilet paper because they had run out.

After his cleaning duties were finished, Barry took a break at the same time as the headmistress, as usual. He made tea for himself and the headmistress, because he got to the common room first. If the headmistress had arrived first, she would have prepared the tea. Barry would have read a book during the break, like he usually does, but he forgot to bring one, so he listened to the radio.

After his break, Barry focused on more varied tasks. Firstly, he completed repairs on doors, furniture and fences. If it were winter, Barry would spread grit outside to stop the paths getting slippery. As it is summer, he cut weeds and pruned hedges.

Barry would normally finish work at 9 p.m., but he stayed later because there were extra tasks to do. A teacher needed help moving furniture and preparing equipment for a class. The teacher and Barry did these tasks together. He will get paid extra for this.

18.16 Present Tenses in Use: Live Reporting

Choose the best **present** form (**simple**, **continuous**, **perfect** or **perfect continuous**), without contractions, using the information provided in brackets and the context of the text. Note that there is flexibility between the **present simple** and the **present perfect** for reporting stories live; mostly the present perfect is used when we reflect on the result of an action, rather than what is happening in the moment.

Doves United vs The Firecats: Live Commentary

You (1) _____ (to join) us live for an exciting match between two women's soccer teams, Doves United and The Firecats. They (2) _____ (to field) strong teams today, and both teams (3) _____ (to perform) brilliantly to reach this semi-final. They (4) _____ (to compete) since June 1st for a chance at the championship trophy, and today's match decides who (5) _____ (to qualify) for the final!

Doves United (6) _____ (to open) the game: they (7) _____ (to take) the kick-off now. The Firecats (8) _____ (to chase) them right away; oh my, these women (9) _____ (to move) fast!

United's captain, Morales, (10) _____ (to have) the ball, and she (11) _____ (to sprint) up the right flank. But she (12) _____ (to face) trouble! Firecats defender Lux (13) _____ (to close) on Morales. They (14) _____ (to clash)! Lux (15) _____ (to steal) the ball and she (16) _____ (to make) a break. The United team (17) _____ (to be) spread out; they (18) _____ (to let) her through!

Lux (19) _____ (to race) into the penalty box – only the keeper to beat!

Oh no! Lux is down! United's centre-half (20) _____ (to hit) her from behind. An awful foul! Lux (21) _____ (to roll) on the floor, she could be injured. The referee (22) _____ (to stop) play, and The Firecats (23) _____ (to gather) in their opponent's half. Someone is shouting – someone else is on the floor. Another player (24) _____ (to push) her over! Things (25) _____ (to get) out of hand.

The referee (26) _____ (to blow) her whistle! She (27) _____ (to show) the red card to United's centre-half. And to a Firecats player! (28) _____ (the referee / to handle) this well? Yes. It (29) _____ (to seem) she has everything under control again.

The players (30) _____ (to calm) down. Play will resume with a penalty.

Lux (31) _____ (to go) to the penalty spot, apparently she (32) _____ (to break / not) any bones. This is an exciting pairing – Lux (33) _____ (to score) eight out of her last nine penalties in this tournament, but the United keeper (34) _____ (to save) nine out of her last ten! No doubt they (35) _____ (both / to practise) very hard. Lux (36) _____ (to step) back from the ball, ready to strike! She (37) _____ (to shoot) – she (38) _____ (to score)!

One minute in, The Firecats (39) _____ (to take) the lead! This game (40) _____ (to promise) to be thrilling.

18.17 Present Tenses in Use: Rules and Instructions

Choose the best **present** form (**simple**, **continuous**, **perfect** or **perfect continuous**) using the information provided in brackets and the context of the text. Note that there can be some flexibility between the **present simple** and the **present perfect** for following instructions; mostly the present perfect is used when it is important that the action is completed. Use contractions where possible.

How to Bake a Perfect Loaf

(1) _____ (you / to want) to make a perfect loaf of bread? This recipe (2) _____ (to deliver) great results.

To make life easier, (3) _____ (to prepare) your ingredients in advance: 500g of strong flour, 8g of yeast, 300ml of water and 10g of salt. These simple ingredients (4) _____ (to combine) for a basic but delicious loaf.

Before you (5) _____ (to begin), a word about temperature. When it is hot, the mixture (6) _____ (to react) faster. On colder days, the recipe (7) _____ (to take) longer to complete. For balance, we (8) _____ (to want) the mixture to be about 75 degrees. If you (9) _____ (to warm) the water, you can manage this temperature.

Step one: combine the water and the yeast in a bowl. The flour (10) _____ (to go) in next, then the salt on top of the flour. This order is important, because the salt (11) _____ (to affect) the yeast if they (12) _____ (to touch) directly.

Mix the ingredients: you can use a spoon, but hand mixing (13) _____ (to give) you a better feel for the results.

(14) _____ (you / mix) it thoroughly now?

(15) _____ (you / to create) a dough! Leave it for about 20 minutes: during this time, the flour (16) _____ (to absorb) water.

Next: how (17) _____ (we / to develop) gluten? This recipe (18) _____ (to require / not) kneading, but uses folding instead. (19) _____ (to place) the dough on a floured counter and fold one side to about halfway in. Turn 90 degrees and fold again. It (20) _____ (to take) two or three turns, usually, until you have a tight ball. (21) _____ (to be / not) that easy?

(22) _____ (to put) the dough back in the bowl, covered by a towel, and leave it to rise for about 90 minutes. When the dough (23) _____ (to become) light and airy, it is ready. Back on the counter, where it (24) _____ (to need) to be folded again, like a letter. Fold to the centre, then turn, until (25) _____ (you / to form) a tight parcel.

Now, the dough (26) _____ (to rise) one more time – leave it for another hour to 90 minutes. When you press it with a finger, (27) _____ (the dough / spring) back? Then it is ready.

We (28) _____ (to use) a Dutch Oven to do the cooking, preheated to 475 degrees. A Dutch Oven (29) _____ (to trap) steam with a lid, for the best results. The dough (30) _____ (to go) in seam side up. The seam (31) _____ (to open) during cooking to give a nice rustic look.

Put the Dutch Oven and dough in the oven for 25 minutes, then (32) _____ (to remove) the lid. Another 15–20 minutes in the oven (33) _____ (to produce) a golden loaf with a firm crust. A properly cooked loaf (34) _____ (to make) a hollow thump when you tap the base.

(35) _____ (it / to sound) done? (36) _____ (to

eat / not) it yet! (37) _____ (to rest) the loaf on a wire rack for 30 minutes, so the interior crumb can set, making it easier to cut. Congratulations: (38) _____ (you / to bake) a perfect loaf!

19. The Future in Use

19.1 Future Simple *Will* or *to Be Going to*

Complete the following sentences by putting the verb in brackets in either the **will** or **to be going to** future simple forms, without contractions. Remember, **will** is mostly used for recently decided actions and predictions, while **to be going to** is used for planned events and to emphasise determination.

For example:

Q: Someone is calling – I _____ the phone.

A: Someone is calling – I **will answer** the phone.

1. Because Lucas is tired, Regina _____ him a tea. (to make)

2. This Halloween, Tina _____ as a zombie. (to dress)

3. My brother is outside, _____ him in? (you / to let)

4. Those men have used the wrong timber. The house _____. (to collapse)

5. Claire thinks her boss _____ her latest report. (to like)

6. Is that a woodpecker in the tree? I _____ my binoculars to check. (to get)

7. Despite the cold summer, the building managers _____ the heating until October. (not / to activate)

8. We've been looking forward to our train journey; we _____ across the Swiss Alps. (to travel)

9. When Paul gets back from Scotland, he _____ a new job. (to start)

10. Tim's parents said he cannot go outside for a month, so he _____ computer games every weekend. (to play)

11. I was planning to go climbing, but I _____ and see if this rain stops! (to wait)

12. The swimming pool is always busy; it _____ busy today, I am sure. (to be)

13. "Where are you going with that knife?"

    "I _____ a piece of birthday cake." (to cut)

14. "What drink would you like?"

    "I _____ a cocktail." (to have)

15. "Where can I complain about the smell in our room?"

    "The lady behind the counter _____ you." (to help)

19.2 Future Simple with Present Simple or Continuous

Complete the following sentences by putting the verb in brackets in either the **present simple** or **present continuous** for future simple meaning, without contractions. Remember, **the present simple** is mostly used for scheduled events, while **the present continuous** is used for arrangements.

For example:

Q: I need a new computer, _____ tomorrow? (the shop / open)

A: I need a new computer, **is the shop open** tomorrow?

1. Dawn _____ her parents next Tuesday. (to visit)

2. Our bus _____ at 12 noon. (to arrive)

3. The family _____ home next Christmas. (to stay)

4. Ian _____ during the following three weekends. (to work / not)

5. The meeting this afternoon _____ every department. (to involve)

6. Hurry, the play _____ at 8 p.m. and I don't want to be late! (to start)

7. Everyone is waiting for Cathy, because she _____ champagne. (to bring)

8. The ghost _____ at sundown, we must be ready. (to appear)

9. Construction work _____ on the new apartment block tomorrow. (to begin)

10. _____ to the dance on Thursday? (you / to come)

11. _____ the speech this evening? (Adrian / to give)

12. _____ for a piano class in the morning? (we / to meet)

13. _____ at three or four? (the train / to leave)

14. _____ us for dinner? (your new girlfriend / to join)

15. _____ today? (the post office / to deliver)

19.3 Mixed Future Simple

Complete the following sentences by putting the verb in brackets in the most appropriate **future simple** form: **present simple**, **present continuous**, **will** or **to be going to**. Use contractions where possible.

For example:

Q: There is a terrible draft here – I _____ to sit somewhere else. (to move)

A: "There is a terrible draft here – **I'll move** to sit somewhere else."

1. "We need volunteers to clean the beach."

   "I _____ it if I have time." (to do)

2. "Izzy is on holiday next week."

   "Oh, _____ somewhere nice?" (she / to travel)

3. "Will our bus get to the airport in time?"

   "I think so, check in _____ in half an hour." (to close)

4. "Have you heard the weather forecast?"

   "Yes, they said it _____." (to rain)

5. "My aunt is in town this Friday. What should we do?"

   "The museum _____ an exhibition on Victorian clothes, you could try that." (to run)

6. "What time should we leave for the game on Saturday?"

   "Early – the rail workers _____ on strike this weekend."

   (to be)

7. "I need to go home and feed my cats. What time does this show

   _____?" (to finish)

8. "Do you know we've run out of printer paper?"

   "Yes, I _____ some this afternoon." (to buy)

9. "Are you okay? You look very pale."

   "No, I _____ sick!" (to be)

10. "Can you come with me to the ballet performance?"

    "Unfortunately not, I _____ golf this afternoon." (to play)

11. "Have you seen the mess on our window?"

    "No, I _____ it in a minute." (to clean)

12. "Why are you writing in such a rush?"

    "Because the show _____ in half an hour!" (to start)

13. "Shall we check out Dover Castle tomorrow?"

    "I can't, I _____ all day tomorrow." (to work)

14. "Does anyone want to go for an ice cream?"

    "Me, I _____!" (to come)

19.4 Future Processes

Complete the following sentences by putting the verb in brackets in either the **future simple** or **future continuous** form, without contractions. Remember, the future simple is mostly used for planned or expected actions while we use the future continuous for ongoing or interrupted temporary processes. For the future simple, **will**, **to be going to** or **the present continuous** can mostly be used flexibly here.

For example:

Q: Theo _____ across Devon all spring. (to cycle)

A: Theo **will be cycling** across Devon all spring. (or **is going to be cycling**)

1. I _____ you in the park later. (to meet)
2. He _____ me his car. (to sell)
3. They _____ hockey for hours. (to play)
4. It _____ colder over the next two weeks. (to get)
5. The college _____ new students in September. (to accept)
6. We are meeting up and travelling together – our friends _____ at the station for us. (to wait / already)
7. Rebecca _____ in the Hilton while she's in town. (to stay)
8. The mayor _____ the new leisure centre this Wednesday. (to open)
9. My wife _____ dinner this evening, as I won't come back until late. (to cook)
10. Sean cannot visit his gran until 6 p.m. because she _____ before then. (to eat)
11. _____ this Sunday? (you / to work)
12. _____ all the bread before 6 a.m.? (they / to deliver)
13. _____ at 3 p.m., in case we need to call? (she / to drive)
14. _____ in Scotland all weekend? (Frank / to hike)
15. _____ the right choice next time? (I / to make)

19.5 Future Sequences

Complete the following sentences by putting the verb in brackets in either the **future simple** or **future perfect** form, without contractions. Remember, the future perfect indicates an action will be completed at a particular point in the future.

For example:

Q: We will _____ the door by lunchtime. (to paint)

A: We will **have painted** the door by lunchtime.

1. Shirley will _____ her exams in June. She will _____ by August. (to take / to graduate)

2. Our parents will _____ at Christmas. They will _____ presents. (to visit / to bring)

3. You are going to _____ some new shoes. Will you _____ enough money? (to buy / to earn)

4. The tide will _____ highest at 11 a.m., because it will _____ all the way in. (to be / to come)

5. Brenda is going to _____ a cake before the party. She will _____ it from scratch. (to bake / to make)

6. Ulrich will _____ his test by 1 p.m. We are going to _____ him a party. (to pass / to throw)

7. Workers will _____ the high street this evening. They are going to _____ traffic. (to close / to divert)

8. I hope the weather will _____ tomorrow. They say it is going to _____ in the morning. (to improve / to rain)

9. Are you going to _____ Jon about the wedding soon? By next week, he will _____ it from someone else. (to tell / to hear)

10. Will you _____ your door before you go away? You will not _____ with it in that state, will you? (to repair / to leave)

19.6 Duration in the Future 1

Complete the following sentences by putting the verb in brackets in either the **future continuous** or **future perfect continuous** form, without contractions. Remember, the future perfect continuous is used to indicate duration with reference to a specific point of future time.

For example:

Q: By the time they arrive, they will _____ for three hours. (to drive)

A: By the time they arrive, they will **have been driving** for three hours.

1. My parents will _____ together for 20 years this October. (to live)

2. The fishermen will _____ in 15 minutes. (to return)

3. You are going to _____ all evening. (to study)

4. He will _____ to fix the sink all day before he admits he needs help. (to try)

5. By the time of the competition, Sally is going to _____ for eighteen months. (to train)

6. I am going to _____ for three days, so I won't be able to call. (to travel)

7. The cat will _____ in the loft during the party. (to sleep)

8. Inflation will _____ for five months by February. (to rise)

9. Colin is going to _____ all day if he reaches the seaside by sunset. (to walk)

10. At midnight, we will _____ the fireworks. (to watch)

11. At noon, we will _____ for Robert for an hour. (to wait)

12. The days will _____ shorter in September. (to get)

19.7 Duration in the Future 2

Complete the following sentences by putting the verb in brackets in either the **future perfect** or **future perfect continuous** form, without contractions. Remember, the future perfect continuous is used to indicate an ongoing future process, while the future perfect tells us an action will be completed.

For example:

Q: The guard will _____ for seven hours by the end of his shift. (to work)

A: The guard will **have been working** for seven hours by the end of his shift.

1. The eggs will _____ in the fridge for a month by the weekend. (to sit)

2. I will _____ my essay by 5 p.m. (to write)

3. Eric will _____ Vikings for two years before he writes his book. (to research)

4. The tourists will _____ all the pubs in town before they go home. (to visit)

5. You won't see any birds, because they will _____ south for the winter. (to migrate)

6. Before long, Ola will _____ for her missing sock for a week. (to search)

7. We will _____ for two hours when Jim joins us. (to talk)

8. If it survives much longer, the tree will _____ for fifteen years. (to grow)

9. By the time we leave school, our teacher will _____ us everything. (to teach)

10. Peggy will _____ a pony for three months by her birthday. (to demand)

19.8 Mixed Future Matching

Form logical **future** tense sentences using the fragments below. Each collection of eight fragments forms four complete sentences. Note that some clauses may fit flexibly, but only one combination should satisfy all four sentences of each question.

For example:

a. We will cook dinner	for an hour when your father gets back.
b. We will be cooking dinner	and have it ready before your father arrives.
c. We will have cooked dinner	during the radio broadcast.
d. We will have been cooking dinner	after your father gets back.

    a.   We will cook dinner after your father gets back.

    b.   We will be cooking dinner during the radio broadcast.

    c.   We will have cooked dinner and have it ready before your father arrives.

    d.   We will have been cooking dinner for an hour when your father gets back.

1.

a. I am going to buy a house	all summer – I'll be exhausted in autumn!
b. I am going to have bought a house	this summer, so won't have much free time.
c. I am going to be buying a house	once I save up enough money.
d. I am going to have been buying houses	by September, you can come visit in October!

2.

a. Clarence is joining us	on the way, he won't want dinner.
b. Clarence will have been driving	this evening – shall we make a soup?
c. Clarence will have eaten	in the guest room – please prepare the bed.
d. Clarence will be staying	all day – will he want to rest when he gets here?

175

3.

a. The post office is going to open	new stores all year, come New Year.
b. The post office is going to have moved	their new store to serve customers.
c. The post office is going to be too busy opening	to a new store by June.
d. The post office is going to have been opening	a new store in June.

4.

a. The new phone will have	selling for two months by January.
b. The new phone will be	sold out by Tuesday.
c. The new phone will	impressing customers all month.
d. The new phone will have been	come with a velvet carry case.

19.9 Future Time Sequences

The following sentences include multiple **future** tense clauses. Put the subjects and verbs into the order of which will start first, or indicate if the first action is unknown.

For example:

Q: We will buy a new boat after our old one breaks.

A: A) our old one breaks B) we will buy

1.   They will come inside after they finish playing.

A) _____ B) _____

2.   The party will end once the last guest leaves.

A) _____ B) _____

3.   We will have been married for ten years if we last another summer!

A) _____ B) _____

4.   If the van is fixed by tomorrow, Tim is going to drive.

A) _____ B) _____

5. When the company releases the game, they will have been working on it for three years.

A) _____ B) _____

6. She will visit her grandmother while she is studying in York.

A) _____ B) _____

7. If the banks calls, tell them I will come back in an hour.

A) _____ B) _____

8. The match will start as soon as the referee arrives.

A) _____ B) _____

9. They will deliver the table while we are preparing dinner.

A) _____ B) _____

10. Our luggage will be cleared after they have inspected it.

A) _____ B) _____

11. Why are you going to Scotland while we will be in England?

A) _____ B) _____

12. Will Larry collect the painting before the shop closes?

A) _____ B) _____

13. Who is attending the conference in spring? Your passes will have been ordered by next week.

A) _____ B) _____

14. Does the train leave after 9 a.m.? Otherwise we will have to pay for a peak ticket.

A) _____ B) _____

15. When Aunt Gina leaves, will she have seen everyone in town?

A) _____ B) _____

19.10 Mixed Future Tenses 1

Complete the following sentences by putting the verb in brackets into the most appropriate **future** form, without contractions (including present tenses for future meaning).

1. After you take a nap, you _____ a lot better. (to feel)
2. You need to finish your work before you _____ home at 6 p.m. (to go)
3. I think I _____ bread from the corner shop when it opens. (to buy)
4. We _____ a garden party on Sunday, weather permitting. (to have)
5. Before we start our lesson, we _____ yesterday's class. (to review)
6. We _____ in the shelter when the bus comes. (to sit)
7. I'm very sorry, it seems Dr. Jones _____ back until 2 p.m. (to come)
8. I don't think you _____ any problems when you land in Boston. (to have)
9. On Friday at 8 o'clock, I _____ my friend. (to meet)
10. The English lesson _____ at 8:45. (to start)
11. Look at the clouds – it _____ in a few minutes. (to rain)
12. When you get off the train, I _____ for you by the ticket machine. (to wait)
13. You _____ your children with you to France, aren't you? (to take)
14. This time next week, I _____ in Switzerland! (to ski)
15. Now I _____ my answers. (to check)

19.11 Mixed Future Tenses 2

Complete the following sentences by putting the verb in brackets into an appropriate **future** form, without contractions. Remember that unless we have a specific reason to use certain future tenses, simpler forms are often preferred. In some cases, more than one option is possible.

1. The train _____ at 12:30. (to arrive)
2. We _____ dinner at a seaside restaurant on Sunday. (to eat)
3. It _____ in Brighton throughout the parade. (to snow)
4. By the time we get home, they _____ football for 30 minutes. (to play)
5. Paul _____ to London on Monday morning. (to fly)
6. Wait! I _____ you to the station. (to drive)
7. This summer, I will _____ in Goring for four years. (to live)
8. The baby should be due soon; next week Erin _____ pregnant for nine months. (to be)
9. Are you still writing your essay? If you finish by 4 p.m., we _____ for a walk. (to go)
10. I _____ my mother in April. (to see)
11. In three years, I _____ in a different country. (to live)
12. When they get married in March, they _____ each other for six years. (to know)
13. You're carrying too much. I _____ the door for you. (to open)
14. Do you think the teacher _____ our homework by Monday morning? (to mark)
15. When I see you tomorrow, I _____ you my new book. (to show)

19.12 Future Tenses in Use: Schedule 1

Listed below is the Robinson family's schedule for a trip to Winchester. Indicate which statements are true at the listed times.

- 06:30: Breakfast and washing
- 07:30: Start journey by car
- 09:30: Arrive in Winchester and walk into town
- 10:15: Tea in "Frieda's Tearoom"
- 10:45: Explore town
- 11:30: Tour of cathedral
- 12:30: Lunch at "The Old Vine"
- 13:45: Visit the castle ruins, then explore more of the town
- 15:00: Visit the old mill on the way back to the car
- 15:45: Travel back by car
- 18:00: Home in time for dinner!

For example:
At 07.30, the Robinsons ...
    a. **... will leave home. – TRUE**
    b. ... will have travelled by car.
    c. **... are starting their journey. – TRUE**
    d. ... are going to have breakfast.

1. At 10.35, the Robinsons ...
    a. ... will be parking the car.
    b. ... will have walked into town.
    c. ... will be having tea.
    d. ... are seeing the cathedral.

2. At 12.40, the Robinsons ...

    a. ... will be in "The Old Vine".

    b. ... will have been touring the cathedral for an hour.

    c. ... are going to explore the town.

    d. ... are going to have finished lunch.

3. At 15.15, the Robinsons ...

    a. ... will be heading home.

    b. ... are going to be seeing the old mill.

    c. ... will have been exploring Winchester for over three hours.

    d. ... will have eaten lunch.

4. At 18.00, the Robinsons ...

    a. ... are going to be driving.

    b. ... will arrive home.

    c. ... will have eaten dinner.

    d. ... will have travelled for two hours or more.

19.13 Future Tenses in Use: Schedule 2

Roger and Mandy are planning their wedding. They have a timetable set out below. Complete the sentences about the day in the **future** tense, without contractions, using the **will** form.

- 09:00 – Wedding party arrives at St Christopher's Church. System checks and final run-through with priest.
- 10:00 – Guests start to arrive. Ushers and bridesmaids help seat guests while bride and groom get ready for ceremony.
- 10:30 – Ceremony begins.
- 11:30 – Ceremony ends. The couple sign documents, followed by photos and a champagne reception.
- 12:30 – Guests driven by bus to McGruber House. Bride and groom greet guests with welcome drinks in the Library Hall.
- 13:30 – Everyone is moved to the Banquet Hall and seated. Lunch is served, with the jazz band playing.
- 15:00 – Speeches given by groom, father-of-the-bride, and best man. Gifts and thanks are also given.
- 16:00 – Guests return to the Library Hall where the jazz band play again. Magician performs tricks.
- 18:00 – Rock band arrives, with dance floor cleared.
- 18:15 – The married couple's first dance, followed by general dancing.
- 19:30 – Taco van arrives for evening snacks.
- 22:00 – Party finishes, with bus to take everyone home.

For example:

Q: At 09:15, the wedding party _____ and they _____ a final run-through. (to arrive / to do)

A: At 09:15, the wedding party **will have arrived** and they **will be doing** a final run-through.

1. At 10:00, the guests _____ to arrive. (to start)

2. Between 10:00 and 10:30, the ushers _____ guests to find their seats. (to help)

3. When the ceremony begins, the bride _____ about 30 minutes to get ready. (to have)

4. By 11:20, the ceremony _____ for almost an hour. (to run)

5. At 11:35, the ceremony _____ and the couple _____ their documents. (to end / to sign)

6. All the guests _____ to McGruber House after the photos have been taken. (to move)

7. The couple _____ welcome drinks in the Library Hall. (to host)

8. Everyone _____ a seat in the Banquet Hall before lunch is served. (to take)

9. The jazz band _____ during lunch. (to play)

10. At 15:00, the groom _____ his speech. The other speeches _____. (to give / to follow)

11. A magician _____ tricks while the jazz band is playing in the Library Hall. (to perform / to play)

12. Someone _____ the dance floor before the couple's first dance. (to clear)

13. A taco van _____ more food later in the evening, in case guests get hungry. (to provide)

14. When the party finishes, people _____ for hours. (to dance)

15. The bus _____ guests to their hotels at the end of the night. (to return)

19.14 Future Tenses in Use: Making Plans

In the following dialogue, Lucy and Charles make plans for the day. Complete the sentences by putting the verbs in brackets into the most appropriate **future** form. Use contractions where possible.

Plans for the Day

Lucy: (1) _____ (you / to come) with me to the lake today?

Charles: I've finished my work, so (2) _____ (I / to join) you, yes. Shall I drive?

Lucy: No, (3) _____ (we / to take) the bus. The car is making funny noises.

Charles: (4) _____ (I / to check) it out, maybe I can fix it.

Lucy: Oh, don't – (5) _____ (you / to work) on the car for hours!

Charles: (6) _____ (it / to take / only) a few minutes, I'm sure.

Lucy: The bus (7) _____ (to arrive) before you finish.

Charles: But (8) _____ (I / to use) the car this evening, too. I'd best get it working.

Lucy: This evening? Where (9) _____ (you / to go)?

Charles: (10) _____ (I / to play) poker at Gilbert's, from 8 o'clock until late.

Lucy: (11) _____ (you / to meet) your friends? What (12) _____ (I / to do)?

Charles: (13) _____ (you / to see / not) a play this evening?

Lucy: Oh no, that was cancelled weeks ago. Perhaps (14) _____ (I / to invite) Janet round. (15) _____

(she / to come) back from Ireland today.

Charles: Great! (16) _____ (she / to have) lots of stories, I would like to see her.

Lucy: But (17) _____ (you / to enjoy) your game instead.

Charles: Maybe she could come another day. (18) _____ (she / to be / not) tired this evening?

Lucy: Ireland isn't far – (19) _____ (she / to travel / not) too long. And (20) _____ (I / to make) her some dinner.

Charles: A meal, too? No – (21) _____ (I / to cook) this evening, and (22) _____ (I / to prepare) more for you two.

Lucy: (23) _____ (you / to start / barely) before you have to go to poker, I'm sure! It's fine. (24) _____ (we / to order) a takeaway, if we have to. Now, are you coming to the lake? (25) _____ (the bus / to leave) in around ten minutes.

Charles: Okay, okay! (26) _____ (I / to look) at the car later.

19.15 Future Tenses in Use: Narrative 1

Complete the following passage by putting the verb in brackets into the most appropriate **future** form (**present simple**, **future simple**, **future continuous**, **future perfect** or **future perfect continuous**), without contractions. There may be more than one option with **will / to be going to / present continuous** forms.

Summer Plans

Amber (1) _____ (to finish) school in the middle of July. She (2) _____ (to have) three months of holiday, then she (3) _____ (to go) university in the autumn. She

(4) _____ (to study) Law at Oxford. The course

(5) _____ (to last) four years, and once she

(6) _____ (to qualify) Amber (7) _____ (to get) a

job in London.

Over the summer, Amber (8) _____ (to work) in the local

garden centre. She (9) _____ (to save) money for university, and

also to travel. The garden centre (10) _____ (to let) her take two

weeks off in August. During that break, she (11) _____ (to

travel) to France with her friends, Holly and Jaime.

All three friends have different plans for the trip. Holly

(12) _____ (to work / not) this summer, and

(13) _____ (to explore) Europe for two months. When Amber

(14) _____ (to meet) her in France, she (15) _____

(to travel) for three weeks already. She (16) _____ (to visit)

Germany and Italy, and after France she (17) _____ (to

continue) to Spain.

Jaime only has one week of holiday, so she (18) _____ (to

come) later, after Amber and Holly (19) _____ (to see) Paris.

They (20) _____ (to travel) south together, to stay by a lake.

Amber hopes it (21) _____ (to make) her fit before university, as

the girls (22) _____ (to swim) and (23) _____ (to

hike) every day – as long as the weather (24) _____ (to stay)

good. She (25) _____ (to read) books to prepare for her course,

too. By the time Amber (26) _____ (to move) to Oxford, she

(27) _____ (to complete) all the advance reading.

Unless she (28) _____ (to meet) a nice young man to distract

her!

19.16 Future Tenses in Use: Narrative 2

Complete the following passage by putting the verb in brackets into the most appropriate **future** form (**present simple**, **future simple**, **future continuous**, **future perfect** or **future perfect continuous**), without contractions. There may be more than one option with **will / to be going to / present continuous** forms, as illustrated in the answers.

An End in Sight

The computer game *Badger Spies* (1) _____ (to hit) the shelves in three months. Over the next month, the developers (2) _____ (to finish) building the game so they can test it. Beta players (3) _____ (to study) the game in detail, trying to spot problems. While they (4) _____ (to test) the game, the marketing team (5) _____ (to finalise) an ambitious marketing campaign.

   Badger Spies (6) _____ (to go) on sale in thirteen countries, to start with, including the USA, the UK and Germany. The developers (7) _____ (to host) a big launch party for the many releases, where they (8) _____ (to serve) food and drinks inspired by the game. The staff at the party (9) _____ (to wear) costumes from the *Badger Spies* world.

   Not everyone is in a party mood, though. One designer, Rupert, worries they (10) _____ (to complete / not) the game in time. He expects he (11) _____ (to make) improvements until the last minute, which means the beta players (12) _____ (to play) an incomplete version for months before they report. He (13) _____ (to complain / not) to the team leader about it, though. They (14) _____ (to release) the game on the set date, even if the mistakes (15) _____ (to correct / not). The company

(16) _____ (to invest) too much time and money in the marketing to slow down.

Rupert worries about the marketing campaign, too. It (17) _____ (to give) people the wrong impression of the game, he thinks. The marketing team (18) _____ (to try / not) the game themselves, and have not discussed it with the design team. The boss announced, with great determination, that they (19) _____ (to make) it sexy. Rupert does not think *Badger Spies* (20) _____ (to be) a sexy game.

Maybe he just feels negative because he is tired. By the time the game is out, Rupert and his team (21) _____ (to work) on the project for almost three years. Whether the game is good or not, he (22) _____ (to celebrate) finally being able to do something else. But the rest of the team are optimistic. The boss says *Badger Spies* (23) _____ (to change) everything – children (24) _____ (to dress) in badger costumes and movie producers (25) _____ (to ask) for the rights to make a film. Rupert does hope that all of that (26) _____ (to happen). Mostly, though, he hopes the game (27) _____ (to entertain) people, and that by the release day they (28) _____ (to fix) all the errors.

20. Mixed Tenses in Use

20.1 Simple Tenses Uses

Read the mixed simple tense statements below. Identify the **simple tense uses** from following options:

- Completed action
- Past state
- Present rule
- Present state
- Future action
- Future state

For example:
Q: Edgar washed his hands twice, to be sure.
A: Completed action

1. Bryony queued for hours at the ticket office.

   _____

2. It will arrive in a week's time.

   _____

3. Unemployment will fall after the factory opens.

   _____

4. You never answer your phone.

   _____

5. Snails sleep under rocks.

   _____

6. It is very cold outside.

   _____

7. She gave the boys a very angry look.

   _____

8. Luke always asks about trains.

    _____

9. The mayor will resign because of the scandal.

    _____

10. They went to Dallas for his birthday.

    _____

11. I will go for a walk later.

    _____

12. On the seafront, it was incredibly windy.

    _____

13. We like dancing.

    _____

14. She will get married in the summer.

    _____

15. The men had pie for lunch.

    _____

16. Our parents will love this painting.

    _____

17. Tulips grow here each spring.

    _____

18. He will want to share that doughnut.

    _____

19. Someone took the sandwich I wanted.

    _____

20. We were ready for trouble.

    _____

20.2 Continuous Tenses Uses

Read the mixed continuous tense statements below. Identify the **continuous tense uses** from following options:
- Temporary / ongoing process
- Process of change
- Emphatic repeated action
- Future arrangement

For example:
Q: The sea level is rising because of global warming.
A: Process of change

1. The Robertsons are staying in Bermuda next August.

   _____

2. My cousin is riding a bike to work from now on.

   _____

3. She is waiting in the hallway right now.

   _____

4. Sally was resting under the tree while reading her book.

   _____

5. It was getting harder to find a decent bagel in town.

   _____

6. I am moving to Mexico in two months.

   _____

7. Erin is forever complaining that no one listens to her.

   _____

8. His motorbike was constantly breaking down.

   _____

9. Mr Taylor is meeting us after his flight gets in.

   _____

10. Victor is dating the girl from the coffee shop.

   _____

11. People will be protesting outside when they pass the new law.

   _____

12. They were pulling the cart when the wheel fell off.

   _____

13. The plumber is repairing our toilet tomorrow.

   _____

14. I made lunch while the boys were playing in the garden.

   _____

15. With better tools, the factory will be expanding.

   _____

16. Our neighbourhood is becoming busier as more people move in.

   _____

17. The managers are hiring a new team of coders.

   _____

18. Justin is studying for a diploma.

   _____

19. My new toothbrush is arriving this afternoon.

   _____

20. Paige and Greg are working on their communications skills.

   _____

20.3 Perfect Tenses Uses

Read the mixed perfect tense statements below. Identify the **perfect tense uses** from following options:

- Completed at a past time
- Past state duration
- Past affecting the present
- Ongoing state / activity
- Duration of ongoing activity
- Completed at a future time

For example:

Q: Rhona has filled in this form five times already.

A: Ongoing activity

1. Foxes have raided our bins; there is garbage everywhere.

    _____

2. The astronomy club has enlisted six new members this year, and it's only March.

    _____

3. I have found some old books, do you want them?

    _____

4. The man had understood nothing the entire time he was studying.

    _____

5. Juliet has learned to sing, which is very distracting.

    _____

6. My son has watched many cartoons.

    _____

7. She had added the ingredients in the wrong order – the biscuits were ruined.

    _____

8. We cannot swim later, the escaped crabs will have infested the beach.

    _____

9. It was warm when Jared got home because he had forgotten to turn off the radiator.

    _____

10. Snakes have got into the shed – run!

    _____

11. The committee have met once a week for two years.

    _____

12. The couple had known each other for five years before marrying.

    _____

13. The offer will have ended before tomorrow.

    _____

14. Winston has spotted 50 different species of butterfly.

    _____

15. Hazel will have submitted her thesis by this evening.

    _____

16. Lydia had been the head chef since Rupert retired.

    _____

17. The ducks had stolen all the bread before we realised they were there.

    _____

18. Margret and Clive have travelled by train for twelve hours so far.

    _____

20.4 Perfect Continuous Tenses Uses

Read the mixed perfect continuous tense statements below. Identify the **perfect continuous tense uses** from following options. Note that completed past processes often also include a duration; both uses may apply, depending on the emphasis on the activity or the time taken.

- Completed past process
- Duration of present process
- Present process started in the past
- Duration of future process

For example:
Q: The seals will have been bathing here all summer.
A: Duration of future process

1. Adrian has been collecting names for his new club.

   _____

2. My parents have been warning me to wrap up since August.

   _____

3. The artist had been painting the mural when he ran out of paint.

   _____

4. The doctor will have been seeing patients for 30 years when he retires.

   _____

5. Wendel has been spending a lot of time worrying about earthquakes.

   _____

6. Shops will have been selling Christmas presents for months before the holiday.

   _____

7. This computer has been loading for an hour already!

   _____

8.   We had been cooking all morning and the dinner was finally ready.

_____

9.   Richard has been swimming every day for a year.

_____

10. Lily was tired because she had been listening to reggae music all night.

_____

11. Christopher will have been writing letters to her all summer before she replies.

_____

12. She had been running daily before she twisted her ankle.

_____

13. You will have been designing that website for a decade before you finish.

_____

14. I have been looking for a new window cleaner, but haven't found one I trust.

_____

15. The ladies have been discussing Ancient Greece for 50 minutes.

_____

16. The windows are open because my apartment has been getting too hot.

_____

17. The children will have been opening jars all afternoon.

_____

18. The car has been making strange noises, so he's taking it to a mechanic.

_____

19. Michelle has been reading that book since January.

_____

20. The inspector had been scanning documents for hours before he spotted the mistake.

_____

20.5 Past Present Matching

Form logical past and present sentences using the fragments below. Each collection of eight fragments forms four complete sentences. Note that some clauses may fit flexibly, but only one combination should satisfy all four sentences of each question.

For example:

a. As Howard got home,	his wife had cooked dinner.
b. Before Howard got home,	he found dinner on the table.
c. Howard has got home,	dinner is always ready.
d. When Howard gets home,	so we are having dinner.

a. As Howard got home, he found dinner on the table.
b. Before Howard got home, his wife had cooked dinner.
c. Howard has got home, so we are having dinner.
d. When Howard gets home, dinner is always ready.

1.

a. Dave is driving to work,	and has parked under the tree.
b. Dave drove to work	when he heard the news on the radio.
c. Dave was driving to work	most days, but not today.
d. Dave drives to work	so he cannot answer his phone.

2.

a. The museum opened	a new wing where you can see old costumes.
b. The museum opens	late on Thursdays until funding ran out.
c. The museum has opened	to the public last December.
d. The museum was opening	on Tuesdays at 8 a.m.

3.

a. The student has read	what looks like a very long book.
b. The student is reading	the book before class started.
c. The student read	everything on the reading list already.
d. The student had read	ten books last month.

4.

a. Becca wanted to travel	through Spain when her car broke down.
b. Becca has wanted to travel	around Europe right now.
c. Becca is travelling	but could not afford it.
d. Becca was travelling	since she was very young.

20.6 Past Present Cloze 1

Complete the following sentences by putting the information in brackets into the most appropriate **past** or **present** form.

For example:

Q: Harry _____ all his money, so he cannot buy the football. (to spend)

A: Harry **has spent** all this money, so he cannot buy the football.

1.   They _____ the pier every year. (to paint)

2.   Norman _____ his house this week. (to clean)

3.   I _____ to classical music since I was a child. (to listen)

4.   The fisherman _____ a huge salmon last night. (to catch)

5.   We _____ philosophy, but it became too confusing. (to discuss)

6.   You _____ a funny tune when you came in, what was it? (to whistle)

7.   Look, the gardener _____ the heads off the roses! (to cut)

8.   Mr Willis _____ two bags of potatoes but left one in the shop. (to buy)

9.   _____ outside when it rained? You look absolutely soaked. (you / to be)

10. Can you pass me the sugar? I _____ an apple pie. (to bake)

11. The dogs _____ holes again; look at that mess. (to dig)

12. Why _____? Stop her – we have dessert! (Susan / to leave)

13. The reporter _____ tired, but kept talking anyway. (to appear)

14. Someone _____ my socks. They were here a second ago. (to steal)

15. When I met the twins, I thought I _____ double. (to see)

20.7 Past Present Cloze 2

Complete the following sentences by putting the information in brackets into the most appropriate **past** or **present** form.

For example:

Q: I am walking to work today, because I _____ the bus. (to miss)

A: I am walking to work today, because I **missed** the bus.

1. Can I borrow your pen? I _____ mine at home. (to leave)

2. A crowd _____ in town because the council raised taxes. (to protest)

3. My sister _____ me to tea, so I am buying flowers for her. (to invite)

4. Has Bob finished that book he _____? (to read)

5. The children were excited to see Aunt Maggie, as she always _____ them chocolate. (to give)

6. Vivian always _____ late, that's why she wasn't home when we called. (to work)

7. School tests _____ harder, so students have started complaining. (to get)

8. The door was locked earlier, so I still _____ how the burglar got in. (to know / not)

199

9.   Robert is upset because _____ the game when his team scored. (to watch / not)

10. We started running in the summer, but we _____ less often as the weather has worsened. (to go)

11. Are the potatoes not ready yet? _____ the oven before we went out? (you / to turn on / not)

12. Is Sue coming to the cinema? She _____ us for months. (to join / not)

13. I washed the dishes yesterday. I _____ them again today. (to wash / not)

14. Frank's son wants to drive to Scotland, but he _____ his driving test yet. (to pass / not)

15. Is that woman climbing a tree now? She _____ us all morning! (to distract)

20.8 Present Future Cloze

Complete the following sentences by putting the information in brackets into the most appropriate **present** or **future** form.

For example:

Q: Now that I have a degree, I _____ a job. (to find)

A: Now that I have a degree, I **am going to find** a job.

1.   We are building a tree house so the children _____ outside more often. (to play)

2.   Daisy is coming home tomorrow, because her flight _____. (to delay)

3.   Howard is waiting for the bus that _____ at eleven. (to arrive)

4.   I have a book in my bag, which I _____ when you arrive. (to read)

5. The men _____ the truck already, so it will definitely get there on time. (to load)

6. Will it rain later? I _____ a coat. (to take / not)

7. _____ tea after you wash those mugs? (you / to make)

8. The phone _____ all morning, I am going to disconnect it soon! (to ring)

9. Who will win the race? It _____ too close to tell. (to look)

10. I am going to the shop later. What _____ me to get? (you / to want)

11. Tyler is learning to ski but he _____ ready in time for the holiday. (to be / not)

12. He _____ that old guitar for a year this October, I think it's time he got a new one. (to play)

13. Brittany washes her hair every day – she _____ well when they go camping. (to cope / not)

14. Look, the horses _____ across that field – we will never catch them! (to race)

15. The men will be delivering our new fridge in an hour, so I _____ to finish my work quickly. (to try)

20.9 Present Future Narrative

Using the following schedule, complete the passage below in the most appropriate **present** or **future** form.

The Jolly Clown Conference

09.00 – Registration
09.30 – Talk: Modern Clowning in Practice
11.00 – Tea and Coffee
11.30 – Workshop: Working with Children
13:00 – Lunch
14:00 – Workshop: Advanced Physical Comedy
15:00 – Break
15:30 – Talk: A History of Clowns – Learn from the Best
17:00 – End of Day

It's 13.45 and Bilbo and Jam (1) _____ (to eat) lunch together. Bilbo (2) _____ (to praise) the clown convention for twenty minutes already.

"The day (3) _____ (to be) wonderful so far," he says.

"But I (4) _____ (to get) tired," Jam says. "I (5) _____ (to fall asleep) during the afternoon talk."

"Nonsense! There (6) _____ (to be) a break before it. And the workshop after lunch (7) _____ (to revive) you."

"I (8) _____ (to know / not) about that. Physical comedy (9) _____ (to make) me very nervous."

"Why (10) _____ (to worry) so much? The information pack (11) _____ (to state) that you can watch if you don't want to join in."

"But I (12) _____ (to want) to take part, right now. I only fear I (13) _____ (to want / not) to when everyone (14) _____ (to run) around hitting their heads on planks."

"Well, by 2 p.m. we (15) _____ (to finish) this hearty meal and perhaps your spirits (16) _____ (to lift). I (17) _____ (to feel) much livelier already, myself."

"You (18) _____ (to feel / always) lively, Bilbo. It might be because you (19) _____ (to eat) too much sugar."

"Ha! I (20) _____ (to eat / not) any sugar for two months, in fact. I am lively because this conference (21) _____ (to inspire) me. The workshop on children (22) _____ (to give) me lots of new ideas, and the talk on clown history (23) _____ (to teach) us about what it takes to really succeed."

"Okay, okay. I (24) _____ (to try) to enjoy the afternoon. Look, I think that while we (25) _____ (to talk), they (26) _____ (to set up) the workshop. Why (27) _____ (that man / to carry) two buckets of water?"

"We (28) _____ (to find out) soon!"

20.10 Future in the Past

Convert the following past sentences into **past future** forms, using the information in brackets.

For example:

Q: She wanted to leave by 9 a.m., but was too busy.

A: She **was going to leave** by 9 a.m., but was too busy.

1. He almost ate all the cake, but it was too much. (to eat)

   _____

2. They were planning to buy a hot tub until they saw the running costs. (to buy)

   _____

3. Shirley intended to go to university if she got the grades. (to go)

     _____

4. She needed to learn to dance before the end of the year. (to learn)

     _____

5. We asked our neighbours to repair the fence and they agreed. (our neighbours / to repair)

     _____

6. I thought of travelling to Germany for Oktoberfest. (to travel)

     _____

7. The poster gave a starting time of 7 p.m. (the poster said / it / to start)

     _____

8. I arranged to meet Geoff in the park.

     _____

9. The forecast was for rain. (they said / it / to rain)

     _____

10. Uncle Jim agreed to supply beer for the party. (to supply)

     _____

11. Luke promised not to drink my tea. (Luke said / to drink / not)

     _____

12. Sam did not expect to pass her exams. (Sam / to think / she / to pass)

     _____

20.11 Time Sequences: Past and Present

The following sentences include multiple **past** and **present** tense clauses. Put the subjects and verbs into the order of which will start first.

For example:

Q: I am working today because I had yesterday off.

A: A) I had B) I am working

1. My boss has asked for a new report, even though I wrote one two days ago.

    A) _____ B) _____

2. Tess has been learning to dance since she saw the Nutcracker ballet.

    A) _____ B) _____

3. It has been getting harder to find work, so I am starting my own company.

    A) _____ B) _____

4. Brian and Freda are arguing about who left the oven on.

    A) _____ B) _____

5. Because it rained, the bench is too wet to sit on.

    A) _____ B) _____

6. Our company is moving offices because they found a better site.

    A) _____ B) _____

7. Jenny drives very well as she started at an early age.

    A) _____ B) _____

8. The woodland animals were so noisy last night that Bernice has barely slept.

    A) _____ B) _____

9. My family came from Hungary originally, but have lived in Denver for five years.

    A) _____ B) _____

10. She was having a warm shower but has stopped because the hot water ran out.

    A) _____ B) _____ C) _____

11. Have they brought the cocktail sausages we asked for?

    A) _____ B) _____

12. What are you drinking? I didn't see that on the menu.

    A) _____ B) _____

13. The driver said we must exit at the front of the train, are we riding in the right carriage?

    A) _____ B) _____ C) _____

14. Who has completed their homework since we studied last night?

    A) _____ B) _____

15. If the dog was here before, where is it now?

    A) _____ B) _____

20.12 Time Sequences: Present and Future

The following sentences include multiple **present** and **future** tense clauses. Put the subjects and verbs into the order of which will start first.

For example:

Q: Naomi is mending her kite because she is taking it to the park later.

A: A) Naomi is mending B) she is taking

1. Even though we are going to a restaurant for dinner, Dad is eating a doughnut.

    A) _____ B) _____

2. They will be expecting a good performance, so he is practising very hard.

    A) _____ B) _____

3. The price seems to be fair, I will buy this jacket.

    A) _____ B) _____

4. Tyler is going to get some cheese from that man who is preparing a stall.

    A) _____ B) _____

5. She will spend all the money she is earning.

    A) _____ B) _____

6. I love chocolate but it will make me fat.

    A) _____ B) _____

7. Will you wear the scarf I am making you?

    A) _____ B) _____

8. Are the police investigating the burglary or will the thief escape punishment?

    A) _____ B) _____

9. Is the table big enough? Perhaps not everyone will fit.

    A) _____ B) _____

10. Does the flight leave soon? I have not checked in.

    A) _____ B) _____

20.13 Time Sequences: Mixed Tenses

The following sentences include multiple mixed tense clauses. Put the subjects and verbs into the order of which will start first, or indicate if the first action is unknown.

For example:

Q: I was surprised to learn that the mayor will be opening our shop.

A: A) I was surprised B) the mayor will be opening

1. We are peeling potatoes so they will be ready for mashing.

    A) _____ B) _____

2. The spiders have been hiding in shadows – that's why you have not seen them.

        A) _____ B) _____

3. Ron is going to introduce his parents to the girl he met last week.

        A) _____ B) _____

4. Mia is taking her test tomorrow, and she has been studying hard since she failed last time.

A) _____ B) _____ C) _____

5. That sign was not here before, someone has put it there.

        A) _____ B) _____

6. The dark clouds suggest a storm is coming, but will it strike before noon?

A) _____ B) _____ C) _____

7. When Wendy gets here, we will ask if she ate the last ham sandwich.

A) _____ B) _____ C) _____

8. The chef admits that he added cumin to the soup, but he claims he will not do it again.

A) _____ B) _____ C) _____

D) _____

9. The boys are not playing in the tournament this evening because they broke the rules and they have not apologised.

A) _____ B) _____ C) _____

10. Tina is publishing a book on relationships soon, as she has been happily married for thirteen years.

        A) _____ B) _____

11. What did that man say to you? You have been sitting in silence ever since.

        A) _____ B) _____

12. Is Dermot ready for the triathlon or is he going to train for longer?

        A) _____ B) _____

13. Does Cindy have the pen I gave you? My uncle gave it to me.

        A) _____ B) _____ C) _____

14. Had Pat tried spicy food before he visited India? He orders it all the time now.

        A) _____ B) _____ C) _____

15. Will you come with me to Florence or have you seen everything already?

        A) _____ B) _____

20.14 Mixed Tenses 1: Narrative

Complete the text below by putting the verbs in brackets into the most appropriate **past**, **present** or **future** forms.

Emily's Piano

Emily (1) _____ (to learn) to play the piano for eight months. It (2) _____ (to be) a dream of hers for many years, but she never (3) _____ (to think) it would be possible until last November. She (4) _____ (to live) with her parents in a small house and, for now, she (5) _____ (to work) as a waitress before she (6) _____ (to go) to university. Her father (7) _____ (to drive) buses and her mother (8) _____ (to teach) in the local school. The family live comfortably, but her father (9) _____ (to say) they had no space or money for a piano.

    Still, Emily (10) _____ (to listen) to piano concertos since she was a child, and (11) _____ (to enjoy) reading books about musicians and music theory. She (12) _____ (to watch) all the online videos about piano tuition that she can find. When she was little, her parents (13) _____ (to buy) her a miniature keyboard. She (14) _____ (to play) on it every day for years when the keyboard broke. But by then she (15) _____ (to enjoy) school and parties too much to care.

As Emily got older, she (16) _____ (to yearn) to play music again. While she (17) _____ (to save) money to continue her education, she secretly (18) _____ (to wish) for a piano instead. She (19) _____ (to earn / not) enough for both, though. Then, in November, her father revealed that he (20) _____ (to collect) extra money himself. Emily's parents (21) _____ (to plan) to buy her a piano as a gift before university, all along! They even paid for lessons, and now Emily (22) _____ (to do) so well that they (23) _____ (to help) her to continue once she moves to university. She (24) _____ (to have / not) space at university for a piano, but (25) _____ (to come) home every other weekend, and is sure she (26) _____ (to find) a piano somewhere on campus. In fact, Emily is certain she (27) _____ (to play) piano for many years to come.

20.15 Mixed Tenses 2: Narrative

Complete the text below by putting the verbs in brackets into the most appropriate **past**, **present** or **future** form.

Wizards and Dragons

For the past few weeks, Bernice (1) _____ (to watch) a new television show about wizards and dragons. Such fantasy shows (2) _____ (to get) more popular in recent years. This is partly because technology (3) _____ (to improve) enough to make fantasy more realistic. But attitudes to fantasy (4) _____ (to change / also). Bernice (5) _____ (to like / not) fantasy before; she and her friends usually (6) _____ (to prefer) shows about crime and mysteries. They (7) _____ (to follow) a seaside detective drama for five years, before this fantasy show (8) _____ (to come) along. None of them (9) _____ (will / to consider) fairy tales seriously before.

Then, everyone (10) _____ (to start) talking about this new show. It (11) _____ (to spread) across the internet, and (12) _____ (to continue) to spread even more when the new series arrives. The popularity of the show (13) _____ (to make / quickly) it cool to like fantasy. Bernice (14) _____ (to like) that, because she really (15) _____ (to enjoy) the show.

In fact, Bernice and her friends (16) _____ (to buy / already) all the books that accompany the show. She (17) _____ (to read / not) any yet, but (18) _____ (to look) forward to them. Their group (19) _____ (to meet) and discuss the books, once everyone (20) _____ (to have) a chance to read some. The books

(21) _____ (to help) them understand the wider story of the television show, and (22) _____ (to give) them an idea of what to expect in future. Bernice (23) _____ (to think) that the wizards (24) _____ (to turn / not) evil, and she (25) _____ (to believe / not) the theories that zombies (26) _____ (to invade) the fantasy world. That (27) _____ (to sound) be silly.

Whatever happens next, Bernice is sure they (28) _____ (to talk) about this show for many years to come!

20.16 Mixed Tenses 3: Narrative

Complete the text below by putting the verbs in brackets into the most appropriate **past**, **present** or **future** form.

A New Library

The Worthing Library (1) _____ (to be) relocated later this year. It (2) _____ (to move / not) far, and it (3) _____ (to return) soon enough – new and improved. The reason: the existing building (4) _____ (to get) renovated. The current library (5) _____ (to serve) the community since 1975, so locals are happy that it (6) _____ (to close / not) for good. With the improvements, it (7) _____ (to upgrade) its status to a "community hub". What (8) _____ (this / to mean)?

This concept (9) _____ (to put) public buildings at the heart of the community; the council (10) _____ (to bring) many services together in one place. This (11) _____ (to strengthen) the community aspect of the library, although buildings offering other services (12) _____ (to close).

In remodelling the library, the designers (13) _____ (to give) consideration to quiet and private spaces, but the "hub" (14) _____ (to buzz) with other activity. Sarah Blemming, involved in the project, said, "Libraries (15) _____ (to form) the heart of a community. We (16) _____ (to create) something that embraces and celebrates that."

During the public consultation, the council (17) _____ (to listen) to various proposals for how to remodel the library. The public (18) _____ (to respond) very favourably, and now (19) _____ (to await / eagerly) the results. By the time the community hub is complete, the council (20) _____ (to close) the library for six months. But the relocated services (21) _____ (to sit) just across the road. Meanwhile, the council (22) _____ (to work) with more partners to identify other locations for community hubs.

20.17 Mixed Tenses 5: Narrative

Complete the text below by putting the verbs in brackets into the most appropriate **past**, **present** or **future** form.

Holiday Plans

Gerry Davies (1) _____ (to host) family Christmas celebrations at his mountain lodge for the past twelve years. The lodge is in the French Alps and (2) _____ (to look) beautiful surrounded by snow. Gerry (3) _____ (to buy) it in 1973, and (4) _____ (to maintain) it himself ever since. He (5) _____ (to raise) two children who have married and (6) _____ (to raise / now) his five grandchildren. The extended family (7) _____ (to spread) out across Europe: Gerry lives in England, but his son's family (8) _____ (to settle) in Scotland, and his daughter's family (9) _____ (to live) in Ukraine while she completes a teaching contract.

Gerry was worried that his family (10) _____ (will / to come / not) to France this Christmas. Last year, his children said that it (11) _____ (to become) less and less desirable to travel for the holiday, as they (12) _____ (to learn) terrible things about global warming. His daughter says frequent flying damages the planet, and it (13) _____ (will / to recover / not). They (14) _____ (to fly) to France every Christmas for thirteen years, next year! How much damage (15) _____ (they / to do) by then?

But Gerry (16) _____ (to want / not) to lose these special times with his family, and he (17) _____ (to come up with) a solution. He (18) _____ (to work / not) anymore, so he has lots of free time. For the past few months, he (19) _____ (to study) all the latest information about the healthiest ways to travel. He (20) _____ (to buy) an electric car last week and for the next Christmas he (21) _____ (to arrange) for his family to meet him via train at convenient locations. He (22) _____ (will / to drive) them the rest of the way to the mountain lodge. By the time everyone (23) _____ (to gather) for Christmas, he (24) _____ (to travel) for two weeks himself, but it (25) _____ (to cause) minimal harm to the environment. And Gerry (26) _____ (to mind / not) collecting everyone. It means he (27) _____ (to be going to / spend) even more time with his family!

20.18 Mixed Tenses 3: Narrative

Complete the text below by putting the verbs in brackets into the most appropriate **past**, **present** or **future** form.

Murder Mystery

Detective Stevens (1) _____ (to gather) the manor guests in the games room, along with the butler, the cleaner and the cook. There were eight people left, now that three others (2) _____ (to be) killed.

"People (3) _____ (to hide) their true identities," Detective Stevens announced.

"Yes!" the butler said. "Dr Julian (4) _____ (to lie) about being a heart surgeon!"

"How insulting!" said Dr Julian. "I (5) _____ (to practise) surgery for ten years!"

"When I phoned the hospital this morning, they (6) _____ (to hear / not) of him."

Dr Julian was trapped. "Very well. But I (7) _____ (to be going to / to reveal) the truth before leaving, honestly. I am a bank clerk – I only (8) _____ (to want) to impress Miss Tatiana! But I (9) _____ (to murder / not) her! And if we (10) _____ (to search) for liars, what about the cook? He (11) _____ (to make / not) a good meal all weekend!"

"I (12) _____ (to feel) unwell," the cook said. "But I (13) _____ (to work) here since the manor opened, I (14) _____ (to swear)."

"He (15) _____ (to work) here when I arrived," the cleaner confirmed. "And what reason (16) _____ (he / to have) to kill

215

Miss Tatiana, Mr Fredericks or the manager, Mr Bollier?"

"Ah ha!" Detective Stevens said. "I thought you (17) _____ (will / to defend) him. You (18) _____ (to conspire / all) together. The house staff and ... Colonel Stamp! (19) _____ (you / to be going to / to explain), or shall I?"

Colonel Stamp, who (20) _____ (to avoid) attention until then, looked worried. He said, "I (21) _____ (will / to tolerate / not) this, no. I (22) _____ (to leave) as soon as my driver arrives."

"But your driver (23) _____ (to come / not)," Detective Stevens said. "I (24) _____ (to instruct) him to take the night off. You see, Colonel Stamp is, in fact, Lemuel Bollier!"

"Bollier?" said the final guest, Mrs Smythe. "(25) _____ (he / to relate) to the manager?"

"(26) _____ (you / will / to talk), now, Lemuel? Your secret is out."

"How (27) _____ (you / to find) out?" Colonel Stamp – actually Lemuel Bollier – said.

"Simple," Detective Stevens said. "When we dined on Friday night, you (28) _____ (to ask) many strange questions about the manor. And you (29) _____ (to say / not) anything about your own history. While we (30) _____ (to drink) brandy in the parlour, Miss Tatiana saw you talking with the cook and the butler. What (31) _____ (you / to discuss), I wonder?"

"I (32) _____ (to discover) a draught in my room and wished to be moved!"

"There (33) _____ (to be) no other rooms available, until Mr Fredericks died. Indeed, you requested a change because you

216

(34) _____ (to be going to / to pour) poison through the floorboards, onto the manager while he slept! Your father, who (35) _____ (to see / not) you since childhood, and (36) _____ (to know / not) you (37) _____ (will / to inherit) his manor. Having promised to reward all the house staff!"

Lemuel Bollier (38) _____ (to pull out) a gun. "Very well, it is all true. But no one (39) _____ (will / to survive) to tell the story."

The doors burst open. Police officers (40) _____ (to wait) in the hall, and (41) _____ (to hear) everything. The criminals were trapped. Detective Stevens said, "Lemuel Bollier, I (42) _____ (to arrest) you for murder."

Infinitives and Participles

The following section is designed to drill awareness of the grammar words which are necessary to accurately form the tenses. These are not essential exercises for using the tenses, but help to develop a clear impression of English structure and practice.

21. Identifying Bare Infinitives

21.1 Past Bare Infinitives

Read the sentences below. Is the underlined verb in the **past simple** (**regular** or **irregular**) or a **bare infinitive**?

1. Did he <u>buy</u> a new pair of trousers?
2. We <u>waited</u> for hours, but no one came.
3. I've eaten all of the chocolates, they <u>were</u> really good.
4. What did you <u>say</u> to the mayor when you met him?
5. When their team scored, the home team <u>cheered</u> loudly.
6. Lady Taylor didn't <u>share</u> her stamp collection with just anyone.
7. When did your foot <u>get</u> better?
8. They <u>lived</u> on a houseboat for three months.
9. Who <u>came</u> to your most recent party?
10. Where did that pile of newspapers <u>disappear</u> to?
11. He sent her flowers because he didn't <u>want</u> to seem ungrateful.
12. When she left, he <u>cried</u>.

21.2 Present Bare Infinitives

Read the sentences below. Is the underlined verb in the **present simple** or a **bare infinitive**?

1. Wilson <u>tends</u> to his garden every day.
2. Do they <u>want</u> any more beans?
3. How far does he <u>run</u> each morning?
4. I don't know what she <u>needs</u>.
5. The dog <u>sleeps</u> under the table.

6. The boat does not <u>float</u> any more.

7. It does <u>seem</u> strange, doesn't it?

8. What <u>is</u> that new perfume you are wearing?

9. Does Mr Carpenter <u>live</u> here?

10. Let him <u>see</u> the documents.

11. He <u>lives</u> on the trains, always moving, never stopping.

12. Don't <u>waste</u> paper, re-use some of the scrap.

21.3 Mixed Bare Infinitives

Read the sentences below. Is the underlined verb in the **present simple** or **past simple**, or is it a **bare infinitive**?

1. We will <u>go</u> to the lakes in summer.

2. Did they <u>have</u> a good time at the opera?

3. What movies <u>are</u> on TV this evening?

4. Many sweets that I <u>enjoyed</u> when I was young are no longer available.

5. Do you <u>remember</u> which room the toilet is in?

6. I always <u>thought</u> he walked with a slight limp.

7. Do you know why they <u>forbid</u> the banjo in my school?

8. We often <u>watch</u> the swans in the park.

9. Can she <u>walk</u> now?

10. There didn't <u>appear</u> to be anything wrong with him.

11. If you <u>boil</u> vegetables for too long, they lose their nutrients.

12. Towards the end of Saturday's race, people <u>became</u> very tired.

22. Participles

22.1 Past Participles

Complete the following sentences using the verb in brackets in either the **past participle** or another verb form. Remember, the past participle is typically used in perfect tenses.

For example:

Q: Oh no, I have _____ my glasses again! (to break)

A: Oh no, I have **broken** my glasses again!

1. We have _____ living here for twenty years. (to be)

2. What kind of nuts did you _____ in this meal? (to use)

3. I will _____ waiting for your return. (to be)

4. They _____ had enough of the loud music. (to have)

5. The internet has _____ a huge impact on the way we interact. (to have)

6. Will you _____ me to the nearest post office? (to direct)

7. I have _____ the eggs; now to complete the cake. (to beat)

8. The criminal had _____ the window twice before they found him. (to break)

9. We will have _____ Grandma before Christmas Day. (to visit)

10. You must _____ the garden shed before it collapses. (to mend)

11. When they have _____ the art of dancing, they will try fencing. (to master)

12. Julio ran through the bath-house naked, because Frank had _____ his robe. (to steal)

22.2 Present Participles

Complete the following sentences using the verb in brackets in either the **present participle** or another verb form. Remember, the present participle is the -**ing** form of the verb, typically used in continuous tenses.

For example:

Q: They are _____ to regret opening that door. (to go)

A: They are **going** to regret opening that door.

1. He had _____ all the potatoes, ready for dinner. (to peel)

2. We were _____ too loudly, that's why they complained. (to sing)

3. Have they been _____ us for long? (to watch)

4. Give me a hand with this log – I can't _____ it myself. (to move)

5. The plumber had _____ on the sink all morning. (to work)

6. I have been _____ for hours; I need a break. (to study)

7. She will _____ on the ice, in those silly shoes. (to slip)

8. Hans was _____ when his chair collapsed. (to read)

9. Are you seriously _____ that jacket again? (to wear)

10. _____ is not allowed here. (to smoke)

11. Will the game have _____ by the time we get there? (to finish)

12. I will be there in a minute, I am just _____ this cup! (to clean)

23. Mixed Verb Types

23.1 Identifying Bare Infinitives and Participles

Read the mixed tenses statements below. Is the underlined word a **bare infinitive** or a **verb participle**?

1. Did he <u>wash</u> the dishes?
2. We have <u>gone</u> to the theatre three times this week.
3. I might <u>buy</u> some dungarees.
4. Next Tuesday, Margie and I will <u>see</u> a movie together.
5. The little dogs are <u>barking</u> again.
6. Playing the piano is <u>done</u> on Sundays.
7. We should <u>go</u> now.
8. Does your mother <u>know</u> our priest?
9. Had they <u>known</u> what happened all along?
10. Did they <u>hear</u> what we said?
11. Won't they be <u>waiting</u> for us?
12. She has <u>been</u> here for a very long time.
13. Have you <u>seen</u> the weather in Idaho?
14. It might <u>rain</u> later.
15. Does the driver <u>have</u> enough fuel?
16. This woman has <u>had</u> too much fun for one day.
17. My favourite necklace was <u>being</u> repaired.
18. Did that <u>make</u> much sense?
19. I could <u>drink</u> another cup of tea.
20. There are some strange people <u>watching</u> us.

23.2 Mixed Infinitives and Participles 1

Complete the following sentences using the verb in brackets, in either the **bare infinitive**, **past participle** or **present participle** form.

    For example:

    Q: Have you been _____ this soup for long? (to cook)

    A: Have you been **cooking** this soup for long?

1.   When will you be _____ the train? (to catch)

2.   Jamie can't _____, she's too old! (to dance)

3.   I have never _____ so many sandwiches in all my life. (to make)

4.   What did he _____ you about? (to ask)

5.   Is this group of gymnasts _____ all month? (to perform)

6.   Why Kylie had _____ the biscuits, no one knew. (to take)

7.   The canaries will have _____, the cage door was left open! (to escape)

8.   You will have been _____ all this for nothing, if you don't apply it later. (to learn)

9.   I cannot _____ to think about the war. (to bear)

10. Can you _____? (to whistle)

11. It was _____ when we left the house, but it has _____ now. (to snow, to stop)

12. Why did that shop assistant _____ you so much trouble? (to give)

13. Have you been _____ for these hairclips? (to look)

14. She couldn't _____ any more pork scratchings. (to afford)

15. Has your business _____ much since we last met? (to grow)

16. That man has _____ his last game of chess, he's banned now. (to play)

17. It was tragic that the game was cancelled when they were
    _____. (to win)
18. Do you think you will _____ all of your modules at
    university? (to pass)
19. We are _____ our assignments next week. (to complete)
20. Have I _____ enough about the seaside? (to write)

23.3 Mixed Infinitives and Participles 2

The following ten sentences have been split and scrambled. Match the first part to the second by looking for patterns in **bare infinitive** and **participle** uses.

1.	I don't	flying to Norway.
2.	He is	seen this new chair I bought?
3.	Jane will	you broken my favourite mug?
4.	The students have	want any more muesli.
5.	What do	thinking of phoning her mum.
6.	Why have	be very happy with the results.
7.	Where are	the parrots look like?
8.	It must have	you going to put your bag?
9.	Have you	handed in their final project.
10.	She was	been difficult to learn Chinese.

A Note from the Author

Dear student,

I hope that this book has helped develop your skills for applying the English tenses. It has been designed merely to test and apply your grammar knowledge, but was produced following *The English Tenses Practical Grammar Guide*. If you have not read that book, it may provide additional insights into the tenses. Both these books were produced independently, and I have also been sharing English tips and exercises through the website *English Lessons Brighton* since 2012. I take great joy in being able to help learners everywhere advance in English, so the ability to reach more students through my books is wonderful.

If you found this book useful, please leave a quick star rating and a short review online. It helps others discover my books, which is essential for me to keep producing them!

Thank you in advance,

Phil Williams

Acknowledgements

It takes a team to produce any book, and that is more true than ever with the independently produced ELB guides. My great thanks goes out to my supportive wife Marta, who always helps test my language material ahead of release, and my editor Caroline Hynes, whose keen eye helps keep everything in order. These books are also bolstered by the support of my large and very positive reading group on the ELB mailing list, whose words of encouragement always help motivate me.

For *The English Tenses Exercise Book*, I had the help of a great team of students and teachers who helped identify problem areas in the final book, including Andre Bianconi, Cheryl Butterfield, Annaliza Davis, Maria Eugenia del Valle, André Juilly, Howat Labrum, Jim Lindsay, Tamsyn Mott, Jaime Sanchez Rivera, Marta Stanowska, and Jennifer Tan. Thank you to everyone involved!

Answers

1.1 Answers

1. The postman was late again.
2. Felicity grew tomatoes in her garden.
3. He did not understand the project.
4. We failed to finish in time.
5. They did not give us the bag of flour.
6. Liam did not ask the question politely.
7. The hummingbirds built a nest in our attic.
8. The piano looked too old to use.
9. She said we were wrong.
10. I did not pick the right flowers.
11. Our cake did not taste right.
12. We drove all the way to Scotland.
13. You did not bring the green umbrella.
14. They arrested the wrong man.
15. The lady of the manor did not write a convincing memoir.

1.2 Answers

1. Were your dogs very messy?
2. Did the chef cook something spectacular?
3. Did you read all three of your textbooks this weekend?
4. Did she ask him to go on a date?
5. Did you know about the rotten fruit?
6. Did the priests demand that the film be banned?
7. Did you buy a new bicycle?
8. Did he hoover the house because of the dust?
9. Did the children play on the swings?
10. Was she very disappointed with the presentation?
11. Did you misjudge the time it would take to get to the party?
12. Did you lose your keys again?
13. Did the story get a lot more interesting after the main character died?
14. Did they send a replacement cabinet after yours broke?
15. Did the council ban parking on your road?
16. Did she run a marathon last spring?
17. Was it the hottest day of the year?
18. Did Ulric visit the doctor for the first time?
19. Did your computer stop working?
20. Did they prepare for the storm months in advance?

1.3 Answers

1. Where did you help the old man?
2. What did Julian sing?
3. Where did you search for the doctor?
4. Why was she very angry?
5. When did everyone go for ice cream?
6. Which necklaces did they steal?
7. How much did you give the homeless man?
8. What did the critic hate?
9. Who did he have a disagreement with? (or Who had a disagreement with the man who sold him his car?)
10. What was cut down yesterday?
11. What did Tyler want to free? (or What did Tyler want to do?)
12. Where did the family take the bottles?
13. What did the girl believe in?
14. How did you tie the knots?
15. Who ate her last cupcake?

1.4 Answers

1. What did he not tell us?
2. Did it not seem like an easy task?
3. Where did Mindy not take the students?
4. Why was the door not locked?
5. How did you not get there in time?
6. Did they not bring any water on the hike?
7. Was she not supposed to be in Italy this week?
8. Did the spiders not live for very long?
9. Were you not sad about the game being cancelled?
10. When did the football team not have a manager?

1.5 Answers

1. We were not very good at sports.
2. The Morrisons owned too many chickens.
3. Herman did not get on with his neighbours.
4. Where did I park my car?
5. Did you see that new ballet?
6. The builders ate a large breakfast.
7. Was she not a good swimmer?
8. The lady did not decide to buy the dress. (*or* The lady decided not to buy the dress.)
9. Did they not listen to the radio?
10. She ran all the way around the park.

2.1 Answers

1. The giraffe was lying down.
2. They were not drawing pictures of fruit.
3. It was getting dark outside.
4. You were telling me about your new phone.
5. They were not flying over Mongolia.
6. I was cleaning the pans when the police arrived.
7. The animals were digging a hole.

8. Kyle was not reading novels this summer.
9. We were painting the house all day.
10. No one was helping with the display.
11. The computer was not loading properly.
12. You were not sleeping in the right room.
13. She was brushing her teeth.
14. I was testing the light switch.
15. The rodents were planning something.

2.2 Answers

1. Were they building a new school?
2. Was Lily hiding something?
3. Were the days getting longer?
4. Were you asking about my van?
5. Was the light working when you got home?
6. Was his father trying to play the piano?
7. Were the students travelling through Bolivia?
8. Was everyone waiting for me?
9. Was I saying the right word?
10. Were the sailors loading the correct boat?
11. Was the bus stopping everywhere?
12. Were we singing in tune?
13. Were Rupert and Jim fighting again?
14. Was the sun shining on your wedding day?
15. Were the trains arriving on time last weekend?

2.3 Answers

1. How (well) were the students doing?
2. What was Tim studying?
3. Where were you flying (to)?
4. Why was the cat running away?
5. What were they singing?
6. How long were you living in America (for)?
7. Who was leaving dirty dishes out?

8. What was her husband watching (on TV)?
9. Where was the tour guide taking them (to)?
10. Why was Hailey smiling?
11. Who were the Japanese investors meeting with? (or Who was meeting the Japanese investors?)
12. Why was the restaurant getting crowded?
13. When were the new shoes arriving?
14. What was Alison preparing (for the carnival)?
15. What were you picking up (from your friends)?

2.4 Answers

1. Were you not enjoying the party?
2. What was the man not showing them?
3. Was I not holding the right pen?
4. Why was the weather not getting warmer?
5. Where was the boat not stopping during the cruise?
6. Were you not using the correct ingredients?
7. When was the bell not ringing?
8. Were they not bringing more sandwiches?
9. Was he not sitting at the back of the class?
10. Why were the children not following the teacher?

2.5 Answers

The complete correct text follows the numbered answers below.
1. was driving
2. Were they selling
3. it was playing
4. Was the van going
5. the driver wasn't heading (or the driver was not heading)
6. was he planning

7. Wasn't something happening (or Was something not happening)
8. They were opening
9. was thinking
10. you weren't expecting (or you were not expecting)

The Ice Cream Van

Simon: Do you know what I just saw? An ice cream van **(1) was driving** down our road.

Carl: Really? **(2) Were they selling** ice cream? It's November!

Simon: Well, **(3) it was playing** music, so I think they wanted customers.

Carl: **(4) Was the van going** to the beach?

Simon: It couldn't have been; **(5) the driver wasn't heading** (or **the driver was not heading**) in the right direction.

Carl: Then where **(6) was he planning** to park?

Simon: Hmm. **(7) Wasn't something happening** (or **Was something not happening**) in the town centre earlier today?

Carl: Of course! **(8) They were opening** a new sports shop this morning!

Simon: Oh! I **(9) was thinking** about going to that, but I decided not to.

Carl: But **(10) you weren't expecting** (or **you were not expecting**) ice cream! Let's go!

3.1 Answers

1. They had started the party early.
2. It had snowed overnight.
3. The delivery truck had parked outside.
4. I had not heard about the Incas before.
5. You had warned me not to go there, but I did.
6. She had arrived too late for the exam.

7. Simone realised she had not listened to this tune yet.
8. Before finding the lecture hall, we had gone to Room 2b.
9. We had not agreed on a price for the painting by noon.
10. He had read the book thirteen times.
11. The picnic was ruined; the rats had eaten everything.
12. The shop had closed down for good.
13. I had not asked for a map, because I knew the way.
14. She had forgotten where the cups were kept.
15. Ryan went to see a film, but they had sold all the tickets.

3.2 Answers

1. Had they been to California before?
2. Had you already asked me about my toe?
3. Had he worn his coat to the park?
4. Had the horse eaten already?
5. Had someone broken the window?
6. Had the mice infested the house?
7. Had you ever been able to juggle?
8. Had Roger repaired the bicycle?
9. Had Jonas taken the wrong bag?
10. Had the cleaners emptied the bins?

3.3 Answers

1. What had Lisa added to the soup?
2. How had the cows escaped from the field?
3. What had you discussed in the previous two lessons?
4. Where had you put your glasses?
5. When had the clock stopped?
6. When had she changed her clothes?
7. Who had the President appointed? (or Who had been appointed by the President?)
8. What had Harry heard (behind the shed)?
9. Where had all the eggs gone?
10. Where had you stayed last time?

3.4 Answers

1. Had he not told her about the invitation?
2. Where had Charlene not been in Boston?
3. Had the team not worked together?
4. Had I not turned off the cooker before going out?
5. Had the plumber not set the radiator to the right temperature?
6. What had the night manager not included in his report?
7. Why had the alarm not gone off at 7 a.m.?
8. What had the chef not added to the soup?
9. Had I not explained the situation clearly?
10. Why had they not checked the car's engine before travelling?

3.5 Answers

The complete correct text follows the numbered answers below.
1. He had left
2. Stephen had started
3. his wife had suggested
4. she had found
5. He had not planned
6. they had bought
7. they had not made
8. He had measured
9. why had he not used
10. Had he read
11. Stephen had wrestled
12. It had turned out
13. why had he not tried
14. the kitchen had started
15. the cake had risen
16. it had developed
17. his wife had been

A Fresh Cake

Stephen was looking forward to a freshly baked cake. **(1) He had left** it baking for

45 minutes now. This was the final step in a process **(2) Stephen had started** four hours earlier, after **(3) his wife had suggested** that he try a new recipe **(4) she had found. (5) He had not planned** to spend the day baking, but **(6) they had bought** all the ingredients already, and **(7) they had not made** homemade cake for a long time, so he agreed to give it a go.

Once he started, he realised it was actually good fun. **(8) He had measured** everything carefully before combining the ingredients, and then made a terrible mess mixing the batter. It was too sticky. His wife asked: **(9) why had he not used** more flour? **(10) Had he read** the recipe correctly?

Eventually, **(11) Stephen had wrestled** the mixture under control, and he cleaned the whole kitchen while they waited for it to rise. **(12) It had turned out** to be quite simple really. When he put the mix in the oven, he asked himself, **(13) why had he not tried** this sooner?

After half an hour, **(14) the kitchen had started** to smell amazing.

Finally, 45 minutes were almost over, and Stephen's mouth was watering. He opened the oven to find **(15) the cake had risen** beautifully, and **(16) it had developed** a firm, golden top. They would definitely enjoy this, and Stephen admitted, **(17) his wife had been** right. It was a good idea.

4.1 Answers

1. They had been travelling all night.
2. I had not been listening during the lecture.
3. She had been dancing with Raul.
4. The bird had been singing for hours.
5. It had not been snowing before they left the hotel.
6. The traffic lights had not been working that morning.
7. Sidney had been learning to play the bassoon.
8. Strange symbols had been appearing all over town.
9. The price of cauliflower had been rising throughout January.
10. Tina had been waiting for the right man.
11. We had been going to the same holiday villa for years.
12. Wild dogs had been stealing from the pantry.
13. The children had not been practising their handwriting.
14. They had not been camping in Wales before.
15. I had been hoping for a good result.

4.2 Answers

1. Had you been watching Channel 4?
2. Had Jim been watering the garden?
3. Had the cat been sleeping in the bedroom?
4. Had they been training together for a long time?
5. Had the carpenter been making new chairs?
6. Had you been snoring in your sleep?
7. Had she been listening to their phone call?
8. Had the door been closing on its own?
9. Had Winston been helping with her studies?
10. Had the bracelet been sitting on the table all along?

4.3 Answers

1. Where had she been hiding the cake?
2. What had you been listening to in the car?
3. What had the dog been barking at?
4. When had Clive been planning to go on holiday?

5. How long had the man been playing the trumpet (for)?
6. What had Mum been preparing for dinner?
7. Where had you been sitting?
8. Why had you been working at the weekend?
9. What had they been thinking about (banning)?
10. How had Fiona been cooking bagels (before she bought the toaster)?

4.4 Answers

1. Had we not been parking in the right space?
2. Where had the boys not been making a mess?
3. Had she not been listening to the teacher?
4. Why had the water not been boiling?
5. Had I not been walking fast enough?
6. Had it not been raining all day?
7. Why had Lily not been reading the books I gave her?
8. When had the politician not been telling the truth?
9. Had they not been running in the morning?
10. Why had the gardener not been trimming the roses?

4.5 Answers

The complete correct text follows the numbered answers below.
1. It had been raining
2. Had I not been warning
3. they had been doing
4. the potatoes had not been growing
5. The weather had been getting
6. people had been saying
7. I had not been listening
8. Why had I not been paying
9. Things had been going

A Ruined Allotment

(1) It had been raining all night, we could tell. The allotment was flooded. **(2) Had I not been warning** everyone about this for months? If they had listened, we could have built a shelter. But **(3) they had been doing** other things, like swimming in the lake. Besides, Barry kept arguing, **(4) the potatoes had not been growing** anyway. Why bother?

(5) The weather had been getting more unpredictable, that was the main problem. Some months we had no rain at all. As much as two months ago, **(6) people had been saying** we might have a completely dry season. But I remembered the storms three years ago, when I lost everything. **(7) I had not been listening** when the forecasts offered warnings that time. **(8) Why had I not been paying** more attention during that period? Back when it would have helped ... The same reason no one listened to me this time. **(9) Things had been going** so well!

5.1 Answers

1. Billy likes cats.
2. Trains in Japan always run on time.
3. Tina does not drink banana milkshakes.
4. The shopping centre opens every day at 6 a.m.
5. All cookies taste amazing.
6. I find biology interesting.
7. Fred and Shirley do not eat after midnight.
8. Unhappy employees are not good for business.
9. The last house on my street looks haunted.
10. My car has climate control, but it does not work.
11. Flocks of birds fly in interesting formations.

12. Peanut butter and cheese do not go well together.
13. Reading books definitely makes you smarter.
14. We do not travel to the lakes more than twice a year.
15. Grandma's stuffed animal collection scares everyone who comes to visit.

5.2 Answers

1. Are you hungry?
2. Does Lily listen to heavy metal music?
3. Do all parrots have colourful feathers?
4. Is the carnival safe for children?
5. Does Uncle Jeff know the way to the beach?
6. Do you speak a foreign language?
7. Do you want another cup of tea?
8. Are you sure this milk is non-dairy?
9. Does Howard always talk during class?
10. Do your parents live near your house?
11. Is exercise important to you?
12. Do the campers sleep in tents?
13. Does your cat seem fat because he is so fluffy?
14. Do good grades matter if you want to be an artist?
15. Is the path under the bridge safe at night?
16. Does Abigail work in the library?
17. Do you need to keep taking these pills? or Do you need to keep taking those pills?
18. Does this cauliflower smell strange?
19. Are glass bottles good for storing hot liquids?
20. Is that man a friend of yours?

5.3 Answers

1. What is (there) in your backpack?
2. When does the sun rise?
3. How do you boil perfect eggs?
4. Where does Brianne buy her hats?
5. Where do the boys play every Tuesday?
6. Why do you always visit the same café?
7. How does Michael always know the answers to these questions?
8. When do you want to go to the cinema?
9. Where does your father work?
10. When does the running club meet?
11. Why do those teachers wear such smart clothes?
12. What do you have to do to open this tin of beans? or What do you have to do to open that tin of beans?
13. How often do the gardeners cut the grass?
14. Which drawer does the cutlery go in?
15. When do the children get home from school?

5.4 Answers

1. Does that chocolate not contain milk?
2. Is he not the owner of this car?
3. Which hotel does not have a swimming pool?
4. Are the guests not expected before 7 p.m.?
5. When is not a good time to visit?
6. Why does Ben not play more tennis?
7. Do they not like the colour of their bedroom?
8. Why is she not the boss already?
9. What does not look right in this picture?
10. Does it not matter if we go to the beach this weekend?

5.5 Answers

The complete correct text follows the numbered answers below.
1. Lewes hosts
2. Some people call
3. What is

4. The festivities mark
5. Seven local societies run
6. they are not
7. The town draws in
8. The evening is not
9. the town welcomes
10. the trains take
11. why do these people not go
12. the market town does not have
13. Why do so many people travel
14. The history goes
15. we see
16. the evenings stir
17. the societies do not burn
18. is it not inevitable

Bonfire Night in Lewes

Every year on November 5th, **(1) Lewes hosts** one of the largest bonfire nights in the UK. **(2) Some people call** Lewes the "Bonfire Capital of the World". **(3) What is** so special about these evenings?

(4) The festivities mark Guy Fawkes Night by bringing together bonfire societies from across Sussex. **(5) Seven local societies run** six separate parades and firework displays, but **(6) they are not** alone. **(7) The town draws in** as many as 30 other societies from across Sussex to join in. **(8) The evening is not** a small event: up to 5,000 people take part in the celebrations, and **(9) the town welcomes** tens of thousands of spectators; as many as 80,000 one year!

On these evenings, **(10) the trains take** a long time to queue for, and the locals might complain: **(11) why do these people not go** somewhere else?! With a population of only 17,500, after all, **(12) the market town does not have** the facilities for so many people.

(13) Why do so many people travel so far for these parades? **(14) The history goes** back a long way. In the past, the celebrations were more

like riots, which only gradually became the processions **(15) we see** today. Even now, **(16) the evenings stir** controversy: many people ask that **(17) the societies do not burn** effigies that cause offence. Between the many memorable evenings, the rich history and the media attention, **(18) is it not inevitable** that so many people should visit?

6.1 Answers

1. My mother is watching the television.
2. The cat is sleeping on the sofa.
3. It is not raining anymore.
4. The phone is ringing.
5. You are learning very fast.
6. We are not working together today.
7. The tap is dripping again.
8. I am not writing about the Egyptians.
9. The nuns are dancing to disco music.
10. She is singing far too loudly.
11. The plants are not growing very fast.
12. Oliver is not sleeping in his own bed.
13. Raccoons are stealing from our bins.
14. That man is staring at you.
15. You are not sitting in the right seat.

6.2 Answers

1. Are you writing an essay?
2. Are the council building a new swimming pool?
3. Is he avoiding his boss?
4. Are you heading north?
5. Is that girl carrying too many books?
6. Is your son behaving well at school?
7. Are you catching a cold? or Do you feel like you are catching a cold?
8. Are Chelsea winning the match?
9. Is Melissa eating healthy food?
10. Are there buns baking in the oven?
11. Is her pregnancy showing?
12. Are the walls in your building getting dirty?
13. Is your creative team generating a lot of ideas?

14. Is Henry sharing his cake with everyone?
15. Are you looking at this picture the wrong way around? or Are you looking at that picture the wrong way around?

6.3 Answers

1. What are you trying to do?
2. Why is he drilling into that wall?
3. What is Nancy thinking about?
4. Where are you walking (to)?
5. How are they investing their savings?
6. Why is the business expanding slowly?
7. Where is Hank storing his old photos?
8. What is drawing lots of birds to the garden?
9. Which direction is the wind blowing (from)?
10. Why are the councillors insisting on raising taxes?
11. How many guests are the kitchen staff preparing food for?
12. Where is Lula parking the car?
13. What is the nurse giving you?
14. What is making that awful sound?
15. How many visitors are waiting in the hall?

6.4 Answers

1. Is Charles not bringing his dog?
2. Are the teachers not setting enough homework?
3. Which ingredient am I not tasting?
4. Where is she not taking the children?
5. Why are my children not drinking their juice?
6. Are the bikes not getting wet in the rain?
7. Which places are you not visiting on your honeymoon?
8. Why are the towels not drying in this room?
9. Is she not missing her boyfriend?

10. Are Joe and Kyle not entering the poetry competition?

6.5 Answers

The complete correct text follows the numbered answers below.

1. Mr Duff is building
2. He is borrowing
3. they are not working
4. The shed is falling
5. Are things not going
6. he is not admitting
7. his wife is asking
8. Winter is coming
9. the family are storing
10. You are doing
11. What are you talking
12. The situation is worrying
13. Her husband is getting
14. he is spending
15. How is she going
16. Mr Duff is not taking
17. the tools are making
18. Why is the man not charging
19. her husband is not watching
20. Everything is coming

Proud Mr Duff

(1) Mr Duff is building a new shed in his garden. **(2) He is borrowing** tools from his neighbour, Mr Benton, but **(3) they are not working** well because Mr Duff has not fully charged them. **(4) The shed is falling** behind schedule. Mr Duff's wife has asked, "**(5) Are things not going** to plan?"

Mr Duff is a proud man. Though the problem persists, **(6) he is not admitting** it, so over time **(7) his wife is asking** lots more questions about the delayed shed. **(8) Winter is coming**, and while Mr Duff works on the shed **(9) the family are storing** their outdoor things under the porch.

235

"**(10) You are doing** something wrong," Mrs Duff insists.

"**(11) What are you talking** about?" Mr Duff replies, stubbornly.

(12) The situation is worrying Mrs Duff. **(13) Her husband is getting** upset and **(14) he is spending** too much time out there. **(15) How is she going** to help? She decides to ask Mr Benton.

Mr Benton suggests that **(16) Mr Duff is not taking** proper care of the tools. He listens, and realises **(17) the tools are making** the wrong noises. **(18) Why is the man not charging** them properly?! Knowing Mr Duff is proud, Mr Benton suggests Mrs Duff charge the tools at night, when **(19) her husband is not watching**. She does, and soon the construction speeds up. **(20) Everything is coming** together – just in time.

7.1 Answers

1. Remi has chosen her dress carefully.
2. The sailors have painted the boat bright green.
3. The dentists have ordered a new chair.
4. My father has not retired yet.
5. You have created a wonderful display.
6. The table has not been prepared for dinner.
7. We have paid the delivery man for the pizza.
8. I have refused to take part in the parade.
9. The police have not identified the thief.
10. She has mentioned her family's wealth many times.
11. Edward has not believed in Santa since he was young.
12. The bus service has not improved.
13. I have recommended this movie many times.
14. The storm has destroyed our fence.
15. My parents have not decided which house to buy.

7.2 Answers

1. Have you seen the newspaper this morning?
2. Has the weather improved?
3. Have they taken all the boxes?
4. Have you got any bread?
5. Has Drew told you about her exam results?
6. Has the postman delivered your package?
7. Has your wife agreed to a colour for the walls?
8. Have you brought enough cheese?
9. Has the teacher set some homework? or Has the teacher set any homework?
10. Has the gardener cut the grass?
11. Have Carl and Harry spent all their holiday money?
12. Have you heard this new song?
13. Has your mother gone to the market?
14. Have you understood this correctly?
15. Have all the teams submitted their final answers?

7.3 Answers

1. Why have you received this package? or Why have you received that package?
2. Where have you been this month?
3. What has Rebecca done with her hair?
4. What has fallen out of the basket?
5. How many pigs has the farmer raised?
6. Why has the club closed?
7. Where have my sweets gone?
8. Which socks have you chosen to wear?
9. When has the scientist ever been wrong?
10. Which paper has the company supplied you with?
11. Why has she failed to convince them?

12. How has this musician remained unknown?
13. Where have you put my violin?
14. What have you fed to those ducks?
15. Why has Sally flown to Portugal?

7.4 Answers

1. Have you not heard the news?
2. Why has his sister not forgiven him?
3. What have the mice not eaten?
4. Has the meeting not finished yet?
5. Which rooms have they not cleaned?
6. Have these people not suffered enough?
7. Why has the store not sold more umbrellas?
8. What problems have the team not analysed in this report?
9. Has Terry not replied about the cinema?
10. What have we not thought of?

7.5 Answers

The complete correct text follows the numbered answers below.
1. Molly has returned
2. She has brought
3. Where has she been
4. has she seen
5. I have experienced
6. I have not wasted
7. Have you not read
8. her Dad has not found
9. have you tried
10. I have written
11. One blog post has reached
12. why have so many people visited
13. Australia has stolen
14. I have not enjoyed
15. My new friends have invited
16. Has she made
17. Travelling has changed
18. Where has his shy little girl gone
19. where has she not been
20. he has learned

Molly's Travels

(1) Molly has returned after a year of travelling. **(2) She has brought** her family many gifts, but they are more interested in her stories. **(3) Where has she been**? What fascinating sights **(4) has she seen**?

"**(5) I have experienced** many things," Molly says. "**(6) I have not wasted** the time I had. **(7) Have you not read** my blog about it?"

Most of her family read the blog, but **(8) her Dad has not found** time yet. He asks, "What exotic foods **(9) have you tried**?"

"**(10) I have written** so many things about the dishes in China already!" Molly says. "**(11) One blog post has reached** 5,000 visitors so far."

Everyone congratulates her. Dad wonders, **(12) why have so many people visited** Molly's blog? He did not know she was a talented writer.

"Which country did you like most?" Mum asks.

"America is nice," Molly says, "but **(13) Australia has stolen** my heart for good. **(14) I have not enjoyed** better weather anywhere else in my life! **(15) My new friends have invited** me back to Melbourne already."

(16) Has she made new friends across the world, to go with this successful blog? **(17) Travelling has changed** his daughter, Dad can see. **(18) Where has his shy little girl gone**? Perhaps now the better question is, **(19) where has she not been**? He is happy for her, though, and **(20) he has learned** his lesson. Next time she goes away, he will pay more attention!

8.1 Answers

1. We have been living here for eight years.
2. I have been listening to pop music.
3. It has been getting harder to park on my road.
4. Those boys have been sitting there for hours.
5. Ferdinand has not been taking French lessons.
6. Our car has been making strange noises.
7. He has been talking for 30 minutes.
8. Pigeons have been nesting on our roof.
9. The pie shop has been turning people away.
10. She has been selling her paintings cheaply.
11. You have not been watching TV all morning.
12. Eric has not been drawing funny cartoons.
13. The phone has been ringing non-stop.
14. I have been reading a book about trees.
15. More raccoons have been stealing from our bins.

8.2 Answers

1. Have you been practising hard enough?
2. Have you been making too much noise?
3. Has she been swimming in the lake?
4. Have you been listening?
5. Has it been getting dark earlier?
6. Has anyone been watering the plants?
7. Have they been waiting for a long time?
8. Has Tim been working for your father?
9. Have you been paying too much for soap?
10. Has the fox been sleeping in the garden?

8.3 Answers

1. Where has this story been going?
2. Why has your computer been heating up?
3. How long has Oliver been riding horses (for)?
4. Why has she been sending out invitations?
5. What has been happening in town this weekend?
6. Where have they been delivering your mail?
7. What have the trucks been carrying this week?
8. Which club has been exploring in a jungle?
9. What has Mr Jones been teaching you?
10. How long have the batteries been charging (for)?

8.4 Answers

1. What has Len not been telling us?
2. Has anyone not been studying?
3. Who has not been reading this weekend?
4. What has she not been doing right?
5. Have you not been going to dance class regularly?
6. Have I not been giving Wanda enough attention?
7. Why has the wind not been blowing this spring?
8. What questions have the reporters not been asking?
9. Has that sound not been worrying you?
10. Why has the team not been working harder?

8.5 Answers

The complete correct text follows the numbered answers below.

1. The council has been making
2. the beach has been suffering
3. The daily tests have not been meeting

4. What has been causing
5. holiday-makers have not been picking up
6. people have not been cleaning up
7. What has the council been doing
8. Visitors have been collecting rubbish
9. The council has been providing
10. Children have been treating
11. Dog walkers have been ignoring
12. Beach patrols have been warning
13. Why have they been focusing
14. I have been watching
15. the truth has been coming out
16. the water company has been dumping
17. Why has the council not been focusing
18. the beach has finally been getting

Cleaning the Beach

(1) The council has been making efforts to improve Worthing's beach. For a long time, **(2) the beach has been suffering** from soiled water. **(3) The daily tests have not been meeting** expected levels of cleanness. **(4) What has been causing** this?

There are two main problems with the water. One is waste from people, where **(5) holiday-makers have not been picking up** after themselves. Another is waste from animals – where **(6) people have not been cleaning up** after their dogs.

(7) What has the council been doing to change this?

"Litter pick" stations have been set up. **(8) Visitors have been collecting rubbish** whilst walking on the beach. **(9) The council has been providing** bags and "grab sticks" to encourage this. **(10) Children have been treating** this as a game: how much litter can they pick up in an hour?

Meanwhile, dogs are no longer allowed on the beach during summer. **(11) Dog walkers have been ignoring** the signs, so there are now big fines in place. **(12) Beach patrols have been warning** dog walkers not to use certain areas to avoid being fined. Not everyone is happy about this. Hillary Menrose complained, "**(13) Why have they been focusing** so hard on dogs, when seagulls make just as much mess. We always pick up after Fluff Doogle on our walks, but **(14) I have been watching** those birds, and they drop litter, too!"

There were big protests when the council wished to further limit dog walkers, and **(15) the truth has been coming out**. Actually, there is a third reason that the sea is dirty: **(16) the water company has been dumping** waste into the sea. Why **(17) has the council not been focusing** on them? One thing's for sure: **(18) the beach has finally been getting** the attention it deserves!

9.1 Answers

1. The final exam will be difficult.
2. Our friends will come for dinner.
3. They are not going to watch the show together.
4. Sasha will not buy the next round of drinks.
5. Amy is going to regret her decision.
6. My shoes are not going to last another winter.
7. You will not agree with me.
8. The church bells are going to ring today.
9. Those geese will steal your bread.
10. The client will approve these new designs.
11. I am not going to lend Charles any more money.
12. Mrs Freda will not teach noisy children.
13. The festival is going to include a lot of musicians.

14. Your new table will arrive tomorrow.
15. This course is not going to take very long.

9.2 Answers

1. Are you going to the party on Saturday?
2. Is he going to give back your book?
3. Will the actor remember his lines?
4. Is this bus going to stop in Portsmouth?
5. Will the performance start on time?
6. Will Vera meet the man of her dreams?
7. Are the Olympics going to be held in Italy?
8. Will Tom admit that he ate the cake?
9. Is your house going to sell by September?
10. Are you (not) going to finish your coffee?
11. Will the old bicycle need to be repaired?
12. Will James bring his wife to the concert?
13. Are the doors going to be replaced?
14. Is that truck going to fit in the parking space?
15. Is the T-shirt going to shrink in the washing machine?
16. Will you split the bill evenly?
17. Will she learn these words by Tuesday?
18. Are you going to see my cousins at the weekend?
19. Will your town change over the next five years?
20. Is that young man going to propose to his girlfriend?

9.3 Answers

1. Who is going to pay for this damage?
2. When will the builders finish the roof?
3. What is going to happen to the vacant beach huts?
4. How is Harry going to climb that tree?
5. What will the papers write about the new President?
6. Why are you going to lose your job?
7. When will your father return from his holiday?
8. Why is the barbecue going to be held in the park?
9. Where are you going to find a good carpet?
10. How will the mice cause havoc?
11. What will you do while your computer is updating?
12. What is she going to cook for her lunch?
13. When is the new product going to be ready?
14. Who will volunteer to take your Saturday shift?
15. Where will you go for your summer holiday?

9.4 Answers

1. Will you not return next year?
2. When are they not going to be at home?
3. What is Drew not going to take on his trip?
4. How will I not watch TV for a week?
5. Are we not going to prepare pasta for dinner?
6. Why is their mother not going to buy them more toys?
7. What terms will they not agree to?
8. Who will not come with us to Kent?
9. Is that tall cake not going to fall over?
10. Who will she not invite to her wedding?

9.5 Answers

The complete correct text follows the numbered answers below.

1. We are going to build
2. It will not be
3. My Uncle Jimmy will help
4. he is going to need
5. he will say
6. are we going to share
7. he will agree
8. The rocket will fly
9. It is not going to cost
10. my dad will find
11. how many people will fit
12. Is the government going to notice
13. they will not allow
14. our rocket is going to reach
15. We will discover
16. What will you use
17. It is going to work
18. we will persuade
19. the adults will build
20. Uncle Jimmy is not going to steal

The Spaceship

(1) We are going to build a spaceship in our back garden. **(2) It will not be** easy, but we have the plans and the right tools. **(3) My Uncle Jimmy will help** put it together, as **(4) he is going to need** to earn his keep while he stays with us this summer. We haven't asked him yet, but **(5) he will say** yes, I am sure. But **(6) are we going to share** all our plans with him? I hope **(7) he will agree** without knowing how valuable the project is.

(8) The rocket will fly faster and higher than any before. **(9) It is not going to cost** much to make, because **(10) my dad will find** good materials in the dump. I do have some unanswered questions, though: **(11) how many people will fit** inside? **(12) Is the government going to notice** what we are doing? If they hear about our amazing rocket, **(13) they will not allow** us to succeed. The government does not want competition – **(14) our rocket is going to reach** Venus. **(15) We will discover** valuable diamonds before they do.

Mum thinks I can't do it. She says, **"(16) What will you use** to fuel the rocket?"

"Hope," I tell her. **"(17) It is going to work** because we have hope."

And anyway, **(18) we will persuade** Jimmy to deal with the other problems. We are the brains and the planners, after all: **(19) the adults will build** it. As long as **(20) Uncle Jimmy is not going to steal** our ideas.

10.1 Answers

1. I will be asking everyone two questions.
2. The days are going to be getting longer.
3. My friend will be driving us to Oxford.
4. We will be playing football all morning.
5. You are going to be waiting for hours.
6. Richard is not going to be researching traffic control this week.
7. She will be sweeping the floor.
8. The company is going to be organising a trip soon.
9. I am not going to be working this afternoon.
10. Penny will be aiming for the best results.
11. He is going to be adding songs to his playlist all night.
12. The bank will not be opening a new branch in Rye.
13. We are going to be dancing on stage this Friday.
14. You are not going to be sitting there when I get back.
15. The baby will be waking up soon.

10.2 Answers

1. Are you going to be washing these dishes?
2. Will Jools be taking the train to Detroit?
3. Will they be supplying you with milk?
4. Is Eric going to be expanding his gallery?
5. Is she going to be speaking on the panel?
6. Will the badgers be sleeping during the day?
7. Will the producers be continuing the radio show?
8. Are they going to be closing more stores?
9. Will the planes be landing at this airport?
10. Is Mrs Antwerp going to be spending time here during her visit?
11. Is the Duke going to be announcing his retirement this week?
12. Will you be meeting the neighbours together?
13. Will they be collecting the sofa today?
14. Is the farmer going to be planting wheat in that field?
15. Are you going to be performing at the Royal Albert Hall?

10.3 Answers

1. Where will everyone be sitting this evening?
2. What are you going to be doing in Bali?
3. How often is Tristan going to be exercising this month?
4. What will Greta be talking about on Wednesday?
5. Who are you going to be sharing a room with?
6. When is she going to be jogging?

7. When will they be clearing away this mess?
8. What will you be reading next week?
9. Where will the barman be hanging his new fairy lights?
10. How long is Clive going to be fixing that van (for)?
11. Where are you going to be skating tomorrow?
12. Who will be wearing the best costume?
13. What is the school going to be teaching this spring?
14. When are the bakers going to be selling their doughnuts?
15. Who is going to be accepting the award?

10.4 Answers

1. When will you not be studying this week?
2. Are the girls not going to be swimming tomorrow?
3. Where is he not going to be riding the horse?
4. Why will they not be attending the party?
5. Will the chef not be preparing a new dish?
6. Is the flag not going to be flying for the President's arrival?
7. Why will they not be looking for the escaped mongoose with us?
8. What will Liz not be bringing on this trip?
9. Why are you not going to be joining the badminton club?
10. Is the plumber not going to be repairing the boiler over lunch?

10.5 Answers

The complete correct text follows the numbered answers below.
1. scouts will be going
2. They are going to be camping

3. The children are not going to be lazing
4. They will be challenging
5. What will the scouts be doing
6. The children will be making
7. They will be hiking
8. they will not be resting
9. everyone is going to be cooking
10. the children will not be calling
11. What else is going to be happening
12. the weather will be changing
13. Mr Ryan will not be letting
14. will it not be raining
15. their activities are going to be occurring
16. I will be preparing
17. What will we be doing

The Scout Trip

The Wood Row **(1) scouts will be going** to the New Forest for four days next week. **(2) They are going to be camping** in a field where they will study the local wildlife. Their leader, Mr Ryan, said, "**(3) The children are not going to be lazing** about. **(4) They will be challenging** themselves all weekend, so they can learn more."

What **(5) will the scouts be doing** on their adventure? A full itinerary has been prepared:

(6) The children will be making notes about the animals they see. **(7) They will be hiking** for three hours each day, and **(8) they will not be resting** much at camp, as **(9) everyone is going to be cooking** two meals each day. Phones are banned, so **(10) the children will not be calling** home.

(11) What else is going to be happening over the weekend? Well, **(12) the weather will be changing** on Saturday morning – from sunny to rainy – but **(13) Mr Ryan will not be letting** that stop them. He asked himself, "When **(14) will it not be raining**?" and made sure that **(15) their activities are going to be occurring** at those times.

"**(16) I will be preparing** alternative indoor activities, too," he said. "**(17) What will we be doing** while it's raining? Well, there's a nice old car museum to explore, for starters."

One thing is for sure: the young scouts are going to be tired.

11.1 Answers

1. We will have decided by 1 p.m.
2. She will have sold the dress before noon.
3. I am not going to have finished this book by nightfall.
4. The workers will have painted our bedroom.
5. You will have accepted my proposal by Friday.
6. Regina is going to have designed a new logo before the meeting.
7. The champion is going to have played his last game by December.
8. The scientists will have added the new planets to the map.
9. The council will have cleared the roads for the festival.
10. Our neighbours are to going to have replaced their windows by Monday.
11. The keys will not have been found by then.
12. The university will have awarded my niece a prize.
13. Victor is going to have escaped before we get back.
14. The groundsmen will have planted new grass over the old field.
15. The eggs will not have gone bad.

11.2 Answers

1. Will they have replaced the batteries by tomorrow?
2. Are you going to have measured the temperature?

243

3. Will you have washed the dishes in time for dinner?
4. Will the dentist have raised her prices?
5. Are they going to have fixed the leaking sink by 10 a.m.?
6. Are you going to have managed this project well?
7. Are the new batteries going to have arrived in time?
8. Will the hats have sold?
9. Will Billie have brought her best socks?
10. Is Mrs Carter going to have visited her daughter?
11. Will petrol prices have risen again?
12. Is the priest going to have learned to dance before the ball?
13. Are the geese going to have left the park?
14. Will you have made enough scones for everyone?
15. Will the panel have discussed the important issues?

11.3 Answers

1. Who is going to have eaten before the party?
2. What will have happened to the wall?
3. Where are you going to have stayed this summer?
4. When is Manny going to have returned that book?
5. Where will the pirates have hidden the treasure?
6. How will the manager have handled his own accounts?
7. When are your clients going to have paid you?
8. What will you have learned on the course?
9. When will the sandwiches have been prepared?
10. Where are the traders going to have docked the ship?

11.4 Answers

1. Where is Darren not going to have been?
2. What will the gerbils not have bitten through?
3. Why will they not have learned from their mistakes?
4. How many cakes are you not going to have made by Saturday?
5. Will the reporter not have written her article on time?
6. Who is not going to have solved this puzzle before the bell?
7. Why is Mrs Harris not going to have fixed her dress before tomorrow?
8. Will the traffic not have caused a delay?
9. Where am I not going to have spoken by the end of my reading tour?
10. Why will they not have delivered the bad news before he arrives?

11.5 Answers

The complete correct text follows the numbered answers below.
1. German clients will have arrived
2. They will have finished
3. they are not going to have processed
4. Bob will have started
5. What will he have done
6. he is going to have called
7. What will he not have completed
8. she will have created
9. She will have prepared
10. she is not going to have eaten
11. The pair will have polished
12. they will have sealed

The Big Presentation

Bob and Charlotte are giving a big presentation tomorrow at 2 p.m. Their **(1) German clients will have arrived** by then, and it is important to impress them. There is lots to do. **(2) They will have finished** the overall report by this evening, but the graphs will be incomplete as **(3) they are not going to have processed** all the data in time. Charlotte is worried because she has to take her children to school before work, but **(4) Bob will have started** on the graphs before she arrives.

(5) What will he have done? She hopes **(6) he is going to have called** the research department and compiled their data. **(7) What will he not have completed?** The graphs themselves. Unfortunately, Bob is not very good with graph software. But Charlotte imagines **(8) she will have created** all the necessary graphs before noon. That will give them time to prepare to greet the clients.

Charlotte will be so busy, she will not have time for lunch. **(9) She will have prepared** smoothies in the morning, though. Hopefully the clients won't notice **(10) she is not going to have eaten** lunch. **(11) The pair will have polished** their presentation to such a high standard, they should be too impressed to care about anything else. By tomorrow afternoon, Charlotte imagines **(12) they will have sealed** the deal.

12.1 Answers

1. I will have been learning Mandarin for a month by this Friday.
2. Soon, the couple will have been arguing for 20 minutes.
3. We are going to have been dancing all night long.
4. You will have been choosing the flowers carefully.
5. The storm clouds are going to have been gathering for a while.
6. Georgie will have been listening to pop music again.
7. Our dog will have been sleeping while we were out.

8. I am going to have been cycling all morning, so I'll need a shower.
9. Carl will have been practising for the Olympics.
10. The boats will have been bumping into each other overnight.
11. The spies will have been listening.
12. My uncle is going to have been researching our family history ahead of the reunion.
13. It will have been getting hotter before we go on holiday.
14. The tree will have been shedding its leaves for weeks.
15. She is going to have been laughing at her own radio show.

12.2 Answers

1. Are you going to have been waiting all morning?
2. Will Nancy have been singing throughout the first act?
3. Will they have been baking a cake?
4. Are you going to have been wasting your time?
5. Are the shoppers going to have been queueing for hours?
6. Will Charlie have been shaving regularly during the holiday?
7. Will we have been writing to each other for a long time?
8. Is Sally going to have been working in insurance for two years?
9. Is the tide going to have been going out?
10. Will the grapes have been getting mouldy?

12.3 Answers

1. How long will she have been practising (for)?
2. Where will Jim have been swimming?
3. How far are you going to have been travelling?
4. What are the trucks going to have been carrying?

5. Why will the children have been walking home?
6. How long are you going to have been working on this project (for)?
7. What are they going to have been waiting for?
8. Why will the foxes have been gathering in the garden?
9. Who is he going to have been asking for help?
10. What is the intern going to have been saying about his job?

12.4 Answers

1. Where will the tractor not have been going (to)?
2. Am I not going to have been participating enough?
3. How long is your aunt not going to have been working for?
4. What are we not going to have been seeing?
5. Will they not have been losing hope?
6. Why is he not going to have been preparing for the test?
7. Which buildings will the company not have been developing?
8. Are the coats not going to have been hanging in the right places?
9. Will the guard not have been standing upright?
10. What will our friends not have been showing us?

12.5 Answers

The complete correct text follows the numbered answers below.
1. things will have been changing
2. they will have been building
3. we will not have been sleeping
4. the population will have been growing
5. new shops will have been opening
6. I will have been living
7. I will not have been working

8. are these outsiders not going to have been hovering
9. we will have been getting
10. they are not going to have been expecting
11. local researchers will have been applying
12. we are not going to have been wasting

The Fish of Mugrub

Things have been changing in the fishing village of Mugrub. By November, **(1) things will have been changing** for five years. Lots of new buildings have been built there; some residents feel that when the next few projects begin **(2) they will have been building** apartments forever. Resident Liam McDonald said, "And because of the noise, when they finish, **(3) we will not have been sleeping** for years!"

Tourists and researchers have been coming to Mugrub to see a new glowing fish, discovered almost five years ago. If projections are met this December, **(4) the population will have been growing** by 25% each year. Should the latest tackle shop get permission, **(5) new shops will have been opening** at a rate of four a year. But has happiness been increasing in the same way?

"**(6) I will have been living** here for three decades this August," McDonald said. "And **(7) I will not have been working** for almost half of that. I liked the peace and quiet before. The mayor says it will calm down, but **(8) are these outsiders not going to have been hovering** around for five years, soon?"

Not everyone is as unhappy with the changing village. Shop owner Jenny McCluck looks forward to the future: "I imagine **(9) we will have been getting** visitors from all over the world during the summer. They cannot resist the village, and though **(10) they are not going to have been expecting** to stay long, they will do. It's good for business."

It's also good for the glowing fish. This summer, **(11) local researchers will have been applying** for grants each year for the past five years – and they are confident Mugrub's popularity will finally secure funding this time. Dr Bailey said, "Next year, we expect to uncover the mysteries of the glowing fish, as **(12) we are not going to have been wasting** time searching for funding!"

13.1 Answers

1. Isn't this easy?
2. There were too many people on the boat.
3. Does Paul not seem quiet today?
4. Swans are very loud.
5. It is not a good day to go swimming.
6. What will you wear to the gala?
7. We waited for hours.
8. They will be at the dock before noon.
9. Does this photo look real to you?
10. When did Nina buy her house?
11. She went to the shop for more mushrooms.
12. I always leave my wallet behind.
13. Won't you tidy your room later?
14. You look too tired to swim.
15. How did the fisherman buy a new boat?
16. This tie appeals to me most.
17. Who did not take their medicine this morning?
18. The President will not give up on this reform.
19. Our house fell apart over a period of many years.
20. Practice makes perfect.

13.2 Answers

1. Do rabbits eat grass?
2. Did Jimmy fall in the mud?
3. Do you (always) enjoy the circus?
4. Will Wendy be in the market tomorrow?
5. Where does the river run through?
6. How many men waited in the street?
7. Did he sit on the bench for two hours?
8. Will there be twenty people at dinner?
9. What time will the delivery arrive?
10. When do they study very hard?
11. Which was the busiest city that year? or Which city was the busiest that year?
12. Who will watch your child tomorrow?
13. Are men less healthy than women?
14. Will the squirrels steal those nuts?
15. Did the radio's battery run out?
16. Is the marigold her favourite flower?
17. Does Polly own a bicycle?
18. Who saved all the children? or Who did the lifeguards save?
19. When you are older, will you get twenty cats? or Will you get twenty cats when you are older?
20. Before the war, did this shop sell fresh bread? or Did this shop sell fresh bread before the war?

13.3 Answers

1. Does Robert not eat meat? (*or* Doesn't Robert eat meat?)
2. Did the investigator not understand the report? (*or* Didn't the investigator understand ...)
3. Why won't people give your charity donations? (*or* Why will people not give ...)
4. Will she not visit her mother again? (*or* Won't she visit ...)
5. Do you not like the bagpipes? (*or* Don't you like ...)
6. Will Harry not go to school tomorrow? (*or* Won't Harry go ...)

7. Did your friends not meet until college? (*or* Didn't your friends meet ...)
8. Are these questions not very strange? (*or* Aren't these questions ...)
9. Will running every day not make you fit? (*or* Won't running every day make ...)
10. Did you not feed the ducks again? (*or* Didn't you feed ...)
11. Who does not practise guitar very often? (*or* Who doesn't practise ...)
12. Why did the council not remove your rubbish this week? (*or* Why didn't the council remove ...)
13. Will they not be able park their car? (*or* Won't they be able to ...)
14. Did Simon not pass his driving test? (*or* Didn't Simon pass ...)
15. What does not look right? (*or* What doesn't look ...)

13.4 Answers

1. Correct
2. Incorrect – I do not live there anymore. (or I don't live there anymore.)
3. Incorrect – The kitchen smells like sweet apple pie.
4. Correct
5. Incorrect – Herman and Claire enjoy playing chess on Saturdays.
6. Correct
7. Correct
8. Incorrect – This aeroplane will fly if it is repaired.
9. Incorrect – He did not arrive in time for the show last night.
10. Incorrect – The greyhounds returned after they escaped.
11. Correct
12. Incorrect – The car looks dirty now.
13. Incorrect – The toaster worked when we tried it earlier.
14. Correct
15. Correct

13.5 Answers

The complete correct text follows the numbered answers below.
1. Bill lives
2. His house sits
3. He always dreamed
4. he finally has
5. It took
6. he did not believe (or he didn't believe)
7. His friends often asked
8. Why do you want
9. Didn't anyone tell
10. Will you not drown (or Won't you drown)
11. many people said
12. Beach property tends
13. it is not easy (or it isn't easy)
14. These details did not bother (or These details didn't bother)
15. he determined
16. he saved
17. He bought
18. he enjoys
19. The water does not come (or The water doesn't come)
20. Bill is going to invite
21. they will see (or they'll see)
22. what will he do
23. Does he have
24. Bill imagines
25. He is going to study (or He's going to study)
26. he will buy (or he'll buy)
27. Nothing is going to stop

A House by the Sea

(1) Bill lives in a bungalow by the sea, now. **(2) His house sits** opposite the beach. **(3) He always dreamed** of owning a house with a sea view, and **(4) he finally has** it. **(5) It took** him fifteen years to find the right home. At times, **(6) he did not believe (*or* he didn't believe)** it would be possible. **(7) His friends**

often asked, "**(8) Why do you want** a home by the sea? **(9) Didn't anyone tell** you that the sea is dangerous? **(10) Will you not drown** (*or* **Won't you drown**)?"

Indeed, before he moved, **(11) many people said** that storms and floods could damage a seaside home. **(12) Beach property tends** to be expensive, too. And in England, **(13) it is not easy** (*or* **it isn't easy**) to find space along the sea, certainly not near big towns. **(14) These details did not bother** (*or* **These details didn't bother**) Bill. Whatever the price, **(15) he determined**, his dream would come true.

Finally, **(16) he saved** enough money and found exactly the right place. **(17) He bought** his bungalow outright. Now, **(18) he enjoys** sitting on the porch watching the waves. **(19) The water does not come** (*or* **The water doesn't come**) high enough to damage the house. **(20) Bill is going to invite** all his friends down during the summer, and **(21) they will see** (*or* **they'll see**) for themselves how wonderful it is here.

But now Bill has achieved his dream, **(22) what will he do** next? **(23) Does he have** other plans? Yes. **(24) Bill imagines** what life would be like *on* the sea. **(26) He is going to study** (*or* **He's going to study**) to become a boat captain. Then, **(27) he will buy** (*or* **he'll buy**) a boat. **(28) Nothing is going to stop** him.

14.1 Answers

1. He will be coming back here after he buys some wine.
2. Everyone was enjoying themselves before we got there.
3. Rita was sewing a new dress two days ago.
4. Joe is dancing exceptionally well today.
5. You will be performing first tonight.
6. People will be discussing this for a long time to come.
7. I was partying all night, so I needed to rest.
8. She is sitting in the wrong seat – someone tell her. or Someone tell her she is sitting in the wrong seat.
9. We were arguing in the street but got told to stop.
10. The giraffe was standing under the tree while it rained.
11. The defeated team will be licking their wounds later.
12. I am trying to sleep but it is too noisy outside.
13. We will be learning exciting new techniques next week.
14. The cleaners are emptying the bins right now.
15. You are annoying me, please go away.

14.2 Answers

1. How long were you working (for)?
2. When will they be climbing the mountain?
3. Is your boy (not) studying enough?
4. Is Jenny taking her language test again?
5. Where was he fighting with a gorilla?
6. Will she be entering the contest? or Is she entering the contest?
7. Is Rupert doing lots of exercise?
8. Were you talking too loudly?
9. Where was the gang hanging out?
10. Is Charlotte giving out sweets?
11. Why are the police searching for a pink car?
12. Will she be cleaning up this mess for a long time?
13. Will Bob be waiting in the foyer (at 9 p.m.)?
14. Who was gathering below the balcony?
15. Is Charles tying his shoelaces?

14.3 Answers

1. Are you not eating well?
2. Were they not planning to come?
3. Will you not be joining them?
4. Is it not getting warmer?
5. Why are you not recycling more plastic?
6. Where is the coast guard not patrolling?
7. Why is Henry not giving any presents this Christmas?
8. Were the foxes not standing on the roof?
9. Why is the bookshop not opening early today?
10. Is your team not playing in the match this weekend?
11. What was Sheila not revealing (about her birdcage)?
12. Was the girl not standing there when you took the photo?
13. Will the campers not be expecting (you to have) fresh water?
14. Is that lion not getting (too) close to the shelter?
15. Why were you not waiting in the parlour last night?

14.4 Answers

1. Aren't you reading that magazine?
2. Weren't they working during yesterday's storm?
3. Aren't your tissues running out? or Won't your tissues be running out?
4. Won't Danny be waiting at home?
5. How long weren't you studying for?
6. Why aren't you sitting close to the stage?
7. Won't Hailey be skiing with you?
8. Weren't they fighting over the last piece of cheese?
9. Isn't the weather changing rapidly?
10. What weren't they including in the recipe?

11. Aren't the farmers working in the field?
12. Wasn't Howard gathering mushrooms last week?
13. Why isn't the fireman listening?
14. Aren't the tulips turning a curious shade of purple?
15. Weren't you taking notes?

14.5 Answers

1. Incorrect – You were singing the right tune.
2. Correct
3. Correct
4. Incorrect – I am baking a wonderful cake.
5. Incorrect – His parents will be visiting tomorrow.
6. Incorrect – The birds were not sitting there yesterday.
7. Correct
8. Incorrect – We were shopping in the mall when the alarm went off.
9. Correct
10. Correct
11. Incorrect – We will not be waiting very long if you call ahead.
12. Correct
13. Correct
14. Incorrect – The cat is staring out of the window again.
15. Incorrect – They will not be performing this evening, after all.

14.6 Answers

The complete correct text follows the numbered answers below.
1. I'm booking
2. What's playing
3. It won't be showing
4. Why are they still making
5. It's getting
6. I'm not going
7. I'm watching
8. What are you doing

9. I was studying
10. Weren't you revising
11. I'll be reading
12. You're working
13. we're not seeing (*or* we aren't seeing)
14. What are you thinking
15. Bridget was telling
16. I'm driving

Going to the Cinema

Billy: **(1) I'm booking** tickets for the cinema. Do you want to come?
Angela: Hmm. **(2) What's playing**?
Billy: It's a superhero movie. **(3) It won't be showing** for much longer, so we need to go now.
Angela: Another superhero movie! **(4) Why are they still making** them?
Billy: This is the best one yet – **(5) it's getting** amazing reviews.
Angela: I don't care – **(6) I'm not going** to another superhero film.
Billy: Well, **(7) I'm watching** it whether you come or not. **(8) What are you doing**, anyway?
Angela: **(9) I was studying** for my exam on Friday before you interrupted, actually.
Billy: **(10) Weren't you revising** all day yesterday?
Angela: Yes, and **(11) I'll be reading** all day tomorrow, too. So what?
Billy: **(12) You're working** too hard! Come to the cinema and have a break.
Angela: Fine. I'll go to the cinema, but **(13) we're not seeing (*or* we aren't seeing)** that superhero film.
Billy: **(14) What are you thinking** of watching instead?
Angela: There's a new thriller. With a twist. **(15) Bridget was telling** me about it last week.
Billy: Hmm. Fine. But **(16) I'm driving**!

15.1 Answers

1. I had finished my essay but was not happy with it.
2. Ryan has bought a new camera and cannot stop talking about it.
3. The shop will have closed before you get there.
4. You have not prepared the salad, have you?
5. Many artists had recorded the tune before John produced a cover.
6. Has the door been forced open?
7. Our friends will not have arrived yet, by this time tomorrow.
8. Will the weather have changed by the weekend?
9. She had started a new book even though she was still reading one.
10. Sam will have walked home, if he is not at the school.
11. I have not seen this film before; it looks good.
12. Had they eaten so many scones that they could not have cake?
13. The children have built a den, so the living room is a mess.
14. Had the priest gone before she arrived?
15. The restaurant will not have served dinner by 7 p.m., as the chef is missing.

15.2 Answers

1. Have you been to Hungary before?
2. Had they locked the door before going out?
3. Has the chef cooked soup today?
4. Will you have rested before the train comes?
5. Had someone punctured the wheel deliberately?
6. Have you told her this before?
7. Has the water boiled yet?
8. Had the minister taken the wrong backpack?
9. Will the snow have cleared by morning?

10. Have you seen many Japanese films?
11. Has the university received my application?
12. Have they released the lobsters too early?
13. Had she written the right answer?
14. Will Maria have cooked the pies by 2 p.m.?
15. Has it become harder to buy property?

15.3 Answers

1. What has Shirley done?
2. How had he got inside?
3. Where will the courier have left the package?
4. Where has Luke put all the empty milk cartons?
5. What had the man (at the front desk) said?
6. Why has no one opened a window (in here)?
7. Who has drawn all over your papers?
8. Where had the badgers hidden?
9. When will the boats have docked (by)?
10. How had Tim broken his phone?
11. Where has she put the remote control?
12. What had the caretaker cleaned the floor with?
13. When had the package arrived?
14. Who has showed the most potential this year?
15. What (decorations) have we stored in the garage?

15.4 Answers

1. Have you not seen Alfred this month?
2. Has the mail not arrived yet?
3. Had the explorers not taken the correct turn?
4. Will the hosts not have prepared for a hundred guests?
5. Has it not been 45 minutes since you put the bread in the oven?

6. What question had you not asked before?
7. Will they not have reserved their seats at the theatre?
8. Had the cupboard not squeaked as loudly (that morning)?
9. Has her boyfriend not returned yet?
10. Have we not paid for this meal already?
11. Will the shops not have closed by 7 p.m.?
12. Why had Harriette not packed the correct shoes?
13. Had he not rested before he started work?
14. Have you not signed up for lessons?
15. Will the taxi not have arrived by midnight?

15.5 Answers

1. Which goals hasn't the President achieved?
2. Why haven't you heard this tune before?
3. Hadn't the thieves hidden the jewels?
4. Won't the men have distributed the presents in time?
5. What hadn't she wanted (that she received)?
6. Where hasn't the tour group visited?
7. How hadn't they known the door would be locked?
8. What won't our opponents have planned for?
9. Haven't you helped with the dishes?
10. Which chair hasn't the kitten damaged?
11. Hadn't he noticed the creature (was following him)?
12. What won't you have completed by New Year?

15.6 Answers

1. Incorrect – I have not seen that play, but I hear it is good.
2. Correct

3. Correct
4. Incorrect – Victor has not learned to play the piano yet.
5. Correct
6. Incorrect – It had not been easy, but the girls replaced the punctured tyre.
7. Incorrect – We hadn't brought a map and got hopelessly lost.
8. Incorrect – Had Sue fed animals before or not?
9. Incorrect – He will have heard the good news before the meeting.
10. Correct
11. Incorrect – They will have collected all the flowers before the wedding day.
12. Correct
13. Incorrect – She has not lived here for long, has she?
14. Incorrect – I will have recovered by the time they arrive tomorrow.
15. Correct

15.7 Answers

The complete correct text follows the numbered answers below.
1. has been
2. have renovated
3. they have decorated
4. they will have spent
5. the house will have been
6. Why has it failed
7. hasn't sold
8. the owners had painted
9. we'd asked
10. Why had the owners hired
11. they haven't done
12. We've lived
13. the damp has never bothered
14. mushrooms had grown
15. we'd expected
16. Has anyone ever moved
17. Mr Murray hasn't found
18. have become
19. What had they brought
20. how many agents will we have tried

The House that Would Not Sell

The building on Grand Avenue **(1) has been** up for sale for a long time now. The owners **(2) have renovated** it recently: **(3) they have decorated** all the rooms, and are currently building a new garage. They claim **(4) they will have spent** more than £10,000 on these improvements when they are done. But **(5) the house will have been** on the market six months by next week. **(6) Why has it failed** to sell?

The property probably **(7) hasn't sold** because of the damp problems. One couple who went to view it complained that **(8) the owners had painted** over mould on one wall. The real estate agent expressed frustration about this: "I wish **(9) we'd asked** more questions before taking on the house. **(10) Why had the owners already hired** two different estate agents? Because the others quit after they discovered the damp!"

The owners, Jeff and Winn Murray, insist **(11) they haven't done** anything wrong. Jeff said, "**(12) We've lived** here for ten years and **(13) the damp has never bothered** us. When we first moved in, **(14) mushrooms had grown** on the carpet. Did we complain? No, because **(15) we'd expected** a few problems beforehand. **(16) Has anyone ever moved** house without problems?"

(17) Mr Murray hasn't found his potential customers forgiving, however. Buyers can easily to spot damp now, as moisture scanners **(18) have become** so effective. Winn Murray said, "One young couple's clothes beeped while we showed them around. **(19) What had they brought** in their pockets? A damp-measuring device! Perhaps we need a new estate agent, who will bring less devious buyers. But **(20) how many**

agents will we have tried then? Perhaps we should just keep the house!"

16.1 Answers

1. Ben had been watching TV for an hour while the soup simmered.
2. Why has your phone been ringing since you started your shower?
3. Our friends had been visiting us once a week until they left town.
4. The gate has not been opening properly for a week now.
5. You had been studying medicine for two years last time I saw you.
6. They will have been waiting all evening by the time you get to the party.
7. Jason has not been calling the council every day this week.
8. How long will I have been travelling for when I finally get home?
9. We had been seeing each other for a year before we got married.
10. The men will have been climbing for days before they reach the summit.
11. Has she been trying to learn Spanish before her holiday next month?
12. I have been considering whether or not to go out this evening.

16.2 Answers

1. Had he been studying for a long time before the exam?
2. Will they have been building that wall all summer?
3. Had you been sitting or standing when the bell rang?
4. Have you been reading about giraffes this week?
5. Will Ben have been living on a boat for two years this August?
6. Has she been staring at me all morning?
7. Had you been looking for a new bag last time I saw you?

8. Has my wife been cooking something that smells delicious?
9. Had mushrooms been growing under the floorboards?
10. Will our nephew have been walking for months before we see him?
11. Has Hillary been arguing with the neighbours?
12. Will the squirrels have been sleeping all winter?

16.3 Answers

1. Who had been banging on the door that night?
2. Where has she been hiding her silverware?
3. Why has Greg been sending the TV station angry letters?
4. What has the plumber been doing in the basement (for a long time)?
5. How long will Jane have been learning to ride camels (for) (come March)?
6. Who had Simon been talking to before dinner?
7. Where will the cake have been cooling (for three hours) before tea?
8. How long had the birds been flying (for) (before they arrived at the lake)?
9. What have you been writing in your journal?
10. Will you have been practising (that dance) for two weeks (before the show)?

16.4 Answers

1. Have the tomatoes not been growing in this soil?
2. Had Veronica not been sending the letters?
3. Had they not been collecting (any) names during the survey?
4. Will you not have been working here long enough for a raise this month?

5. Had she not been paying attention when the homework was set?
6. Has the old man not been eating his beans?
7. Will the couple not have been renting for long before they buy?
8. Have Roger and Kim not been washing their towels?
9. Had your aunt not been buying anything online?
10. Why will Sandy not have been working today?

16.5 Answers

1. Who hadn't been wearing her crown at night?
2. Won't he have been travelling through Europe (next month)?
3. What hadn't Sally been sharing (with anyone)?
4. Haven't you been using the blue pen?
5. Hadn't Dennis been searching for his wallet all morning?
6. Which cookery shows haven't I been watching?
7. How long hasn't she been replying to my messages (for)?
8. Won't the club have been expanding quickly enough to earn a bonus?
9. Why hasn't the charity been accepting donations since January?
10. Hadn't the cupboard been squeaking last time we were there?

16.6 Answers

1. Correct
2. Incorrect – The Smiths had not been closing their windows at night, even when it rained.
3. Incorrect – The children have been playing outside this week.
4. Correct
5. Incorrect – We have not been meeting as often now as we used to.
6. Correct

7. Incorrect – Mandy had been letting her sister use the computer that summer.
8. Correct
9. Correct
10. Incorrect – She will have been reading the correct book.
11. Incorrect – Jim will have been working for eight days by tomorrow morning.
12. Correct
13. Correct
14. Incorrect – Have our guests been waiting long? They look bored.
15. Incorrect – My car has not been starting since the accident last Thursday.

16.7 Answers

The complete correct text follows the numbered answers below.
1. has been training
2. has been taking place
3. has been running
4. hadn't been swimming
5. had never been climbing
6. will have been learning
7. Why has she been working
8. Janet had been getting
9. She'd been seeing
10. Claude has been competing
11. What had she been thinking
12. she'd been rising
13. Her diet hadn't been helping
14. she's been feeling
15. she hasn't been getting
16. Her life has also been improving
17. she's even been sleeping
18. she's been growing
19. Will she have been practising
20. Janet will have been working

Extreme Endurance

Janet **(1) has been training** to complete the Extreme Endurance Race in July. The race **(2) has been taking place** in Devon for eight years now, and involves swimming, running, cycling and climbing. Janet **(3) has been running** and cycling since she was young, but before last January she **(4) hadn't been swimming** for a long time and **(5) had never been climbing**. By the time of the race, she **(6) will have been learning** to climb for only six months!

(7) Why has she been working so hard for this? Before Christmas, **(8) Janet had been getting** ill frequently. **(9) She'd been seeing** doctors two or three times a week, and all of them said she needed more exercise. Her friend **(10) Claude has been competing** in tough races for decades, and he suggested she try one. So she chose the toughest. **(11) What had she been thinking?**

By February, **(12) she'd been rising** every morning at 5am for two months. **(13) Her diet hadn't been helping**, so she cut out sugar and dairy. The improvements were rapid. Janet has not only lost weight and raised her stamina, **(14) she's been feeling** more awake and alive. What's more – **(15) she's not been getting** ill anymore. **(16) Her life has also been improving** in other ways she did not expect – **(17) she's even been sleeping** better.

But the Extreme Endurance Race is quickly approaching, and **(18) she's been growing** more nervous by the day. **(19) Will she have been practising** for long enough to face it? She isn't sure, but one thing is certain: by the time it's over, **(20) Janet will have been working** hard enough to form a habit. Now she's started getting fit, she doesn't expect to stop.

17.1 Answers

1. Billy completed his homework before tea. *or* Billy was completing his homework before tea.
2. We agreed to meet at 4 p.m.
3. Lynn called while I was waiting for a bus.
4. He is only here because you invited him.
5. We could see that the ship was sinking.
6. John burst into the room to deliver the news.
7. She found her glasses under the sofa.
8. Only three students submitted their essays early.
9. They left early because they were not enjoying the film.
10. The boy cried when a bee stung him.
11. I lost phone while I was relaxing in Spain.
12. Vera forgot to lock the door again.
13. Ruth was caring for her mother, so could not go to the party.
14. The dog snarled because it was protecting its toy.
15. Fred was loading the car when he remembered his goggles.
16. We discovered our parents were paying too much for gas.
17. What were you doing at the time that the fire started?
18. When did she explain how to turn on the fridge?
19. Where did the thieves hide the diamonds?
20. Why was Julia laughing during the meeting?

17.2 Answers

1. "Are you going on holiday this year?" "No, I went on one already."
2. "I heard you gave up science classes." "Yes, I thought I wasn't learning enough."

3. Penny collected model buses for many years. She was trying to get enough to start a museum.
4. "Why did we stop using disposable cups?"
"Because management decided to reduce plastic."
5. Sparrows were nesting in our loft. We could hear them above us.
6. "What did that sign say?"
"I couldn't see, it was swaying in the wind."
7. The new restaurant was a massive success. Hundreds of customers came in the first two days.
8. "You're home early tonight."
"Yes, I hurried back to watch the game."
9. Didn't that man look terribly cold? Wasn't he shaking all over?
10. "Look at how many burgers I have!"
"Wow, did you buy them all?"
11. "Your father called to ask where you were. Didn't you tell him we were going to the beach?"
12. "I heard they gave Michelle a first-class ticket to Bali."
"Yes, I think so – wasn't she consulting on the site of a new hotel?"

17.3 Answers

1. There were no biscuits left because she had eaten them all.
2. The guests surprised her, as their flight had arrived early.
3. Our neighbours had been shouting for hours when we asked them to stop.
4. All our lights went out. I had forgotten to pay the meter.
5. Raccoons had been raiding our bins every night, so we added locks.
6. She had been preparing a presentation but went out before it was finished.
7. He left the café because his friends had been laughing at him.

8. Anna had read all the author's books except one.
9. Which book had she been reading before she found this one?
10. When had they opened the new bar? It looked very vibrant.

17.4 Answers

1. Sheila was ironing her dress during a storm.
2. When we arrived at the hotel, it looked closed.
3. Though they seemed dim, the lights were on.
4. By 3 p.m. all his shares had risen; he was having a good day.
5. No one moved: the man had a gun.
6. Her husband always bought books when he felt bored.
7. You were having a bad dream, so I woke you.
8. At the time, they did not understand the problem.
9. Throughout July, we were often trying to paint our shed.
10. Geoff was listening to the radio at 11 a.m.
11. She had not fully decided, but she preferred the yellow curtains.
12. I was reading War and Peace but took a break to read a comic.
13. The man was choosing a tie for so long that they closed the shop.
14. As she entered the garage, Enid heard a curious sound.
15. Luke studied hard because he was aiming to get top marks.
16. Would work send me to Italy? It was exactly what I wanted.
17. He waited for a decision. Did they believe his story?
18. When we met Lana, did she smell of smoke?
19. The parrots surprised everyone – why did they appear so angry?

20. While I made tea, were you looking in my diary?

17.5 Answers

1. I was tired because I had been studying in the library.
2. Jolene had loved her backpack, but it was time to give it away.
3. We had tasted success while working at the bank.
4. Two wolves had been lurking near the camp at night.
5. Though he had seemed kind when he visited, he stole my ring.
6. The shop had been suffering from a lack of donations, so they ran an advert to help.
7. Marius had lived in Lewes for thirteen years before he moved to Germany.
8. Claude had been living in Lewes for thirteen years when he was asked to move.
9. The cheese had smelled fine in the morning, but was bad by lunch.
10. Tammy had believed it was impossible until she discovered the answer.

17.6 Answers

1. The hotel had cost a lot because it was the height of summer.
2. They exchanged letters only after they had separated.
3. My father had bought a new car two days before he visited us.
4. I passed my driving test once I had taken 40 lessons.
5. She wanted to ride her bike but the chain had broken the day before.
6. Miles had played the guitar for three years before he lost interest in it.
7. Where was the water he had asked for?
8. Shelly left early because she had completed her assignment.

9. The doctor had prescribed some medicine but Jim stopped taking it after a day.
10. By the time the firemen arrived, the building had been evacuated.
11. I had wanted boiled eggs but they gave me beans on toast.
12. The bridge needed repairing because the river had flooded that morning.
13. The children who achieved the best results had studied hardest.
14. By the time the procession started, thousands of people had gathered to see the Queen.
15. Our aunt retired early because she had started saving at an early age.

Note that these answers consider the most appropriate structure grammatically, where the past perfect indicates an earlier past time. However, though the past perfect is used to add clarity, many sequences can be understood without it. For example, sentences 2, 7 and 11 could have both verbs in the past simple.

17.7 Answers

1. They needed to hurry because the ice was melting.
2. Roland could not find the toy because his friend had hidden it.
3. The pie was burning, so I switched the oven off.
4. Grandma had escaped, so we sent out a search party.
5. Hillary knew a lot because she had read all the books in the library.
6. I could not hear the news because my son was talking.
7. Though Tom had repaired his computer, the screen still did not work.
8. She called her mum while she was walking home.
9. The family was planning a garden party until they forecast rain.

10. Claus could not go to the shops because Herman had borrowed his car that morning.
11. Though the game had ended, the crowd did not go home.
12. We sat on the bench as the bus was taking a long time to arrive.
13. Neil stopped studying the letter; he had found the answer.
14. When she was travelling across Europe, Gina visited Switzerland.
15. Because the tree had fallen, the road was blocked.

17.8 Answers

1. By the time I left Romania, I had been teaching there for three years.
2. While Jen was washing the dishes, Roy cleaned the table.
3. We sheltered in the barn because it was raining.
4. The track was impassable as it had been snowing heavily.
5. Alan was speaking to his bank manager all morning. or Alan had been speaking to his bank manager all morning.
6. You would have heard my answer if you had been listening.
7. I didn't use the sink as the tap had been leaking lately.
8. The bus was making funny noises, so we pulled over.
9. He could not drive home because he had been drinking wine.
10. The cleaners had been talking, and decided it was time to take action.

17.9 Answers

The complete correct text follows the numbered answers below.
1. decided
2. wanted
3. was not
4. was not
5. asked
6. did she have
7. said
8. Did you leave
9. did not know
10. had
11. walked
12. remembered
13. found
14. told
15. needed
16. Did you see
17. asked
18. did you not put
19. answered
20. explained
21. was not
22. locked
23. was
24. was
25. sat
26. was not
27. could he do
28. was
29. returned
30. had
31. grabbed
32. charged
33. ran
34. did not
35. arrived
36. were not
37. did they go
38. understood
39. did not like
40. were

Felix and the Umbrella

Felix **(1) decided** to go the park last Saturday. He **(2) wanted** to see the pond and feed the ducks. It **(3) was not** a sunny day, so he needed an umbrella. The umbrella **(4) was not** in its usual place. He **(5) asked** his sister: **(6) did she have** his umbrella? She **(7) said** no.

"**(8) Did you leave** it at school?" she replied.

He **(9) did not know**. He **(10) had** the umbrella when he **(11) walked** home on Thursday. He **(12) remembered** leaving it to dry in the bathroom.

Felix **(13) found** the bathroom door locked. His father **(14) told** him the bath **(15) needed** replacing.

"**(16) Did you see** my umbrella in there?" Felix **(17) asked**.

"Why **(18) did you not put** it back by the door?" his dad **(19) answered**.

Felix **(20) explained** that it had been wet. But the umbrella **(21) was not** in the bathroom when he **(22) locked** the door, his dad **(23) was** sure. **(24) Where was it**?

Felix **(25) sat** on the stairs, sad. It **(26) was not** possible to visit the park without the umbrella. What else **(27) could he do**?

Just as he **(28) was** about to give up hope, his mother **(29) returned** from shopping. She **(30) had** the umbrella!

Felix **(31) grabbed** the umbrella from her startled hands, and **(32) charged** outside, finally ready to visit the park. He **(33) ran** down the road, and **(34) did not stop** for anything on the way. He **(35) arrived** at the pond, at long last. The ducks **(36) were not** there. Where **(37) did they go**?

Of course, Felix **(38) understood**, standing in the rain. The ducks **(39) did not like** the rain either. They **(40) were safe**, inside, out of sight.

He would have to come back another day.

Note that this passage demonstrates a narrative following a clear sequence of completed action. For clarity, the past perfect may be used in some instances here, such as for 21 and 22, but is not essential. The past continuous may also be used in some instances, to focus on the process instead of completion, such as with 10 and 11 – but we can use the past simple because the action was completed.

17.10 Answers

The complete correct text follows the numbered answers below.

1. was searching
2. were running
3. were providing
4. Was the place selling
5. was it offering
6. was trying
7. was not discussing
8. was bustling
9. were not handling
10. were running
11. was not smiling
12. was he wearing
13. were the managers dressing
14. was opening and closing
15. were waiting
16. how were they expecting
17. was rumbling
18. was not listening
19. was watching
20. was he planning
21. was having
22. were swimming
23. were serving
24. were becoming
25. was standing
26. were leaving
27. was eating
28. was not coming
29. were laughing
30. were enjoying
31. Were the chefs putting
32. was everyone not questioning
33. was not fooling
34. was devouring

An Unsatisfactory Restaurant

When I **(1) was searching** for a new restaurant, I discovered Calbini's had opened in the town centre. They **(2) were running** a promotion that week: three courses for £12.95. Very cheap, as others nearby **(3) were providing** a main course for £18! **(4) Was the place selling** itself short? Or **(5) was it offering** a worse service?

I visited on a Wednesday night with my colleague Gunther. He **(6) was trying** to decide what to eat on the way, from the online menu, but he **(7) was not discussing** it with me. Gunther is a quiet man.

On our arrival to the restaurant, the building **(8) was bustling** with people. Very busy for a Wednesday night! And the staff **(9) were not handling** it well: waiters **(10) were running** around, hot-faced, and the man who welcomed us was tired and **(11) was not smiling**. Moreover, what **(12) was he wearing**? Not a smart uniform, but brightly patterned rags covered in stains. Why **(13) were the managers** dressing their staff like clowns?

Our table was at the back of the room, next to the kitchen. The door **(14) was opening and closing** constantly. Even worse, we **(15) were waiting** for fifteen minutes before a waiter gave us a menu. The writing was badly printed: **(16) how were they expecting** anyone to read this?

We used Gunther's online menu instead. By then, my stomach **(17) was rumbling**. We had to give our orders twice because the waiter **(18) was not listening**. He **(19) was watching** the other tables; with so many people there, **(20) was he planning** a route of attack?

Eventually, our order was placed: for the main course, I **(21) was having** the calzone and Gunther chose tortellini.

Our starters arrived – prawns for both of us. The prawns **(22) were swimming** in brine. Undercooked. I stood and demanded to know if they **(23) were serving** us garbage.

The waiters, of course, were too busy to notice. The other customers **(24) were becoming** noisier as the restaurant only got busier. And now, as I **(25) was standing**, I saw the food on other tables. All as bad as ours.

I told Gunther we **(26) were leaving** at once, only to discover he **(27) was eating** the vile prawns!

"It's not bad," he told me. Clearly he **(28) was not coming** with me.

He wasn't the only one happy. Other people **(29) were laughing**. They **(30) were enjoying** this cheap, busy restaurant! **(31) Were the chefs putting** something special in the food? Or **(32) was everyone not questioning** the quality because it was so cheap?

Either way, it **(33) was not fooling** me. I gathered my things and left. The last time I saw him, Gunther **(34) was devouring** my meal, too.

17.11 Answers

The complete correct text follows the numbered answers below.
1. had been looking
2. had prepared
3. had made
4. had been making
5. had reached
6. had disappeared
7. had put
8. had commented
9. had it gone
10. had taken
11. Had someone sneaked
12. had been watching
13. had not heard
14. had not been listening

15. had become
16. had left
17. had not been disturbed
18. had wanted
19. Had a squirrel come
20. Had he not noticed
21. had not found
22. had he been playing
23. had let
24. had received
25. had been dreaming
26. had thought
27. had taken
28. had he not prepared

The Mystery of the Missing Sandwich

Lunch was approaching. Xavier **(1) had been looking** forward to his sandwich all morning. He **(2) had prepared** a special sandwich today: halloumi, salad and hummus that his wife **(3) had made**. She **(4) had been making** her own hummus for years, and now it **(5) had reached** perfection.

But when Xavier opened the fridge, the sandwich **(6) had disappeared**. He stared in disbelief: he **(7) had put** it there last night. His wife **(8) had commented** on it at 9 a.m., when she took milk for her tea, "That looks nice!" Where **(9) had it gone**?

Xavier was alone that morning. His wife **(10) had taken** the train to York for the day. **(11) Had someone sneaked** in while he **(12) had been watching** TV? He **(13) had not heard** anything, but he **(14) had not been listening** carefully.

Xavier searched the house for signs of an intruder – or clues to what **(15) had become** of the missing sandwich. His daughter's room was locked, because she **(16) had left** for university a week ago. The other bedroom and the living room **(17) had not been disturbed**.

The garden door was open, because Xavier **(18) had wanted** some fresh air. He stood checking the trees. **(19) Had a squirrel come** inside and opened the fridge? **(20) Had he not noticed** a genius thief?

After searching the garden for crumbs, Xavier returned to the kitchen. He **(21) had not found** any evidence of an intruder or the sandwich's fate. Why **(22) had he been playing** the TV so loud? His distraction **(23) had let** some terrible person steal his amazing sandwich.

Finally, Xavier decided to call his wife and tell her about this tragedy. But first, he saw he **(24) had received** a message from her already.

"Thank you for preparing that lovely sandwich – it was everything I **(25) had been dreaming** of all morning!"

Xavier stared in horror. His wife **(26) had thought** the sandwich was for her. She **(27) had taken** it with her when she left! But he could only blame himself. Why **(28) had he not prepared** one for her, too?

17.12 Answers

1.
a. Neil was cycling when it started raining.
b. Neil had cycled home in the rain, so he arrived wet.
c. Neil cycled home in the rain yesterday.
d. Neil had been cycling since 9 a.m., so he stopped for lunch.

2.
a. Carla passed the salt to Jeremy after he asked for it.
b. Carla had been passing the same man all year when she walked to work.

c. Carla was passing the shop when a bracelet caught her eye.
d. Carla had passed this shop before, was she going the right way?

3.

a. Our teacher had given us a difficult assignment, so I could not go out.
b. Our teacher gave us too much homework this afternoon.
c. Our teacher had been giving us too much homework ever since term started.
d. Our teacher was giving us an exam when the bell rang.

4.

a. The band played until 3 a.m. last night.
b. The band had been playing for five hours before they had to stop.
c. The band were playing when the lights went out.
d. The band had played all the songs they knew and had to stop.

17.13 Answers

1. A) he ate dinner B) Carl washed
2. A) she was preparing B) the ambassador arrived
3. A) I had been studying B) I took
4. A) Boris closed the door B) the cat slept
5. X – simultaneous
6. A) someone had taken B) we could not enter
7. A) he was fixing B) the post arrived
8. A) she finished B) Kim went
9. A) our neighbours were talking B) they left

10. A) he had borrowed B) Roland returned
11. X – simultaneous
12. X – simultaneous
13. A) had Jim been asking B) you sent
14. X – simultaneous
15. A) what did they put B) the cake tasted

17.14 Answers

1. At 07:55 yesterday ...
a. **... Jen was on the bus. – TRUE**
b. **... Jen was listening to music. – TRUE**
c. ... Jen was checking her make-up.
d. ... Jen arrived at the Friends Centre.

2. At 9:35 yesterday ...
a. ... Jen was entertaining children.
b. **... Jen had drunk a coffee. – TRUE**
c. **... Jen was walking through town. – TRUE**
d. ... Jen had started her second job.

3. At 12:45 yesterday ...
a. **... Jen had eaten a burrito. – TRUE**
b. ... Jen was reading a magazine.
c. **... Jen had been reading a magazine. – TRUE**
d. ... Mary bought a burrito.

4. At 15:30 ...
a. ... Jen was travelling to the Friends Centre.
b. **... Jen had been visiting schools for over two hours. – TRUE**
c. ... Jen was teaching adults.
d. ... Jen finished visiting schools.

5. At 19:30 yesterday ...

a. **... Jen finished work for the day. – TRUE**

b. **... Jen had taught magic to adults. – TRUE**

c. ... Jen was cooking dinner.

d. **... Jen went to get the bus. – TRUE**

6. At 10:30 yesterday ...

a. ... Jen practised new tricks.

b. ... Jen fell asleep.

c. **... Jen had eaten dinner. – TRUE**

d. **... Jen was reading a book. – TRUE**

17.15 Answers

1. Ongoing Past Process
2. Past State
3. Past State
4. Past Action Completed Earlier
5. Past Action Completed Earlier
6. Earlier Ongoing Past Process
7. Past State
8. Past Possession
9. Past Action Completed Earlier
10. Earlier Ongoing Past Process
11. Past State
12. Earlier Past State
13. Earlier Past State
14. Earlier Ongoing Past Process
15. Past Action Completed Earlier
16. Past State
17. Past Action
18. Past Action
19. Ongoing Past Process
20. Ongoing Past Process
21. Past Action
22. Past Action
23. Ongoing Past Process
24. Past Action
25. Ongoing Past Process
26. Past Action Completed Earlier

17.16 Answers

The complete correct text follows the numbered answers below.

1. announced
2. had been meeting
3. submitted
4. loved
5. had been experiencing
6. formed
7. argued
8. had been decreasing
9. was trying
10. had drawn
11. showed
12. had gathered
13. had become
14. (had) got
15. (had) removed
16. could not
17. had improved
18. insisted
19. had asked
20. (had) visited
21. had been researching
22. had not seen
23. persuaded
24. were delaying
25. held
26. had grown
27. gave
28. led
29. was coming

A New Pier

In April, the seaside town of Trilby-on-Sea **(1) announced** plans to build a new pier. Before this decision, Trilby's council **(2) had been meeting** with local charities and tourist organisations for six months. A Scottish architect **(3) (had) submitted** designs including shops and rides. Most of the town **(4) loved** the designs, but the council were unsure. They **(5) had been experiencing** budget cuts for the past few years.

Local residents **(6) formed** a group called Pier Alliance in January to convince the council. They **(7) argued** that the new pier would bring wealth to Trilby. Visitor numbers **(8) had been decreasing** since two summers before, and everyone **(9) was trying** to find a solution. They remembered: Trilby's old pier **(10) had drawn** massive crowds, many decades ago.

Newspaper clippings **(11) showed** that hundreds of people **(12) had gathered** on the pier daily. It **(13) had become** unstable in the 1980s, when the supports **(14) (had) got** damaged in a terrible storm. The council **(15) (had) removed** the pier, saying they **(16) could not** afford to maintain it.

Technology **(17) had improved** a lot since then, so Pier Alliance **(18) insisted** the new pier would be cheaper and safer. By time of the final decision, they **(19) had asked** ten different experts to speak to the council about it. In March, a gentleman from America **(20) (had) visited** the town. He **(21) had been researching** piers for thirteen years and said he **(22) had not seen** a better design than Trilby's new proposal. Slowly, Pier Alliance **(23) persuaded** the council. The men in charge **(24) were delaying** the decision, so the town finally **(25) held** a rally to demonstrate how support **(26) had grown** for the new pier.

Finally, the council **(27) gave** in, and the April announcement **(28) led** to great celebrations. The new pier **(29) was coming** at last!

17.17 Answers

The complete correct text follows the numbered answers below.
1. had taken
2. had disappeared
3. was repairing

4. were you doing
5. were not sitting
6. Were you watching
7. had not been looking
8. had not been working
9. asked
10. was making
11. did not see
12. Had he drunk
13. suspected
14. were wandering
15. had not been
16. (had) caught
17. had told
18. had been enjoying
19. Had she let
20. Did you take
21. looked
22. had been admiring
23. had
24. was not being
25. was getting
26. grabbed
27. cried
28. had been lying
29. ran
30. was already leaving
31. was standing
32. Had he been watching
33. did he steal
34. showed
35. had been getting
36. had exposed

The Pen Thief

Vicky was certain Clive **(1) had taken** her pen. It **(2) had disappeared** while she **(3) was repairing** the printer.

"What **(4) were you doing** ten minutes ago?" Vicky asked. "You **(5) were not sitting** at your desk, I am sure."

"**(6) Were you watching** me?" Clive replied.

She **(7) had not been looking** his way, no. But he **(8) had not been working** when she fixed the printer, not if he stole her pen. She **(9) asked** him to answer her question.

"I **(10) was making** tea," he told her.

Vicky **(11) did not see** a mug of tea on his desk. **(12) Had he drunk** it already? She **(13) suspected** not. "You **(14) were wandering** around my desk, weren't you?"

"Absolutely not!" Clive protested. He **(15) had not been** near her desk since Vicky **(16) (had) caught** him stealing her paper a month ago. She **(17) had told** him to stay away, and she **(18) had been enjoying** the results ever since.

(19) Had she let her guard down too soon?

"**(20) Did you take** my pen?" she asked, plainly.

Clive shook his head, but **(21) looked** scared. "I did not, I would not, I never!"

He **(22) had been admiring** her pen ever since she bought it; it **(23) had** a platinum grip. Vicky decided he **(24) was not being** honest. But she **(25) was getting** nowhere with words. She **(26) grabbed** him quickly, and he **(27) cried** out when she found the pen in a pocket. He **(28) had been lying** all along!

Vicky **(29) ran** towards her manager, but when she got there Clive **(30) was already leaving**. The manager **(31) was standing** nearby. **(32) Had he been watching** all along?

"What **(33) did he steal** this time?" the manager asked.

Vicky **(34) showed** him the pen, and the manager sighed sadly. Clive **(35) had been getting** away with these thefts for too long. But they **(36) had exposed** him, at last.

18.1 Answers

1. My family usually eats dinner at 7 p.m.
2. He is paying for this meal.
3. Jonas teaches at St Mary's High School.
4. Our children do not play any instruments.
5. This bed always creaks noisily.
6. We are buying a new house.
7. Albert is not trying hard enough – he can do better.
8. You are sitting in my chair, please move.
9. Every time I visit Gran, she gives me sweets.
10. Her friends are not helping her this time.
11. This professor's course fills very quickly each year.
12. Sam serves food at the soup kitchen on Tuesdays.
13. I am not studying to become a lawyer anymore.
14. Why do the geese fly south each winter?
15. How is Jenna travelling through the mountains on her trip?
16. Are you choosing a new tie for the wedding ceremony?
17. Which shops do not offer non-dairy chocolates?
18. What is happening on the beach right now?
19. Who owns that bright pink car?
20. Where are your parents staying this weekend?

18.2 Answers

1. Dominic is usually so nice. Why is he being naughty?
2. The sun is setting very late this month. Usually, the sun sets earlier.
3. She refuses to say sorry. She is not apologising.
4. Harry just climbed a tree. He is swinging from a branch.
5. You will love the way Deidre cooks potatoes. She always fries them.

6. Mia has not given an answer yet – she is thinking about it.
7. I never usually buy nectarines for myself, but today I am buying some for my mother.
8. The boy is watching TV. He is not bouncing his ball.
9. "Where is my magazine?"
"I think it is lying by the sofa."
10. "We are decorating our living room."
"Oh, what colour are you painting it?"
11. "Mr Harris is not coming to dinner."
"Strange. He does not cancel often."
12. "The volleyball team surprised everyone by reaching the final."
"Do they not normally win?"
13. "Are you holding a bottle of wine?"
"No, it's a bottle of olive oil."
14. The building supervisor does not allow smoking. We are breaking the rules!
15. "I drew this picture."
"Ah, you are improving quickly!"

18.3 Answers

1. This fish tastes strange, is it old?
2. Caroline looks very elegant in her new dress.
3. My uncle is reading a biography of Julius Caesar.
4. I do not want your banana, thank you.
5. The cows are stomping on all the flowers.
6. Leo is struggling to understand algebra.
7. Our neighbours seem very quiet today.
8. Laila and Howard are not sharing their peanuts.
9. Finley has all the best Xbox games currently available.
10. The customers doubt that they are being given a good deal.
11. Eli is getting everyone a round of beers.

12. I might not go to Calcutta – I am having second thoughts about it.
13. Though she needs a new chair now, Anna is comparing all the options first.
14. We promise to deliver the table by Friday.
15. Why do my hands appear to be so dirty?
16. Does that clock need new batteries too, now?
17. Who is listening to my radio show this week?
18. What are you wearing to school today?
19. Does Maria not hear that singing bird?
20. Why do beavers love building dams?

18.4 Answers

1. She's frustrated because she is always cleaning up. (habitual action)
2. The beach is crowded today. (state)
3. It is getting dark, I don't think we should walk home. (changing state)
4. They usually eat in the dining room. (repeated event)
5. When you flick a switch, the light comes on. (general fact)
6. This cheese smells awful. (state)
7. "Now, I declare this store open!" (spoken action)
8. I am always looking for new books to read. (habitual action)
9. Our grandparents visit twice a month. (repeated event)
10. They say actions speak louder than words. (general fact)
11. The swimmers are competing for the gold medal. (temporary action)
12. I propose we take a different route home. (spoken action)
13. Gary is not home, he is walking the dog. (temporary action)

14. Seagull numbers are increasing because tourists are leaving food around. (changing state, temporary action)
15. Look, that tree is swaying in the wind! (temporary action)

18.5 Answers

1. This bread has gone mouldy.
2. Alison created a website this morning.
3. He did not sweep the floor before dinner.
4. The boiler has broken again, so there is no hot water.
5. I cannot come to class. Last time, Mr Rogers told me not to come back.
6. Nathan has passed his driving test because he did not quit.
7. My cousin hates spiders, so he has sealed all of his windows.
8. The garden has bloomed with the recent hot weather.
9. The sailors moved quickly because the winds were favourable.
10. Chloe is visiting, but she has not said how long she will stay.
11. My phone battery has died, can I use your charger?
12. She could not find her purse, so paid with her credit card.
13. Did you see? My essay has won the competition.
14. Did you receive the coffee machine you ordered?
15. We put our poster up in the hall, have you seen it?
16. Did you buy the candles when you went shopping yesterday?
17. Have you not given in your assignment yet?
18. Why has that woman taken all the baguettes? There are none left!
19. Lola is telling everyone about her new job, has she spoken to you about it?
20. Did the farmer deliver that milk, or have you been to the shop?

18.6 Answers

1. I was going to pottery classes earlier this year.
2. Tristan was printing fake money and now he is in jail.
3. You have been working too hard this month, take a break.
4. She was not helping her dad build the shed until Friday.
5. The teenagers were cleaning the streets last week. Are they back?
6. Hundreds of thousands of people have been signing the petition. It could reach a million by tomorrow.
7. We have been taking lessons since January, to improve our pronunciation.
8. The king was avoiding his responsibilities, so a committee was formed.
9. The ivy has been spreading over our wall. We must cut it back before it gets worse.
10. They have not been opening the window – it stinks in here!
11. Were you waiting here before me?
12. Has the museum been showing this exhibit for long?
13. Have the children been bothering you today?
14. Was the wheel squeaking when you used the bike?

18.7 Answers

1. Who left this bag here? It has left a stain.
2. You have not convinced me to come to the game.
3. I know Germany well, because I lived there for six months last year.
4. The car just made an awful noise – I think we hit a log.

5. She was sure about it: Simon broke the vase.
6. I could not bring the book home. The librarian refused to lend it to me.
7. This kitchen is unsanitary. Rats have infested the cellar.
8. My phone has stopped working. Can I borrow yours?
9. What is in the oven? Have you cooked potatoes?
10. Who designed these wonderful curtains? Did you do them?
11. Someone is stealing my socks. Did Billie take them?
12. How is your degree? Has it got any easier?

18.8 Answers

1. We have been using this washing machine for fifteen years.
2. I am walking to work for the whole week, starting today.
3. She is considering which scarf to buy.
4. The couple have been shopping for a while.
5. William has not been playing computer games for very long.
6. You have been watching me since I came in – stop it!
7. Alice is buying doughnuts every day this week, we have decided.
8. That man is selling hats at a discount for the next two hours.
9. You've been quiet. Have you been reading all morning?
10. I need the car later. Are you using it all day?
11. She has been unwell for weeks. Has she not been taking her medicine?
12. Why is he asking me so many questions right now?

18.9 Answers

1. Martha has opened six shops in Brighton.

2. We have stayed in hotels many times this year.
3. The sea has been getting warmer all summer.
4. He has not gone to class a single time this week.
5. You have washed the dishes twice today.
6. I have not been receiving as many letters as I used to, and hope that will change.
7. Claudia has been spying on her brother for fifteen minutes.
8. Eliot has not watched any television since yesterday.
9. Margaret has been studying her geography textbook since last Wednesday.
10. You have been putting your shoes in the wrong cupboard for months.
11. The boy has given his teacher an apple once a week this year.
12. The girl has been taking the bus to school almost every day this year, but sometimes walks.
13. How many times have they said they would repair the road?
14. Have you been bowling in Oxford recently?
15. Has she been cutting her hair short for a long time?
16. How long have the clients been waiting for? Get them some water!

18.10 Answers

1. We have loved each other for twenty years.
2. They have believed in magic ever since they saw the Great Roberto perform.
3. I have been listening to rap music for the past three weeks.
4. Axel has been tired since he woke up.
5. She has been reading Victorian ghost stories all night.

6. You have not been relaxing during this holiday.
7. Doris has heard all the children's speeches today.
8. What has Carter been doing in his shed all morning?
9. How long have they known about the secret passage for?
10. Why have we not understood everything he has been saying?
11. How long has that fox been sitting on our fence for?
12. Have the villagers seemed restless for long?

18.11 Answers

1. Correct – repetitive action
2. Correct – repetitive action
3. Correct – *let me explain* refers to a perceived temporary problem
4. Incorrect – *never* implies it is timeless
5. Correct – appearances can be temporary
6. Correct – the smell can be temporary
7. Correct – the repeated occurrence can be temporary
8. Incorrect – *flood* implies a general rule, not a temporary situation
9. Correct – an informal question within the moment
10. Incorrect – the belief is not temporary
11. Incorrect – the liking of the gift is not temporary
12. Correct – an informal question within the moment

18.12 Answers

1.
a. The pie is cooling on the shelf.
b. The pie has cooled enough to eat.
c. The pie has been cooling for an hour already.
d. When the pie cools, we can eat it.

2.
a. Tania has had her dinner, and is going to bed.
b. Tania has been having strange dreams constantly this week.
c. Tania has lots of friends, because she is nice.
d. Tania is having a party, so no one can sleep.

3.
a. The professor is studying a new language right now.
b. The professor has studied ten languages already.
c. The professor studies languages as a hobby.
d. The professor has been studying languages for 50 years.

4.
a. What have you done with my pen? I can't find it.
b. What are you doing with my pen? Use your own!
c. What do you do with my pen when you borrow it? It always comes back wet!
d. What have you been doing with my pen? You've had it all morning.

18.13 Answers

1. X – simultaneous
2. A) the teacher has marked B) my sister is asking
3. A) the TV is not working B) he is reading (A caused B)
4. A) we have been visiting B) it is getting more crowded
5. A) which has been B) my mother cooks
6. X – simultaneous
7. A) I have been complaining B) they are repairing
8. A) Lottie has learned B) she is wandering

9. A) have you seen B) what are you watching
10. X – simultaneous

18.14 Answers

The complete correct text follows the numbered answers below.
1. writes
2. is working
3. has become
4. has granted
5. has been researching
6. has
7. is editing
8. include
9. do you like
10. has fame changed
11. do you get
12. have you been writing
13. do you not like
14. is
15. seem
16. Has Reid not heard
17. has been touring
18. has met
19. wants
20. comes
21. has lived
22. gives
23. is now funding
24. fears
25. has not visited
26. frightens
27. do her readers care
28. have only been raising
29. Is Emma making
30. thinks
31. has been
32. has been wasting
33. has been waiting

A Difficult Interview

Emma **(1) writes** for the Daily Sentinel newspaper. She **(2) is working** on a feature article about pop icon, Natalie Reid. It is a very important piece for the newspaper, because Reid **(3) has become** one of the most famous musicians in the world, and she **(4) has granted** Emma an exclusive interview. Emma **(5) has been researching** the singer for a month, to make sure she **(6) has** an informed set of questions to ask.

Today, Emma **(7) is editing** her interview questions. Some of her examples **(8) include**:

What **(9) do you like** to do in your free time?

How **(10) has fame changed** your life?

Where **(11) do you get** your ideas from?

How long **(12) have you been writing** music for?

What **(13) do you not like** about being famous?

Emma **(14) is** worried, because these questions **(15) seem** too ordinary. **(16) Has Reid not heard** them a hundred times before? Reid **(17) has been touring** the world for the past six months. She **(18) has met** thousands of people who probably asked the same things.

Emma **(19) wants** to ask something different. Reid **(20) comes** from an unusual background; she **(21) has lived** in a poor neighbourhood all her life, and **(22) gives** generously to charities. The singer **(23) is now funding** the construction of new housing. But Emma **(24) fears** asking questions about these topics, because she **(25) has not visited** Reid's neighbourhood herself. The area **(26) frightens** her. And **(27) do her readers care** about these things? On social media, Reid's fans **(28) have only been raising** questions about her relationships for the past few months.

(29) Is Emma making things too complicated?

No, Emma **(30) thinks**, now; it's time to get on with it. She **(31) has been** foolish to avoid these topics. And she **(32) has been wasting** time worrying about it. Most likely, Reid **(33) has been waiting** for someone to ask the important questions!

18.15 Answers

Barry **gets** to work at 6 p.m. He **talks** with the teachers, **if they are** still in the school.

Barry **starts** work by vacuuming all the carpets. He **lifts** the chairs onto tables to clear the floors, and **empties** the bins in each room. Barry **wipes** the boards clean, **if it is** necessary.

Then, Barry **sweeps** the tiled floors in the corridors and halls. **On Fridays (or Because it is Friday)**, he **mops** these floors. He **uses** two buckets, one for soapy water and one for rinsing.

Once all the floors **are** finished, Barry **cleans** the washrooms. He **sprays** them with disinfectant and **scrubs** the toilets. He **replaces** the soap and toilet paper **when they run out (or if they have run out)**.

After his cleaning duties **are** finished, Barry **usually takes** a break at the time as the headmistress. He **makes** tea for himself and the headmistress **when (or if) he gets** to the common room first. If the headmistress **arrives** first, she **prepares** the tea. Barry **usually reads** a book during the break, but **if he forgets** to bring one, he **listens** to the radio.

After his break, Barry **focuses** on more varied tasks. Firstly, he **completes** repairs, such as on doors, furniture or fences. **During winter**, Barry **spreads** grit outside to stop the paths getting slippery. **During summer**, he **cuts** weeds and **prunes** hedges.

Barry **normally finishes** work at 9 p.m., but **stays** later **if there are** extra tasks to do. **Sometimes**, teachers **need** help moving furniture or preparing equipment for a class. The teachers and Barry **do** these tasks together. He **gets** paid extra for this.

18.16 Answers

The complete correct text follows the numbered answers below.
1. are joining
2. are fielding
3. have performed
4. have been competing
5. qualifies
6. open
7. are taking
8. chase
9. move
10. has
11. is sprinting
12. faces
13. is closing
14. clash
15. steals
16. is making
17. is
18. are letting
19. races
20. has hit
21. is rolling
22. has stopped
23. are gathering
24. has pushed
25. have got
26. is blowing
27. is showing
28. Is the referee handling
29. seems
30. have calmed
31. goes
32. has not broken
33. has scored
34. has saved
35. have both been practising
36. steps
37. shoots

38. scores
39. have taken
40. promises

Doves United vs The Firecats: Live Commentary

You **(1) are joining** us live for an exciting match between two women's soccer teams, Doves United and The Firecats. They **(2) are fielding** strong teams today, and both teams **(3) have performed** brilliantly to reach this semi-final. They **(4) have been competing** since June 1st for a chance at the championship trophy, and today's match decides who **(5) qualifies** for the final!

Doves United **(6) are opening** the game, they **(7) are taking** the kick-off now. The Firecats **(8) chase** them right away; oh my, these women **(9) move** fast!

United's captain, Morales, **(10) has** the ball, and she **(11) is sprinting** up the right flank. But she **(12) faces** trouble! Firecats defender Lux **(13) is closing** on Morales. They **(14) clash**! Lux **(15) steals** the ball and she **(16) is making** a break. The United team **(17) is** spread out; they **(18) are letting** her through!

Lux **(19) races** into the penalty box – only the keeper to beat!

Oh no! Lux is down! United's centre-half **(20) has hit** her from behind. An awful foul! Lux **(21) is rolling** on the floor, she could be injured. The referee **(22) has stopped** play, and The Firecats **(23) are gathering** in their opponent's half. Someone is shouting – someone else is on the floor. Another player **(24) has pushed** her over! Things **(25) have got** out of hand.

The referee **(26) is blowing** her whistle! She **(27) is showing** the red card to United's centre-half. And to a Firecats player! **(28) Is the referee handling** this well? Yes. It **(29) seems** she has everything under control again.

The players **(30) have calmed** down. Play will resume with a penalty.

Lux **(31) goes** to the penalty spot, apparently she **(32) has not broken** any bones. This is an exciting pairing – Lux **(33) has scored** eight out of her last nine penalties in this tournament, but the United keeper **(34) has saved** nine out of her last ten! No doubt they **(35) have both been practising** very hard. Lux **(36) steps** back from the ball, ready to strike! She **(37) shoots** – she **(38) scores**!

One minute in, The Firecats **(39) have taken** the lead! This game **(40) promises** to be thrilling.

18.17 Answers

The complete correct text follows the numbered answers below.
1. Do you want
2. delivers
3. prepare
4. combine
5. begin
6. reacts
7. takes
8. want
9. warm
10. goes
11. affects
12. touch
13. gives
14. Have you mixed
15. You've created
16. absorbs
17. do we develop
18. doesn't require
19. Place
20. takes
21. Isn't
22. Put
23. becomes
24. needs

25. you've formed
26. rises
27. does the dough spring
28. use
29. traps
30. goes
31. opens
32. remove
33. produces
34. makes
35. Does it sound
36. Don't eat
37. Rest
38. you've baked

How to Bake a Perfect Loaf

(1) Do you want to make a perfect loaf of bread? This recipe **(2) delivers** great results.

To make life easier, **(3) prepare** your ingredients in advance: 500g of strong flour, 8g of yeast, 300ml of water and 10g of salt. These simple ingredients **(4) combine** for a basic but delicious loaf.

Before you **(5) begin**, a word about temperature. When it is hot, the mixture **(6) reacts** faster. On colder days, the recipe **(7) takes** longer to complete. For balance, we **(8) want** the mixture to be about 75 degrees. If you **(9) warm** the water, you can manage this temperature.

Step one: combine the water and the yeast in a bowl. The flour **(10) goes** in next, then the salt on top of the flour. This order is important, because the salt **(11) affects** the yeast if they **(12) touch** directly.

Mix the ingredients: you can use a spoon, but hand mixing **(13) gives** you a better feel for the results.

(14) Have you mixed it thoroughly now? **(15) You've created** a dough! Leave it for about 20 minutes: during this time, the flour **(16) absorbs** water.

Next: how **(17) do we develop** gluten? This recipe **(18) doesn't require** kneading, but uses folding instead. **(19) Place** the dough on a floured counter and fold one side to about halfway in. Turn 90 degrees and fold again. It **(20) takes** two or three turns, usually, until you have a tight ball. **(21) Isn't** that easy?

(22) Put the dough back in the bowl, covered by a towel, and leave it to rise for about 90 minutes. When the dough **(23) becomes** light and airy, it is ready. Back on the counter, where it **(24) needs** to be folded again, like a letter. Fold to the centre, then turn, until you **(25) you've formed** a tight parcel.

Now, the dough **(26) rises** one more time – leave it for another hour to 90 minutes. When you press it with a finger, **(27) does the dough spring** back? Then it is ready.

We **(28) use** a Dutch Oven to do the cooking, preheated to 475 degrees. A Dutch Oven **(29) traps** steam with a lid, for the best results. The dough **(30) goes** in seam side up. The seam **(31) opens** during cooking to give a nice rustic look.

Put the Dutch Oven and dough in the oven for 25 minutes, then **(32) remove** the lid. Another 15–20 minutes in the oven **(33) produces** a golden loaf with a firm crust. A properly cooked loaf **(34) makes** a hollow thump when you tap the base.

(35) Does it sound done? **(36) Don't eat** it yet! **(37) Rest** the loaf on a wire rack for 30 minutes, so the interior crumb can set, making it easier to cut. Congratulations: **(38) you've baked** a perfect loaf!

19.1 Answers

1. Because Lucas is tired, Regina will make him a tea.

2. This Halloween, Tina is going to dress as a zombie.
3. My brother is outside, will you let him in?
4. Those men have used the wrong timber. The house is going to collapse.
5. Claire thinks her boss will like her latest report.
6. Is that a woodpecker in the tree? I will get my binoculars to check.
7. Despite the cold summer, the building managers are not going to activate the heating until October.
8. We've been looking forward to our train journey; we are going to travel across the Swiss Alps.
9. When Paul gets back from Scotland, he is going to start a new job.
10. Tim's parents said he cannot go outside for a month, so he is going to play computer games every weekend.
11. I would like to go climbing, but I will wait and see if this rain stops!
12. The swimming pool is always busy; it is going to be busy today, I am sure.
13. "Where are you going with that knife?"
14. "I am going to cut a piece of birthday cake."
15. "What drink would you like?"
16. "I will have a cocktail."
17. "Where can I complain about the smell in our room?"
18. "The lady behind the counter will help you."

19.2 Answers

1. Dawn is visiting her parents next Tuesday.
2. Our bus arrives at 12 noon.
3. The family is staying home next Christmas.
4. Ian is not working during the following three weekends.
5. The meeting this afternoon involves every department.
6. Hurry, the play starts at 8 p.m. and I don't want to be late!
7. Everyone is waiting for Cathy, because she is bringing champagne.
8. The ghost appears at sundown, we must be ready.
9. Construction work begins on the new apartment block tomorrow.
10. Are you coming to the dance on Thursday?
11. Is Adrian giving the speech this evening?
12. Are we meeting for a piano class in the morning?
13. Does the train leave at three or four?
14. Is your new girlfriend joining us for dinner?
15. Does the post office deliver today?

19.3 Answers

1. "We need volunteers to clean the beach."
   "I'll do it if I have time."
2. "Izzy is on holiday next week."
   "Oh, is she travelling somewhere nice?"
3. "Will our bus get to the airport in time?"
   "I think so, check in closes in half an hour."
4. "Have you heard the weather forecast?"
   "Yes, they said it's going to rain."
5. "My aunt is in town this Friday. What should we do?"
   "The museum is running an exhibition on Victorian clothes, you could try that."
6. "What time should we leave for the game on Saturday?"
   "Early – the rail workers are on strike this weekend."

7. "I need to go home and feed my cats. What time does this show finish?"
8. "Do you know we've run out of printer paper?"
   "Yes, I'm going to buy some this afternoon."
9. "Are you okay? You look very pale."
   "No, I'm going to be sick!"
10. "Can you come with me to the ballet performance?"
    "Unfortunately not, I'm playing golf this afternoon."
11. "Have you seen the mess on our window?"
    "No, I'll clean it in a minute."
12. "Why are you writing in such a rush?"
    "Because the show starts in half an hour!"
13. "Shall we check out Dover Castle tomorrow?"
    "I can't, I'm working all day tomorrow."
14. "Does anyone want to go for an ice cream?"
    "Me, I'll come!"

19.4 Answers

1. I will meet you in the park later. (*or* I am going to meet / am meeting you in the park later)
2. He is going to sell me his car. (*or* He will sell me his car.)
3. They will be playing hockey for hours. (*or* They are going to be playing hockey for hours.)
4. It is going to be getting colder over the next two weeks. (*or* It will be getting colder over the next two weeks.)
5. The college will accept new students in September. (*or* The college is going to accept / is accepting new students in September.)

6. We are meeting up and travelling together – our friends will already be waiting at the station for us.
7. Rebecca will be staying in the Hilton while she's in town. (*or* Rebecca is going to be staying in the Hilton while she's in town.)
8. The mayor is going to open the new leisure centre this Wednesday. (*or* The mayor will open / is opening the new leisure centre this Wednesday.)
9. My wife will cook dinner this evening, as I won't come back until late. (*or* My wife is going to be cooking / is cooking dinner this evening, as I won't come back until late.)
10. Sean cannot visit his gran until 6 p.m. because she will be eating before then. (*or* Sean cannot visit his gran until 6 p.m. because she is going to be eating before then.)
11. Will you be working this Sunday? (*or* Are you going to be / Are you working this Sunday?)
12. Are they going to deliver all the bread before 6 a.m.? (*or* Will they deliver / Are they delivering all the bread before 6 a.m.)
13. Will she be driving at 3 p.m., in case we need to call? (*or* Is she going to be driving at 3 p.m., in case we need to call?)
14. Will Frank be hiking in Scotland all weekend? (*or* Is Frank going to be hiking / Is Frank hiking in Scotland all weekend?)
15. Will I make the right choice next time? (*or* Am I going to make the right choice this time?)

19.5 Answers

1. Shirley will take her exams in June. She will have graduated by August.

2. Our parents will visit at Christmas. They will bring presents.
3. You are going to buy some new shoes. Will you have earned enough money?
4. The tide will be highest at 11 a.m., because it will have come all the way in.
5. Brenda is going to have baked a cake before the party. She will make it from scratch.
6. Ulrich will have passed his test by 1 p.m. We are going to throw him a party.
7. Workers will close the high street this evening. They are going to divert traffic.
8. I hope the weather will improve tomorrow. They say it is going to rain in the morning.
9. Are you going to tell Jon about the wedding soon? By next week, he will have heard it from someone else.
10. Will you have repaired your door before you go away? You will not leave with it in that state, will you?

19.6 Answers

1. My parents will have been living together for 20 years this October.
2. The fishermen will be returning in 15 minutes.
3. You are going to be studying all evening.
4. He will have been trying to fix the sink all day before he admits he needs help.
5. By the time of the competition, Sally is going to have been training for eighteen months.
6. I am going to be travelling for three days, so I won't be able to call.
7. The cat will be sleeping in the loft during the party.

8. Inflation will have been rising for five months by February.
9. Colin is going to have been walking all day if he reaches the seaside by sunset.
10. At midnight, we will be watching the fireworks.
11. At noon, we will have been waiting for Robert for an hour.
12. The days will be getting shorter in September.

19.7 Answers

1. The eggs will have been sitting in the fridge for a month by the weekend.
2. I will have written my essay by 5 p.m.
3. Eric will have been researching Vikings for two years before he writes his book.
4. The tourists will have visited all the pubs in town before they go home.
5. You won't see any birds, because they will have migrated south for the winter.
6. Before long, Ola will have been searching for her missing sock for a week.
7. We will have been talking for two hours when Jim joins us.
8. If it survives much longer, the tree will have been growing for fifteen years.
9. By the time we leave school, our teacher will have taught us everything.
10. Peggy will have been demanding a pony for three months by her birthday.

19.8 Answers

1.
a. I am going to buy a house once I save up enough money.
b. I am going to have bought a house by September, you can come visit in October!

c. I am going to be buying a house this summer, so won't have much free time.

d. I am going to have been buying houses all summer – I'll be exhausted in autumn!

2.

a. Clarence is joining us this evening – shall we make a soup?

b. Clarence will have been driving all day – will he want to rest when he gets here?

c. Clarence will have eaten on the way, he won't want dinner.

d. Clarence will be staying in the guest room – please prepare the bed.

3.

a. The post office is going to open a new store in June.

b. The post office is going to have moved to a new store by June.

c. The post office is going to be too busy opening their new store to serve customers.

d. The post office is going to have been opening new stores all year, come New Year.

4.

a. The new phone will have sold out by Tuesday.

b. The new phone will be impressing customers all month.

c. The new phone will come with a velvet carry case.

d. The new phone will have been selling for two months by January.

19.9 Answers

1. A) they finish playing B) they will come

2. A) the last guest leaves B) the party will finish

3. A) we last another summer B) we will have been married

4. A) the van is fixed B) Tim will drive

5. A) they will have been working B) the company releases

6. X – simultaneous

7. A) the banks calls B) I will come back

8. A) the referee arrives B) the match will start

9. X – simultaneous

10. A) they have inspected B) our luggage will be cleared

11. X – simultaneous

12. A) Larry collect B) the shop closes

13. B) your passes will have been ordered B) who is attending

14. A) we will have to pay B) does the train leave

15. A) will she have seen B) Aunt Gina leaves

19.10 Answers

1. After you take a nap, you will feel a lot better.

2. You need to finish your work before you go home at 6 p.m.

3. I think I will buy bread from the corner shop when it opens.

4. We are having a garden party on Sunday, weather permitting. (*or* We will have / are going to have a garden party on Sunday, weather permitting.)

5. Before we start our lesson, we are going to review yesterday's class. (*or* Before we start our lesson, we will review yesterday's class.)

6. We will be sitting in the shelter when the bus comes.

7. I'm very sorry, it seems Dr. Jones will not come back until 2 p.m.

8. I don't think you will have any problems when you land in Boston. (*or* I don't think you are going to have

any problems when you land in
Boston.)
9. On Friday at 8 o'clock, I am meeting
my friend. (*or* On Friday at 8 o'clock,
I am going to meet / will meet my
friend.)
10. The English lesson starts at 8:45. (as a
schedule)
11. Look at the clouds – it is going to rain
in a few minutes. (*or* Look at the
clouds – it will rain in a few minutes.)
12. When you get off the train, I will be
waiting for you by the ticket machine.
(*or* When you get off the train, I am
going to be waiting for you by the
ticket machine.)
13. You are going to take your children
with you to France, aren't you? (*or*
You are taking your children with you
to France, aren't you?)
14. This time next week, I will be skiing
in Switzerland!
15. Now I will check my answers. (*or* Now
I am going to check my answers.)

19.11 Answers

1. The train arrives at 12:30. (as a
schedule)
2. We are going to eat dinner at a
seaside restaurant on Sunday. (*or* are
eating / will eat)
3. It will be snowing in Brighton
throughout the parade. (*or* is going to
be snowing)
4. By the time we get home, they will
have been playing football for 30
minutes.
5. Paul is flying to London on Monday
morning. (*or* is going to to fly)
6. Wait! I will drive you to the station.
7. This summer, I will have been living
in Goring for four years.
8. The baby should be due soon, next
week Erin will have been pregnant for
nine months.

9. Are you still writing your essay? If you
finish by 4 p.m., we will go for a walk.
10. I am going to see my mother in April.
(*or* I am seeing / will see my mother
in April.)
11. In three years, I am going to live in a
different country. (*or* In three years, I
will be living in a different country.)
12. When they get married in March, they
will have known each other for six
years.
13. You're carrying too much. I will open
the door for you.
14. Do you think the teacher will have
marked our homework by Monday
morning?
15. When I see you tomorrow, I will
show you my new book.

19.12 Answers

1. At 10.35, the Robinsons ...
a. ... will be parking the car.
b. **... will have walked into town.
– TRUE**
c. **... will be having tea. – TRUE**
d. ... are seeing the cathedral.

2. At 12.40, the Robinsons ...
a. **... will be in "The Old Vine". –
TRUE**
b. ... will have been touring the
cathedral for an hour.
c. ... are going to explore the town.
d. ... are going to have finished
lunch.

3. At 15.15, the Robinsons ...
a. ... will be heading home.
b. **... are going to be seeing the
old mill. – TRUE**
c. **... will have been exploring
Winchester for over three
hours. – TRUE**
d. **... will have eaten lunch. –
TRUE**

4. At 18.00, the Robinsons ...
a. ... are going to be driving.
b. **... will arrive home. – TRUE**
c. ... will have eaten dinner.
d. **... will have travelled for two hours or more. – TRUE**

19.13 Answers

1. At 10:00, the guests will start to arrive.
2. Between 10:00 and 10:30, the ushers will be helping people to find seats.
3. When the ceremony begins, the bride will have had about 30 minutes to get ready.
4. By 11:20, the ceremony will have been running for almost an hour.
5. At 11:35, the ceremony will have ended and the couple will be signing their documents.
6. All the guests will move to McGruber House after the photos have been taken.
7. The couple will host welcome drinks in the Library Hall.
8. Everyone will have taken a seat in the Banquet Hall before lunch is served.
9. The jazz band will be playing during lunch.
10. At 15:00, the groom will give his speech. The other speeches will follow.
11. A magician will be performing tricks while the jazz band is playing in the Library Hall.
12. Someone will have cleared the dance floor before the couple's first dance.
13. A taco van will be providing more food later in the evening, in case guests get hungry.
14. When the party finishes, people will have been dancing for hours.
15. The bus will return guests to their hotels at the end of the night.

19.14 Answers

The complete correct text follows the numbered answers below.
1. Are you going to come (*or* Are you coming)
2. I'll join
3. we're taking (*or* we'll take)
4. I'll check
5. you'll be working
6. It'll only take
7. The bus will have arrived
8. I'm going to use
9. are you going
10. I'm playing
11. You're meeting
12. will I do
13. Aren't you going to see (*or* Aren't you seeing)
14. I'll invite
15. She's coming
16. She'll have
17. You'll be enjoying
18. Won't she be
19. she won't have been travelling
20. I'll make
21. I'm going to cook (emphatic)
22. I'll prepare
23. you'll have barely started
24. We'll order
25. The bus leaves
26. I'll look

Plans for the Day

Lucy: **(1) Are you going to come (*or* Are you coming)** with me to the lake today?
Charles: I've finished my work, so **(2) I'll join** you, yes. Shall I drive?
Lucy: No, **(3) we're taking (*or* we'll take)** the bus. The car is making funny noises.
Charles: **(4) I'll check** it out, maybe I can fix it.
Lucy: Oh, don't – **(5) you'll be working** on the car for hours!

Charles: **(6) It'll only take** a few minutes, I'm sure.

Lucy: **(7) The bus will have arrived** before you finish.

Charles: But **(8) I'm going to use** the car this evening, too. I'd best get it working.

Lucy: This evening? Where **(9) are you going**?

Charles: **(10) I'm playing** poker at Gilbert's, from 8 o'clock until late.

Lucy: **(11) You're meeting** your friends? What **(12) will I do**?

Charles: **(13) Aren't you going to see (or Aren't you seeing)** a play this evening?

Lucy: Oh no, that was cancelled weeks ago. Perhaps **(14) I'll invite** Janet round. **(15) She's coming** back from Ireland today.

Charles: Great! **(16) She'll have** lots of stories, I'd like to see her.

Lucy: But **(17) you'll be enjoying** your game instead.

Charles: Maybe she could come another day. **(18) Won't she be** tired this evening?

Lucy: Ireland isn't far – **(19) she won't have been travelling** too long. And **(20) I'll make** her some dinner.

Charles: A meal, too? No – **(21) I'm going to cook** this evening, and **(22) I'll prepare** more for you two.

Lucy: **(23) You'll have barely started** before you have to go to poker, I'm sure! It's fine. **(24) We'll order** a takeaway, if we have to. Now, are you coming to the lake? **(25) The bus leaves** in around ten minutes.

Charles: Okay, okay! **(26) I'll look** at the car later.

19.15 Answers

*The future tenses can be flexible, so the answers below are recommended based on the tense, with explanations. In most cases the **will / to be going to / present continuous** forms may be interchangeable or may not impact the meaning significantly. There is also some flexibility between the **simple** and **continuous** forms shifting focus from the arranged event to the process. This is one reason that the **present continuous** form is so useful for future meanings, as it describes an arrangement and also a process.*

The complete correct text follows the numbered answers below.

1. finishes (present simple – scheduled)
2. has (present simple – scheduled)
3. is going to (future simple – arrangement)
4. is going to study (future simple – arrangement)
5. will last (future simple or present simple – scheduled)
6. qualifies (present simple – time clause)
7. is going to get (future simple – arrangement)
8. is working (future simple or continuous – arrangement / process)
9. is going to save (future simple – determined arrangement)
10. is letting (future simple – arrangement)
11. is travelling (future simple or continuous – arrangement / process)
12. is not working (future simple or continuous – arrangement / process)
13. will be exploring (future continuous – process)
14. meets (present simple – time clause)
15. will have been travelling (future perfect continuous – duration)
16. will have visited (future perfect – completed event)

17. is continuing (future simple or continuous – arrangement / process)
18. will come (future simple – arrangement)
19. have seen (future perfect – completed event)
20. will travel (future simple – arrangement)
21. will make (future simple – arrangement)
22. will be swimming (future continuous – process)
23. hiking (future continuous – process)
24. stays (present simple – time clause)
25. is going to read (future simple – arrangement)
26. moves (present simple – time clause)
27. will have completed (future perfect – completed event)
28. meets (present simple – possibility)

Summer Plans

Amber (1) finishes school in the middle of July. She (2) has three months of holiday, then she (3) is going to university in the autumn. She (4) is going to study Law in Oxford. The course (5) will last four years, and once she (6) qualifies Amber (7) is going to get a job in London.

Over the summer, Amber (8) is working in the local garden centre. She (9) is going to save money for university, and also to travel. The garden centre (10) is letting her take two weeks off in August. During that break, she (11) is travelling to France with her friends, Holly and Jaime.

All three friends have different plans for the trip. Holly (12) is not working this summer, and (13) will be exploring Europe for two months. When Amber (14) meets her in France, she (15) will have been travelling for three weeks already. She (16) will have visited

Germany and Italy, and after France she (17) is continuing to Spain.

Jaime only has one week of holiday, so she (18) will come later, after Amber and Holly (19) have seen Paris. They (20) will travel south together, to stay by a lake. Amber hopes it (21) will make her fit before university, as the girls (22) will be swimming and (23) hiking every day – as long the weather (24) stays good. She (25) is going to read books to prepare for her course, too. By the time Amber (26) moves to Oxford, she (27) will have completed all the advance reading.

Unless she (28) meets a nice young man to distract her!

19.16 Answers

The future tenses can be flexible, so the answers below are recommended based on the tense, with explanations. In most cases the **will / to be going to / present continuous** *may be interchangeable or may not impact the meaning significantly. One form can be more appropriate than another, however, for example when using* **to be going to** *to emphasise determination, or* **will** *to show casual plans that we may not be fully certain about. There is also flexibility between the* **simple** *and* **perfect** *forms, as the perfect tense is rarely absolutely necessary.*

The complete correct text follows the numbered answers below.

1. hits
2. will finish
3. will study
4. are testing
5. are going to finalise
6. will go
7. are going to host
8. will be serving
9. will be wearing

10. will not complete
11. will be making
12. will have been playing
13. is not going to complain
14. are going to release
15. have not been corrected
16. will have invested
17. will give
18. will not have tried
19. are going to make
20. will be
21. will have been working
22. will celebrate
23. will change
24. are going to dress
25. are going to ask
26. will happen
27. will entertain
28. will have fixed

An End in Sight

The computer game *Badger Spies* **(1) hits** the shelves in three months. Over the next month, the developers **(2) will finish** building the game so they can test it. Beta players **(3) will study** the game in detail, trying to spot problems. While they **(4) are testing** the game, the marketing team **(5) are going to finalise** an ambitious marketing campaign.

Badger Spies **(6) will go** on sale in thirteen countries, to start with, including the USA, the UK and Germany. The developers **(7) are going to host** a big launch party for the many releases, where they **(8) will be serving** food and drinks inspired by the game. The staff at the party **(9) will be wearing** costumes from the *Badger Spies* world.

Not everyone is in a party mood, though. One designer, Rupert, worries they **(10) will not complete** the game in time. He expects he **(11) will be making** improvements until the last minute, which means the beta players **(12) will** have been playing an incomplete version for months before they report. He **(13) is not going to complain** to the team leader about it, though. They **(14) are going to release** the game on the set date, even if the mistakes **(15) have not been corrected**. The company **(16) will have invested** too much time and money in the marketing to slow down.

Rupert worries about the marketing campaign, too. It **(17) will give** people the wrong impression of the game, he thinks. The marketing team **(18) will not have tried** the game, and have not discussed it with the design team. The boss announced, with great determination, that they **(19) are going to make** it sexy. Rupert does not think *Badger Spies* **(20) will be** a sexy game.

Maybe he just feels negative because he is tired. By the time the game is out, Rupert and his team **(21) will have been working** on the project for almost three years. Whether the game is good or not, he **(22) will celebrate** finally being able to do something else. But the rest of the team are optimistic. The boss says *Badger Spies* **(23) will change** everything – children **(24) are going to dress** in badger costumes and movie producers **(25) are going to ask** for the rights to make a film. Rupert does hope all of that **(26) will happen**. Mostly, though, he hopes the game **(27) will entertain** people, and that by the release day they **(28) will have fixed** all the errors.

20.1 Answers

1. Completed action
2. Future action
3. Future action
4. Present rule
5. Present rule
6. Present state
7. Completed action

8. Present rule
9. Future action
10. Completed action
11. Future action
12. Past state
13. Present state
14. Future action
15. Completed action
16. Future state
17. Present rule
18. Future state
19. Completed action
20. Past state

20.2 Answers

1. Future arrangement
2. Temporary / ongoing process
3. Temporary / ongoing process
4. Temporary / ongoing process
5. Process of change
6. Future arrangement
7. Emphatic repeated action
8. Emphatic repeated action
9. Future arrangement
10. Temporary / ongoing process
11. Temporary / ongoing process
12. Temporary / ongoing process
13. Future arrangement
14. Temporary / ongoing process
15. Process of change
16. Process of change
17. Temporary / ongoing process
18. Temporary / ongoing process
19. Future arrangement
20. Temporary / ongoing process

20.3 Answers

1. Past affecting the present
2. Ongoing state / activity
3. Past affecting the present
4. Past state duration
5. Past affecting the present
6. Ongoing state / activity
7. Completed at a past time
8. Completed at a future time
9. Completed at a past time
10. Past affecting the present
11. Duration of ongoing activity
12. Past state duration
13. Completed at a future time
14. Ongoing state / activity
15. Completed at a future time
16. Past state duration
17. Completed at a past time
18. Duration of ongoing activity

20.4 Answers

1. Present process started in the past
2. Duration of present process
3. Completed past process
4. Duration of future process
5. Present process started in the past
6. Duration of future process
7. Duration of present process
8. Completed past process
9. Duration of present process
10. Completed past process
11. Duration of future process
12. Completed past process
13. Duration of future process
14. Present process started in the past
15. Duration of present process
16. Present process started in the past
17. Duration of future process
18. Present process started in the past
19. Duration of present process
20. Completed past process

20.5 Answers

1.
a. Dave is driving to work, so he cannot answer his phone.
b. Dave drove to work and has parked under the tree.
c. Dave was driving to work when he heard the news on the radio.
d. Dave drives to work most days, but not today.

2.

a. The museum opened to the public last December.

b. The museum opens on Tuesdays at 8 a.m.

c. The museum has opened a new wing where you can see old costumes.

d. The museum was opening late on Thursdays until funding ran out.

3.

a. That student has read everything on the reading list already.

b. The student is reading what looks like a very long book.

c. The student read ten books last month.

d. The student had read the book before class started.

4.

a. Becca wanted to travel but could not afford it.

b. Becca has wanted to travel since she was very young.

c. Becca is travelling around Europe right now.

d. Becca was travelling through Spain when her car broke down.

20.6 Answers

1. They paint the pier every year.
2. Norman is cleaning his house this week.
3. I have been listening to classical music since I was a child.
4. The fisherman caught a huge salmon last night.
5. We were discussing philosophy, but it became too confusing.
6. You were whistling a funny tune when you came in, what was it?
7. Look, the gardener has cut the heads off the roses!

8. Mr Willis bought two bags of potatoes but left one in the shop.
9. Were you outside when it rained? You look absolutely soaked.
10. Can you pass me the sugar? I am baking an apple pie.
11. The dogs have been digging holes again; look at that mess.
12. Why is Susan leaving? Stop her – we have dessert!
13. The reporter appeared tired, but kept talking anyway.
14. Someone has stolen my socks. They were here a second ago.
15. When I met the twins, I thought I was seeing double.

20.7 Answers

1. Can I borrow your pen? I left mine at home.
2. A crowd is protesting in town because the council raised taxes.
3. My sister has invited me to tea, so I am buying flowers for her.
4. Has Bob finished that book he was reading?
5. The children were excited to see Aunt Maggie, as she always gave them chocolate.
6. Vivian always works late, that's why she wasn't home when we called.
7. School tests have been getting harder, so students have started complaining.
8. The door was locked earlier, so I still do not know how the burglar got in.
9. Robert is upset because he was not watching the game when his team scored.
10. We started running in the summer, but we have been going less often as the weather has worsened.
11. Are the potatoes not ready yet? Did you not turn on the oven before we went out? (or Didn't you turn on the oven before we went out?)

12. Is Sue coming to the cinema? She has not joined us for months.
13. I washed the dishes yesterday. I am not washing them again today.
14. Frank's son wants to drive to Scotland, but he has not passed his driving test yet.
15. Is that woman climbing a tree now? She has been distracting us all morning!

20.8 Answers

1. We are building a tree house so the children will play outside more often.
2. Daisy is coming home tomorrow, because her flight has been delayed.
3. Howard is waiting for the bus that arrives at eleven.
4. I have a book in my bag, which I will be reading when you arrive.
5. The men have loaded the truck already, so it will definitely get there on time.
6. Will it rain later? I hope not as I have not taken a coat.
7. Are you going to make tea after you wash those mugs? (or Will you make / Are you making tea after you wash those mugs?)
8. The phone has been ringing all morning, I am going to disconnect it soon!
9. Who will win the race? It looks too close to tell.
10. I am going to the shop later. What do you want me to get?
11. Tyler is learning to ski but he will not be ready in time for the holiday. (or Tyler is learning to ski but he is not going to be ready in time for the holiday.)
12. He will have been playing that old guitar for a year this October, I think it's time he got a new one.

13. Brittany washes her hair every day – she will not cope well when they go camping. (or Brittany washes her hair every day – she is not going to cope well when they go camping.)
14. Look, the horses are racing across that field – we will never catch them!
15. The men will be delivering our new fridge in an hour, so I am trying to finish my work quickly.

20.9 Answers

The complete correct text follows the numbered answers below.
1. are eating
2. has been praising
3. has been
4. am getting
5. am going to fall asleep (or will fall asleep)
6. is
7. will revive
8. don't know
9. makes
10. are you worrying
11. states
12. want
13. won't want (or will not want)
14. is running
15. will have finished
16. will have lifted
17. am feeling
18. always feel
19. eat
20. have not been eating
21. is inspiring
22. has given
23. will teach (or is going to teach)
24. will try
25. have been talking
26. have been setting up
27. is that man carrying
28. will find out (or are going to find out)

It's 13.45 and Bilbo and Jam **(1) are eating** lunch together. Bilbo **(2) has been praising** the clown convention for twenty minutes already.

"The day **(3) has been** wonderful so far," he says.

"But I **(4) am getting** tired," Jam says. "I **(5) am going to fall asleep** during the afternoon talk."

"Nonsense! There **(6) is** a break before it. And the workshop after lunch **(7) will revive** you."

"I **(8) don't know** about that. Physical comedy **(9) makes** me very nervous."

"Why **(10) are you worrying** so much? The information pack **(11) states** that you can watch if you don't want to join in."

"But I **(12) want** to join in, right now. I only fear I **(13) won't want** to when everyone **(14) is running** around hitting their heads on planks."

"Well, by 2 p.m. we **(15) will have finished** this hearty meal and perhaps your spirits **(16) will have lifted**. I **(17) am feeling** much livelier already, myself."

"You **(18) always feel** lively, Bilbo. It might be because you **(19) eat** too much sugar."

"Ha! I **(20) have not been eating** any sugar for two months, in fact. I am lively because this conference **(21) is inspiring** me. The workshop on children **(22) has given** me lots of new ideas, and the talk on clown history **(23) will teach** us about what it takes to really succeed."

"Okay, okay. I **(24) will try** to enjoy the afternoon. I think that while we **(25) have been talking**, they **(26) have been setting up** the workshop. Why **(27) is that man carrying** two buckets of water?"

"We **(28) will find out** soon!"

20.10 Answers

1. He was going to eat all the cake, but it was too much. (*or* He would have eaten all the cake, but it was too much.)
2. They were going to buy a hot tub until they saw the running costs.
3. Shirley was going to go to university if she got the grades. (*or* Shirley would go to university if she got the grades.)
4. She was going to learn to dance before the end of the year. (*or* She would learn to dance before the end of the year.)
5. Our neighbours were going to repair the fence. (*or* Our neighbours would repair the fence.)
6. I was going to travel to Germany for Oktoberfest. (*or* I thought I would travel to Germany for Oktoberfest.)
7. The poster said it would start at 7 p.m. (*or* The poster said it was going to start at 7 p.m.)
8. I was going to meet Geoff in the park. (*or* I would meet Geoff in the park.)
9. They said it would rain. (*or* They said it was going to rain.)
10. Uncle Jim was going to supply beer for the party.
11. Luke said he would not drink my tea.
12. Sam did not think she would pass her exams. (*or* Sam thought she was not going to pass her exams.)

20.11 Answers

1. A) I wrote B) my boss has asked
2. A) she saw B) Tess has been learning
3. A) it has been getting B) I am starting
4. A) who left B) Brian and Freda are arguing
5. A) it rained B) the bench is
6. A) they found B) our company is moving
7. A) she started B) Jenny drives

8. A) the woodland animals were B) Bernice has barely slept
9. A) my family came B) have lived
10. A) she was having B) the hot water ran out C) has stopped
11. A) we asked B) have they brought
12. A) I didn't see B) what are you drinking
13. A) the driver said B) are we riding C) we must exit
14. A) we studied B) who has completed
15. A) the dog was B) where is
16. 20.12 Answers
17. A) Dad is eating B) we are going
18. A) he is practising B) they will be expecting
19. A) the price seems B) I will buy
20. A) who is preparing B) Tyler is going to get
21. A) she is earning B) she will spend
22. A) I love chocolate B) it will make
23. A) I am making B) will you wear
24. A) are the police investigating B) will the thief escape
25. A) is the table B) not everyone will fit
26. A) I have not checked in B) Does the flight leave

20.13 Answers

1. A) we are peeling B) they will be ready
2. X – simultaneous
3. A) the girl he met B) Ron is going to introduce
4. A) she failed B) she has been studying C) Mia is taking
5. A) that sign was not B) someone has put
6. A) and B) X – simultaneous (dark clouds suggest / storm is coming) C) will it strike
7. A) she ate B) when Wendy gets here C) we will ask

8. A) he added B) and C) X – simultaneous (The chef admits / he claims) D) he will not do
9. A) they broke B) they have not apologised C) the boys are not playing
10. A) she has been happily married B) Tina is publishing
11. A) What did that man say B) You have been sitting
12. A) Is Dermot ready B) is he going to train
13. A) My uncle gave B) I gave C) Does Cindy have
14. A) Had Pat tried B) he visited C) He orders
15. A) have you seen B) Will you come

20.14 Answers

The complete correct text follows the numbered answers below.

1. has been learning
2. has been (or had been)
3. thought
4. lives
5. is working
6. goes
7. drives
8. teaches
9. said
10. has been listening
11. enjoys
12. watches
13. bought
14. had been playing
15. was enjoying
16. yearned
17. was saving
18. wished
19. was not earning
20. had been collecting
21. had planned (or had been planning)
22. is doing (or has been doing)
23. will help (or are going to help)
24. will not have (or is not going to have)

25. is going to come (or will come / will be coming)
26. is going to find (or will find)
27. will be playing (or is going to be playing)

Emily's Piano

Emily **(1) has been learning** to play the piano for eight months. It **(2) has been** (*or* **had been**) a dream of hers for many years, but she never **(3) thought** it would be possible until last November. She **(4) lives** with her parents in a small house and, for now, she **(5) is working** as a waitress before she **(6) goes** to university. Her father **(7) drives** buses and her mother **(8) teaches** in the local school. The family live comfortably, but her father **(9) said** they had no space or money for a piano.

Still, Emily **(10) has been listening** to piano concertos since she was a child, and **(11) enjoys** reading books about musicians and music theory. She **(12) watches** all the online videos about piano tuition that she can find. When she was little, her parents **(13) bought** her a miniature keyboard. She **(14) had been playing** on it every day for years when the keyboard broke. But by then she **(15) was enjoying** school and parties too much to care.

As Emily got older, she **(16) yearned** to play music again. While she **(17) was saving** money to continue her education, she secretly **(18) wished** for a piano instead. She **(19) was not earning** enough for both, though. Then, in November, her father revealed that he **(20) had been collecting** extra money himself. Emily's parents **(21) had planned** (*or* **had been planning**) to buy her a piano as a gift before university, all along! They even paid for lessons, and now Emily **(22) is doing** (*or* **has been doing**) so well that they **(23) will help** (*or* **are going to help**) her to continue once she moves to university. She **(24) will not have** (*or* **is not going to have**) space at university for a piano, but **(25) is going to come** (*or* **will come / will be coming**) home every other weekend, and is sure she **(26) is going to find** (*or* **will find**) a piano somewhere on campus. In fact, Emily is certain she **(27) will be playing** (*or* **is going to be playing**) piano for many years to come.

20.15 Answers

The complete correct text follows the numbered answers below.
1. has been watching
2. have been getting
3. has improved
4. have also been changing
5. did not like
6. prefer
7. had been following
8. came
9. would have considered
10. started
11. spread
12. will continue
13. has quickly made (or is quickly making)
14. likes
15. enjoys
16. have already bought
17. has not read
18. is looking
19. will meet
20. has had
21. will help
22. will give
23. thinks
24. will not turn
25. does not believe
26. are going to invade
27. sounded
28. will be talking

Wizards and Dragons

For the past few weeks, Bernice **(1) has been watching** a new television show about wizards and dragons. Such fantasy shows **(2) have been getting** more popular in recent years. This is partly because technology **(3) has improved** enough to make fantasy more realistic. But attitudes to fantasy **(4) have also been changing**. Bernice **(5) did not like** fantasy before; she and her friends usually **(6) prefer** shows about crime and mysteries. They **(7) had been following** a seaside detective drama for five years, before this fantasy show **(8) came** along. None of them **(9) would have considered** fairy tales seriously before.

Then, everyone **(10) started** talking about this new show. It **(11) spread** across the internet, and **(12) will continue** to spread even more when the new series arrives. The popularity of the show **(13) has quickly made (or is quickly making)** it cool to like fantasy. Bernice **(14) likes** that, because she really **(15) enjoys** the show.

In fact, Bernice and her friends **(16) have already bought** all the books that accompany the show. She **(17) has not read** any yet, but **(18) is looking** forward to them. Their group **(19) will meet** and discuss the books, once everyone **(20) has had** a chance to read some. The books **(21) will help** them understand the wider story of the television show, and **(22) will give** them an idea of what to expect in future. Bernice **(23) thinks** that the wizards **(24) will not turn** evil, and she **(25) does not believe** the theories that zombies **(26) are going to invade** the fantasy world. That **(27) sounded** silly.

Whatever happens next, Bernice is sure they **(28) will be talking** about this show for many years to come!

20.16 Answers

The complete correct text follows the numbered answers below.
1. is being
2. is not moving
3. will return
4. is getting
5. has served
6. is not closing
7. will upgrade
8. does this mean
9. puts
10. are bringing
11. will strengthen
12. will close
13. have given
14. will buzz
15. form
16. are creating
17. listened
18. responded
19. are eagerly awaiting
20. will have closed
21. will sit
22. is working

A New Library

The Worthing Library **(1) is being** relocated later this year. It **(2) is not moving** far, and it **(3) will return** soon enough – new and improved. The reason: the existing building **(4) is getting** renovated. The current library **(5) has served** the community since 1975, so locals are happy that it **(6) it is not closing** for good. With the improvements, it **(7) will upgrade** its status to a "community hub". What **(8) does this mean**?

This concept **(9) puts** public buildings at the heart of the community; the council **(10) are bringing** many services together in one place. This **(11) will strengthen** the community aspect of the library, although buildings offering other services **(12) will close**.

In remodelling the library, the designers **(13) have given** consideration to quiet and private spaces, but the "hub" **(14) will buzz** with other activity. Sarah Blemming, involved in the project, said, "Libraries **(15) form** the heart of a community. We **(16) are creating** something that embraces and celebrates that."

During the public consultation, the council **(17) listened** to various proposals for how to remodel the library. The public **(18) responded** very favourably, and now **(19) are eagerly awaiting** the results. By the time the community hub is complete, the council **(20) will have closed** the library for six months. But the relocated services **(21) will sit** just across the road. Meanwhile, the council **(22) is working** with more partners to identify other locations for community hubs.

20.17 Answers

The complete correct text follows the numbered answers below.
1. has been hosting
2. looks
3. bought
4. has been maintaining
5. raised
6. are now raising
7. has spread
8. have settled
9. are living
10. would not come
11. is becoming (or has been becoming)
12. have learned
13. will not recover
14. will have been flying
15. will they have done
16. did not want
17. has come up with
18. does not work

19. has been studying
20. bought
21. is arranging
22. will drive
23. has gathered
24. will have been travelling
25. will cause
26. does not mind
27. is going to spend

Holiday Plans

Gerry Davies **(1) has been hosting** family Christmas celebrations at his mountain lodge for the past twelve years. The lodge is in the French Alps and **(2) looks** beautiful surrounded by snow. Gerry **(3) bought** it in 1973, and **(4) has been maintaining** it himself, ever since. He **(5) raised** two children who have married and **(6) are now raising** his five grandchildren. The extended family **(7) has spread** out across Europe: Gerry lives in England, but his son's family **(8) have settled** in Scotland, and his daughter's family **(9) are living** in Ukraine while she completes a teaching contract.

Gerry was worried that his family **(10) would not come** to France this Christmas. Last year, his children said that it **(11) is becoming** less and less desirable to travel in the holiday, as they **(12) have learned** terrible things about global warming. His daughter says frequent flying damages the planet, and it **(13) will not recover**. They **(14) will have been flying** to France every Christmas for thirteen years, next year! How much damage **(15) will they have done** by then?

But Gerry **(16) did not want** to lose these special times with his family, and he **(17) has come up with** a solution. He **(18) does not work** anymore, so he has lots of free time. For the past few months, he **(19) has been studying** all the latest information about the healthiest ways to travel. He **(20) bought** an electric car last week and for the next Christmas he **(21) is arranging** for his family to meet him via train at convenient locations. He **(22) will drive** them the rest of the way to the mountain lodge. By the time everyone **(23) has gathered** for Christmas, he **(24) will have been travelling** for two weeks himself, but it **(25) will cause** minimal harm to the environment. And Gerry **(26) does not mind** collecting everyone. It means he **(27) is going to spend** even more time with his family!

20.18 Answers

The complete correct text follows the numbered answers below.

1. gathered
2. had been
3. have been hiding
4. is lying
5. have been practising
6. had not heard
7. was going to reveal
8. wanted
9. did not murder
10. are searching
11. has not made
12. have been feeling
13. have been working
14. swear
15. was working
16. did he have (*or* does he have)
17. were going to defend
18. are all conspiring
19. Are you going to explain
20. had avoided
21. will not tolerate
22. am going to leave
23. is not coming
24. instructed
25. Is he related
26. Will you talk
27. did you find
28. were asking (or asked)
29. did not say
30. were drinking
31. were you discussing
32. had discovered
33. were
34. were going to pour
35. had not seen
36. did not know
37. would inherit
38. pulled out
39. will survive
40. had been waiting
41. had heard
42. am arresting

Murder Mystery

Detective Stevens **(1) gathered** the manor guests in the games room, along with the butler, the cleaner and the cook. There were eight people left, now that three others **(2) had been** killed.

"People **(3) have been hiding** their true identities," Detective Stevens announced.

"Yes!" the butler said. "Dr Julian **is lying** about being a heart surgeon!"

"How insulting!" said Dr Julian. "I **(5) have been practising** surgery for ten years!"

"When I phoned the hospital this morning, they **(6) had not heard** of him."

Dr Julian was trapped. "Very well. But I **(7) was going to reveal** the truth before leaving, honestly. I am a bank clerk – I only **(8) wanted** to impress Miss Tatiana! But I **(9) did not murder** her! And if we **(10) are searching** for liars, what about the cook? He **(11) has not made** a good meal all weekend!"

"I **(12) have been feeling** unwell," the cook said. "But I **(13) have been working** here since the manor opened, I **(14) swear**."

"He **(15) was working** here when I arrived," the cleaner confirmed. "And what reason **(16) did he have** to kill Miss Tatiana, Mr Fredericks or the manager, Mr Bollier?"

"Ah ha!" Detective Stevens said. "I thought you **(17) were going to defend** him. You **(18) are all conspiring** together. The house staff and ... Colonel Stamp! **(19) Are you going to explain**, or shall I?"

Colonel Stamp, who **(20) had avoided** attention until then, looked worried. He said, "I **(21) will not tolerate** this, no. I **(22) am going to leave** as soon as my driver arrives."

"But your driver **(23) is not coming**," Detective Stevens said. "I **(24) instructed** him to take the night off. You see, Colonel Stamp is, in fact, Lemuel Bollier!"

"Bollier?" said the final guest, Mrs Smythe. "**(25) Is he related** to the manager?"

"**(26) Will you talk**, now, Lemuel? Your secret is out."

"How **(27) did you find** out?" Colonel Stamp – actually Lemuel Bollier – said.

"Simple," Detective Stevens said. "When we dined on Friday night, you **(28) were asking** many strange questions about the manor. And you **(29) did not say** anything about your own history. While we **(30) were drinking** brandy in the parlour, Miss Tatiana saw you talking with the cook and the butler. What **(31) were you discussing**, I wonder?"

"I **(32) had discovered** a draught in my room and wished to be moved!"

"There **(33) were** no other rooms available, until Mr Fredericks died. Indeed, you requested a change because you **(34) were going to pour** poison through the floorboards, onto the manager while he slept! Your father, who **(35) had not seen** you since childhood, and **(36) did not know** you **(37) would inherit** his manor. Having promised to reward all the house staff!"

Lemuel Bollier **(38) pulled out** a gun. "Very well, it is all true. But no one **(39) will survive** to tell the story."

The doors burst open. Police officers **(40) had been waiting** in the hall, and **(41) had heard** everything. The criminals were trapped. Detective Stevens said, "Lemuel Bollier, I **(42) am arresting** you for murder."

21.1 Answers

1. Bare infinitive
2. Past simple (regular)
3. Past simple (irregular)
4. Bare infinitive
5. Past simple (regular)
6. Bare infinitive
7. Bare infinitive
8. Past simple (regular)
9. Past simple (irregular)
10. Bare infinitive
11. Bare infinitive
12. Past simple (regular)

21.2 Answers

1. Present simple
2. Bare infinitive
3. Bare infinitive
4. Present simple
5. Present simple
6. Bare infinitive
7. Bare infinitive
8. Present simple
9. Bare infinitive
10. Bare infinitive (imperative)
11. Present simple
12. Bare infinitive (imperative)

21.3 Answers

1. Bare infinitive
2. Bare infinitive

293

3. Present simple
4. Past simple (regular)
5. Bare infinitive
6. Past simple (irregular)
7. Past simple (irregular)
8. Present simple
9. Bare infinitive
10. Bare infinitive
11. Present simple
12. Past simple (irregular)

22.1 Answers

1. We have **been** living here for twenty years. (Past participle)
2. What kind of nuts did you **use** in this meal? (Bare infinitive)
3. I will **be** waiting for your return. (Bare infinitive)
4. They **have** had enough of the loud music. (Present auxiliary)
5. The internet has **had** a huge impact on the way we interact. (Past participle)
6. Will you **direct** me to the nearest post office? (Bare infinitive)
7. I have **beaten** the eggs; now to complete the cake. (Past participle)
8. The criminal had **broken** the window twice before they found him. (Past participle)
9. We will have **visited** Grandma before Christmas Day. (Past participle)
10. You must **mend** the garden shed before it collapses. (Bare infinitive)
11. When they have **mastered** the art of dancing, they will try fencing. (Past participle)
12. Julio ran through the bath-house naked, because Frank had **stolen** his robe. (Past participle)

22.2 Answers

1. He had **peeled** all the potatoes, ready for dinner. (Past participle)

2. We were **singing** too loudly, that's why they complained. (Present participle)
3. Have they been **watching** us for long? (Present participle)
4. Give me a hand with this log – I can't **move** it myself. (Bare infinitive)
5. The plumber had **worked** on the sink all morning. (Past participle)
6. I have been **studying** for hours; I need a break. (Present participle)
7. She will **slip** on the ice, in those silly shoes. (Bare infinitive)
8. Hans was **reading** when his chair collapsed. (Present participle)
9. Are you seriously **wearing** that jacket again? (Present participle)
10. **Smoking** is not allowed here. (Present participle – used as a noun)
11. Will the game have **finished** by the time we get there? (Past participle)
12. I will be there in a minute, I am just **cleaning** this cup! (Present participle)

23.1 Answers

1. Bare infinitive
2. Past participle
3. Bare infinitive
4. Bare infinitive
5. Present participle
6. Past participle
7. Bare infinitive
8. Bare infinitive
9. Past participle
10. Bare infinitive
11. Present participle
12. Past participle
13. Past participle
14. Bare infinitive
15. Bare infinitive
16. Past participle
17. Present participle
18. Bare infinitive
19. Bare infinitive
20. Present participle

23.2 Answers

1. When will you be **catching** the train? (Present participle)
2. Jamie can't **dance**, she's too old! (Bare infinitive)
3. I have never **made** so many sandwiches in all my life. (Past participle)
4. What did he **ask** you about? (Bare infinitive)
5. Is this group of gymnasts **performing** all month? (Present participle)
6. Why Kylie had **taken** the biscuits, no one knew. (Past participle)
7. The canaries will have **escaped**, the cage door was left open! (Past participle)
8. You will have been **learning** all this for nothing, if you don't apply it later. (Present participle)
9. I cannot **bear** to think about the war. (Bare infinitive)
10. Can you **whistle**? (Bare infinitive)
11. It was **snowing** when we left the house, but it has **stopped** now. (Present participle, past participle)
12. Why did that shop assistant **give** you so much trouble? (Bare infinitive)
13. Have you been **looking** for these hairclips? (Present participle)
14. She couldn't **afford** any more pork scratchings. (Bare infinitive)
15. Has your business **grown** much since we last met? (Past participle)
16. That man has **played** his last game of chess, he's banned now. (Past participle)
17. It was tragic that the game was cancelled when they were **winning**. (Present participle)
18. Do you think you will **pass** all of your modules at university? (Bare infinitive)
19. We are **completing** our assignments next week. (Present participle)
20. Have I **written** enough about the seaside? (Past participle)

23.3 Answers

1. I don't want any more muesli.
2. He is flying to Norway.
3. Jane will be very happy with the results.
4. The students have handed in their final project.
5. What do the parrots look like?
6. Why have you broken my favourite mug?
7. Where are you going to put your bag?
8. It must have been difficult to learn Chinese.
9. Have you seen this new chair I bought?
10. She was thinking of phoning her mum.

Also by Phil Williams

The English Tenses Practical Grammar Guide

Quickly discover the many uses of the English tenses. How do English speakers use two tenses to mean the same thing? Why do the rules not always apply?

This comprehensive guide to the usage patterns of all 12 aspects of the English language covers all the rules and grammatical forms. The English Tenses: Practical Grammar Guide *is ideal as either an accompaniment to core texts or as a full self-study guide. It introduces the reader to flexible uses of the English tenses, with simple, easy-to-follow explanations, colourful examples and enlightening comparisons.*

Advanced Writing Skills for Students of English

Want to improve your English writing skills? This guide will clearly teach you how to master written language. You'll learn how to write concisely, how to vary your structure and vocabulary, how to edit your work, and much more!

Presented with a focus on why different styles and techniques work, Advanced Writing Skills *teaches not only what makes writing most effective, but also the reasoning behind its tips, making them easier to remember and apply. As well as covering general writing tips, across all subjects, this book also offers guidance on specific areas of writing, including business, academic and creative writing.*

Word Order in English Sentences

*Want to know what subject-verb-object **really** means? Unsure about where to place your adverbs? Need to rearrange sentences confidently?*

A complete foundation in word order and sentence structure for the English language, Word Order in English Sentences *can be used both for reference and as a full self-study guide. From basic rules through to the many considerations of adverbial phrases, prepositions and complex sentences, with exercises in between, this grammar guide contains everything you need for a strong understanding of how sentences are put together.*

The rules and patterns for forming and reforming phrases and sentences are all presented with easy-to-follow explanations, clear examples and exercises to test understanding. With his engaging style, Phil Williams takes you beyond the basics, making flexible and advanced English accessible to all.

296